ANGER DISORDERS

THE SERIES IN CLINICAL AND COMMUNITY PSYCHOLOGY

CONSULTING EDITORS
Charles D. Spielberger and Irwin G. Sarason

ANGER DISORDERS
Definition, Diagnosis, and Treatment

Edited by
Howard Kassinove, Ph.D., ABPP
Hofstra University

Taylor & Francis
Publishers since 1798

USA	Publishing Office:	Taylor & Francis 1101 Vermont Ave., N.W., Suite 200 Washington, DC 20005 Tel: (202) 289-2174 Fax: (202) 289-3665
	Distribution Center:	Taylor & Francis 1900 Frost Road, Suite 101 Bristol, PA 19007-1598 Tel: (215) 785-5800 Fax: (215) 785-5515
UK		Taylor & Francis, Ltd. 4 John Street London WC1N 2ET Tel: 071 405 2237 Fax: 071 831 2035

ANGER DISORDERS: Definition, Diagnosis, and Treatment

2 3 4 5 6 7 8 9 0 BRBR 0 9 8 7 6 5

This book was set in Times Roman by Brushwood Graphics, Inc. The editor was Heather L. Jefferson. Cover design by Michelle Fleitz. Printing and binding by Braun-Brumfield, Inc.

A CIP catalog record for this book is available from the British Library.
(∞) The paper in this publication meets the requirements of the ANSI Standard Z39.48-1984 (Permanence of Paper)

Library of Congress Cataloging-in-Publication Data

Anger disorders: definition, diagnosis, and treatment/edited by Howard Kassinove.
    p. cm.—(The series in clinical and community psychology)
    Includes index.

    1. Anger 2. Psychotherapy. I. Kassinove, Howard. II. Series.
    [DLM: 1. Anger. 2. Affective Symptoms. 3. Aggression. 4. Hostility.
    WM 171 A587 1995]
RC569.5.A53A54 1995
616.85'82—dc20
DNLM/DLC
for Library of Congress   95-4880
                                              CIP

ISBN 1-56032-352-3 (cloth)
ISBN 1-56032-353-1 (paper)
ISSN 0146-0846

This book is dedicated to those people who, in many different ways, have taught us about anger.

- *To Tina, Andrew, and Jeffrey, who for many years have been incredibly supportive of my work, and have observed, endured, and taught me about my own anger.*
- *To our scientific and professional colleagues, and to our students, who have helped us understand anger and aggression.*
- *To our clients, patients, and research subjects, who have been our real teachers.*

Contents

Foreword

I have to admit I am somewhat prejudiced in favor of this book because it tends to confirm, with support from a considerable number of research studies, many of the views on anger that I expressed almost two decades ago in my book, *Anger: How to Live with and Without It* (Secaucus, NJ: Citadel, 1977). The 1960s and 1970s were the heyday of the let's-let-it-all-hang-out theory and therapy of anger, and I was one of the relatively few dissenters.

My book, which was followed in the 1980s by Carol Tavris' *Anger: The Misunderstood Emotion* (New York: Simon & Schuster, 1983) and several other important articles and books, presented the unpopular view that anger usually does much more harm (especially psychosomatic harm) than good: that honestly and freely expressing it tends to escalate rather than reduce it, that enraged individuals can zero in on their rage-inciting philosophies, and that, if they employ a number of cognitive, emotive, and behavioral methods to interrupt their self-enraging processes, they can learn—and continue to teach themselves—several effective methods for gaining control over their angry eruptions.

Although my book on anger was unusually cognitive for a topic dealing with one of the most emotional of human traits and states, it followed the principles of rational-emotive behavior therapy, which have always emphasized that people's thoughts, feelings, and behaviors are practically never "pure" or disparate but that they accompany and significantly interact with each other. Therefore, when people are "disturbed" or "dysfunctional," changing their disorders to healthier and more functional processes involves using a number of therapeutic methods. The authors of this book's chapters also stress the interrelations of cognition, emotion, and action both in producing and reducing anger. Good!

The one thing I would like to add to Howard Kassinove's well-edited book is a detailed outline of the disadvantages of making oneself angry, enraged, and vindictive. The following is an inclusive list, as I originally proposed in *Anger: How to Live with and Without It*.

1   Anger starts with the notion that other people's thoughts, feelings, and/or actions are "bad"—meaning "unfortunate," "undesirable," or "unfair." This seems "healthy" or "legitimate" because people feel entitled to view others' behaviors as interrupting their own values and interests, and therefore to see them as "bad." But when people are angry, they commonly see others' behaviors as "awful," "horrible," or "terrible"—or as (a) totally bad, (b) more than bad, and (c) badder than they should be or are allowed to be. Defining other people's actions as totally bad is an unlikely overgeneralization, as Alfred Korzybski the well-known general semantics theorist has noted. Defining them as more than or 100% bad is inaccurate. Finally, insisting that because they see them as bad, they must not be as bad as they indubitably are is grandiose.

2   People's anger, when they strongly feel it, holds that they cannot stand, cannot bear other people's "wrong" behavior. But if they really couldn't stand it, they would presumably die because of it—which is rarely the case. If they survive it, they would not be able to have any pleasure at all because of it.

3   People's rage at others stems not only from their strongly disliking their "bad" thoughts, feelings, and acts, but from their disliking or damning them, their totality, their entire personhood for committing "unfair" behaviors.

4   People's rage at others' "unfairness," and at them for "being" this way, will very likely produce these results: (a) People often make themselves obsessed with other people who they think and feel absolutely should not and must not act the way they indubitably do act; (b) they tend to act vindictively and sometimes obsess with thoughts of futile and harm-inciting revenge; (c) their anger, low frustration tolerance, righteous indignation, and impatience easily may spur them to abuse weaker individuals, such as subordinates, family members, and powerless children over whom they have control; (d) anger is one of the main factors leading to rape, assault, homicide, and all kinds of other crimes, as noted by Kassinove and Sukhodolsky in chapter 1 and later by Tsytsarev and Grodnitzky in chapter 6; (e) political, economic, social, and religious violence have many causes, an important one of which is anger and resentment; (f) social, political, ethnic, religious, and other forms of prejudices and bigotry stem from, lead to, and augment anger; (g) when people are angry, they frequently take on some of the worst characteristics of the people they hate, including bullying, prejudice, violence, and arrogance; (h) anger often overlaps with, helps create, and escalates feelings of depression. People who insist that bad behaviors and conditions absolutely should not and must not exist, and that it is awful when they do, often depress as well as enrage themselves when such acts and situations actually exist; and (i) as several chapters in this book show, anger—both suppressed and overt, expressed and unexpressed—is often associated and seems to encourage severe psychosomatic problems, including hypertension, heart problems, ulcers, and other ailments.

These are some of the main disadvantages of human anger and resentment. Of course, this is not the whole story because even neurotic anger includes determination, righteous indignation, fighting for humanitarian causes, motivation to change obnoxious feelings and behaviors, and other advantageous consequences. Anger disorders, however, are common, and require clear definition, specific diagnosis, and effective treatment. The chapters herein cover these areas in an expert and comprehensive manner. Reading them will prove useful to almost any clinician, instructor, and researcher.

Albert Ellis, Ph.D., President
Institute for Rational-Emotive Therapy
New York, NY

Preface

Because all behaviors are multidetermined, I can readily say that a number of factors led to the idea for this book. At the phenomenological level, I have always been fascinated by anger, and I believe this is why I was taken by the idea of an edited book on the subject. I have also been fascinated by the lack of teaching about anger (as opposed to aggression) in undergraduate or graduate school, by the small number of articles about anger that appear in the scientific literature, and by the low number of panels devoted to anger at professional meetings. This lack of attention to anger stands in sharp contrast to the central role given to it by laypersons, artists and writers, and the daily literature of newspapers and magazines. Clearly, psychologists have not been dealing with a phenomenon that is central to everyday experience and that the public wants to understand. At the scientific and professional levels, this book emerged from a series of research projects completed by the chapter authors, and by their work experiences wherein patients and clients often presented with anger-centered problems. At the most immediate level, the idea for this book emerged directly from a symposium on anger given by several of the chapter authors at the annual convention of the American Psychological Association (APA) in Toronto in August 1993 and repeated and extended at the 1994 APA meeting in Los Angeles.

With regard to my own phenomenology, throughout my life I have recognized that anger has been and still is central to my personal, everyday experience. I can remember being occasionally angry at my friends, girlfriends, teachers, and parents. Later, when I reached "mature" adulthood, I was periodically angry at my children, students, neighbors, co-workers, superiors, subordinates, and so on. Sometimes I was angry at people I knew well, such as my best friend, sometimes at people I hardly knew, such as a slow secretary in a colleague's office, and sometimes at people I didn't know personally at all, such as drivers in other cars. I was angry at people such as Hitler, at foreign countries such as Russia and North Vietnam, at social institutions such as religion, at governmental demands such as paying state taxes, and so on. My anger list is long because anger is an

everyday experience. People experience it themselves or are the target of someone else's anger every single day.

With regard to science, anger is not well understood. Thus, clinical practitioners have not gone to the literature to find guidance when working with angry
clients. Clearly, there are a number of basic questions that need to be addressed:
What is anger and how (if at all) is it different from annoyance, rage, or hostility?
How does one know if someone is angry? What causes angry feelings? What
kind of anger is normal, and when and how does one decide that anger is abnormal and that someone has an anger disorder? How does one factor in cultural
norms when working with clients in a multicultural society such as the United
States? How is child/adolescent anger different from adult anger? When, if ever,
does anger lead to aggression? If people don't express their anger, will they
develop medical problems? What if they do express it? Are they then protected
from medical problems? Is it wise to sometimes hold on to anger and *not* try to
make it go away? Finally, what is the best way to help someone with an anger
problem?

I am sure that some of my family members, colleagues, and acquaintances
would surely judge me to be occasionally angry. Yet I do not think I am seen as
aggressive. I have never hit another person, I have never been arrested, and I
have never had to pay a penalty for something I have broken. What then is the
relationship of anger to aggression? What cues do people use to judge that a person is angry? For the practitioner, the most available cues are the client's verbalizations, facial expressions, and body language, as shown in the psychotherapy
office or verbally reported during sessions. How do clinicians use these cues to
understand and help people who go to them for help?

Psychologists, counselors, sociologists, criminologists, psychiatrists, and
anthropologists have devoted much time and journal space to the study of aggression, but relatively little to anger. Is this because aggression is an overt motor
behavior that cannot be counted, measured, and observed? Traditional, logical
positivist leanings certainly point in that direction, and for the many years that
behaviorism had a grip on practitioners they eschewed the use of self-report data
to help understand the human experience. Yet it is self-report data on which the
practicing clinician must typically rely.

Mental health practitioners, teachers, parents, and personnel managers often
must deal with patients, students, colleagues, and others who self-report anger,
not aggression. Psychologists and other mental health practitioners sometimes
listen for weeks or months to clients who report feeling very angry. These persons complain about the unjust, unfair situations in their lives, and almost uniformly whine and moan about how the world should be treating them more fairly,
how it should be easier than it is, or how it should be more pleasant than it is.
Teachers listen to their students' anger each semester, few of whom become
aggressive (although some students actually do become violent with their teachers, and a few even murder their teachers). Is their anger situational, or do some
of these students become angry in almost every frustrating situation of their

lives? What is the relationship of daily frustration to anger, and of anger to aggression? Workers frequently listen to colleagues' job-related anger about salaries, working conditions, and so on, yet only a small percentage actually becomes violent.

Once the basic questions are answered, it becomes important to develop effective treatment programs for the practitioner. Again, some fundamental questions need to be answered. I offer an example from my own life. When I was married 29 years ago, I constantly told my wife how angry I was while caught in traffic jams. I never acted aggressively, in the sense of hitting the car, my dog, or my family members, but I do admit to yelling and sometimes "gunning the engine" when traffic let up. (Isn't *gunning* the engine an interesting phrase?) My anger verbalizations were something like, "I *can't stand* this traffic jam," "This is *awful*," "There *shouldn't* be so much traffic on a Saturday afternoon," or "Those drivers are *total idiots*!" Only my wife knows what my facial expressions and bodily movements (the other cues used by psychotherapists) were like. No one knows about my blood pressure or heart rate, but one can guess.

Later on, after years of marriage to a wife who modeled calm behavior and after years of studying psychotherapy (especially relaxation training and desensitization with Joseph Wolpe and rational-emotive psychotherapy with Albert Ellis, now known as rational-emotive behavior therapy [REBT]), I no longer experience much anger when frustrated in traffic. Why is that? What happened to my anger? Where did it go? It certainly did not get "turned inward," as the psychoanalysts used to say, because I do not get depressed in traffic either. Did my anger disappear because all roads in the New York area are now free of traffic jams? This would be known as changing the "A," or activating event, in REBT terminology, and it is certainly not true. Did my anger disappear because I learned to relax in the presence of the frustrating stimulus, as Wolpe taught me to do? Did it extinguish, as Skinner might have said, because there was little reinforcement of my angry verbalizations and behavior by others in my environment? Did I learn those new rational cognitions, as taught to me by Ellis? It is true that in traffic jams I now say, "This is *unpleasant* and I *wish* there were less traffic, but there is no reason why the world must be as I want it to be; I can easily tolerate it, and other drivers will probably continue to drive inappropriately until forever." Or is it that my wife has been modeling her supportive, calming behaviors for 29 years? It is probably a combination of all these processes. Although scientists argue about the precise causes of behavior, practitioners know that to help people a multifocused approach usually leads to the best results.

This book, then, is written for both the scientist and practitioner, and for students in practitioner-oriented fields. It is intended to be useful to persons who work professionally with angry clients, and those who want to use comprehensive treatment methods based on scientific knowledge and understanding of anger. This joint commitment is to provide scientifically based information that can be used in treatment. In that sense, we hope our readers see the thread of the scientist-practitioner in each chapter.

Kassinove and Sukhodolsky begin in chapter 1 by providing an overview of the concept of *anger* and anger disorders. There is a long, but uneven history of the study of emotions in general, and anger in particular, and anger must be understood in the context of more general emotion theory. As a psychologist educated in Russia, Sukhodolsky adds the first of a number of cross-cultural perspectives that are threaded within most of the chapters. The authors believe that cross-cultural analyses make them aware of the limitations of their findings with American subjects, and show them, and hopefully their clients, how flexible and adaptable human beings really are. They briefly review historical approaches to anger; define basic concepts such as *emotion, feeling, anger, hostility*, and *aggression*; and review the more common theories of anger and aggression. Finally, they examine the social constructivist perspective, which promotes the importance of the self-reported anger experience.

A major problem for the practitioner is the lack of official *DSM* anger categories. In chapter 2, Eckhardt and Deffenbacher review the problems associated with a lack of adequate definitions, present a working model of anger, and propose five specific anger disorders: Adjustment Disorder with Angry Mood, Situational Anger Disorder with Aggression, Situational Anger Disorder Without Aggression, Generalized Anger Disorder With Aggression, and Generalized Anger Disorder Without Aggression.

The next three chapters present different perspectives on anger. In chapter 3, Spielberger, Reheiser, and Sydeman review the psychometric approach to anger, and provide an up-to-date analysis of the experience and expression of anger. History of the state-trait distinction is presented, and state anger is shown to have two components: feeling angry and feeling like expressing anger. New insights on the expression of anger are also presented. In addition to the expressive patterns of anger-in, anger-out, and anger-control, evidence is presented to show that anger-control is subdivided into "anger-control in" and "anger-control out." Spielberger et al. then review the evidence linking anger and hostility to cancer, heart disease, and other severe and life-threatening illnesses.

In chapter 4, Salzinger explains what is probably one of the most misunderstood concepts in American psychology—the radical behaviorist's approach to private events such as anger. He notes that behaviorists are quite able to deal with private events such as anger. Salzinger describes how people learn to respond to anger-evoking stimuli, and how they learn to speak publicly about their private responses to such stimuli.

In chapter 5, Tanaka-Matsumi reviews the cross-cultural literature regarding the antecedents of anger and the various display rules for the kinds of anger behaviors accepted in different cultures. She also discusses problems in the assessment of anger across different cultures, and notes how dysfunctional ways of dealing with anger may be labeled as *aggression* or *depression* in different cultures. She stresses the importance of knowing the cultural background of the client and the display rules accepted in the culture of origin.

In chapter 6, Tsytsarev and Grodnitzky discuss anger and aggression as they are manifest in criminal populations. They examine different types of violent behavior and crimes, and evaluate the role of anger in aggressive criminal behavior. From a motivational perspective, they develop the concept of *affect of anger*; they show how anger may be a central and necessary condition for some types of aggression, and how it may be transformed into aggression. Tsytsarev was educated and practiced in St. Petersburg, Russia for many years, and several clinical cases from America and Russia are reviewed.

Chapter 7 begins the discussion of anger disorder treatments. In this chapter, Tafrate reviews the adult psychotherapy outcome literature on anger treatment, and notes those treatments that have research support, those that do not, and those that have not been adequately studied.

In chapter 8, DiGiuseppe discusses the important role of the interpersonal relationship, and the therapeutic alliance, when working with persons with anger disorders. Using a number of case examples, he presents strategies for identifying and modifying beliefs that stand in the way of developing an appropriate psychotherapy relationship.

Chapters 9 and 10 present ideal anger-treatment packages for the reader. In chapter 9, Deffenbacher presents a comprehensive treatment plan for adults with anger disorders. In chapter 10, Feindler presents a similar package for children and adolescents. Each of these treatment packages is solidly based on experimental psychological knowledge about anger and aggression. Although the authors present the best there is, as of today, they also recognize that problems of noncompliance and recidivism are real and must be dealt with in the treatment package.

In chapter 11, Kassinove and Eckhardt summarize what is now known about anger, and present a model that brings the various perspectives developed in the previous chapters into focus. Then, based on clinical experience, they discuss some of the advantages and disadvantages of practice from the different perspectives.

ACKNOWLEDGMENTS

Many people helped make this book a reality, and, as is often true, they are too numerous to mention. Our students and colleagues and the many known and unknown reviewers of our journal articles and grant proposals have contributed in ways they are unaware of, and we are thankful for their input. A number of people read early versions of some chapters, including Andrew Berger, Andrew Kassinove, Merry McVey, and Stephen Terracciano; and some chapter authors were particularly diligent in reading the other chapters. Chris Eckhardt, my friend and colleague, stands out in this crowd and deserves my special thanks. I also want to thank Dean Robert C. Vogt, Provost Herman Berliner, and other Hofstra University administrators for providing me with a special leave to bring the book to completion, and for their support of psychological science at Hofstra. My editor at Taylor & Francis, Elaine Pirrone, made the process go as smoothly as possible, and was an important source of guidance. Finally, I owe so much to my wife, Tina, for graciously putting up with my affair with "Tillie." You see, I spent so many days and nights alone with Tillie (my laptop computer) that Tina gave her a name. Tina never got angry, even when Tillie joined us in bed.

Howard Kassinove
Hempstead, NY

Contributors

JERRY L. DEFFENBACHER, Ph.D.,
ABPP
Professor of Psychology
Colorado State University
Fort Collins, CO 80523

RAYMOND DIGIUSEPPE, Ph.D., ABPP
Associate Professor of Psychology
St. John's University
Jamaica, NY 11439
    and
Institute for Rational-Emotive Therapy
45 East 65th Street
New York, NY

CHRISTOPHER I. ECKHARDT, Ph.D
Assistant Professor of Psychology
University of North Carolina
at Wilmington
Wilmington, NC 28403

EVA L. FEINDLER, Ph.D.
Associate Professor of Psychology
C.W. Post College/LIU
Brookville, NY 11548

GUSTAVO R. GRODNITZKY, Ph.D.
Department of Psychology
Federal Correctional Institution—Route 37
Danbury, CT 06811-3099

HOWARD KASSINOVE, Ph.D, ABPP
Professor of Psychology
Hofstra University
Hempstead, NY 11550

ERIC C. REHEISER
Department of Psychology
University of South Florida
Tampa, FL 33620

KURT SALZINGER, Ph.D.
Professor of Psychology
Hofstra University
Hempstead, NY 11550

CHARLES D. SPIELBERGER, Ph.D.,
ABPP
Distinguished University Research
Professor
Behavioral Medicine & Health Psychology
University of South Florida
4202 East Fowler Ave.
Tampa, FL 33620-8200

DENIS G. SUKHODOLSKY, M.A., M.S.
Adjunct Instructor of Psychology
Department of Psychology
Hofstra University
Hempstead, NY 11550

SUMNER J. SYDEMAN
Department of Psychology
University of South Florida
Tampa, FL 33620

RAYMOND CHIP TAFRATE, Ph.D.
Department of Psychology
Hofstra University
Hempstead, NY 11550
    and
Institute for Rational-Emotive Therapy
45 East 65th Street
New York, NY

JUNKO TANAKA-MATSUMI, Ph.D.
Associate Professor of Psychology
Hofstra University
Hempstead, NY 11550

SERGEI V. TSYTSAREV, Ph.D.
Associate Professor of Psychology
St. Petersburg State University
St. Petersburg, Russia
    and
Adjunct Associate Professor of Psychology
Hofstra University
Hempstead, NY 11550

Chapter 1

Anger Disorders: Basic Science and Practice Issues

Howard Kassinove and Denis G. Sukhodolsky

Hofstra University, Hempstead, New York

Anger plays a significant role in everyday life. Sometimes it is short-lived, moderate in intensity, and, perhaps, even helpful. At other times it is persistent, severe, and highly disruptive. Overt anger can lead to negative evaluations by others, a negative self-concept, low self-esteem, interpersonal and family conflict, verbal and physical assault, property destruction, and occupational maladjustment (Deffenbacher, 1992). Suppressed anger is related to a number of medical conditions including essential hypertension, coronary artery disease, and cancer (Greer & Morris, 1975; Harburg, Gleiberman, Russell, & Cooper, 1991; Harburg, Blakelock, & Roeper, 1979; Kalis, Harris, Bennett, & Sokolow, 1961; Spielberger, Crane, Kearns, Pellegrin, & Rickman, 1991). These detrimental effects of anger have been known for a long time. More than 60 years ago, Meltzer (1933) reported that, "Anger has been called the worst propensity of human nature, the father and mother of craft, cruelty, and intrigue, and the chief enemy of public happiness and private peace" (p. 285). More recently, Dix (1991) concluded that even the common experience of parenting is constantly associated with anger. He noted that, ". . . average parents report high levels of anger with their children, the need to engage in techniques to control their anger, and fear that they will at some time lose control and harm their children" (p. 3).

Anger is also a frequent experience. According to Averill (1983), "Depending upon how records are kept, most people report becoming mildly to moderately angry anywhere from several times a day to several times a week (Anastasi, Cohen, & Spatz, 1948; Averill, 1979, 1982; Gates, 1926; Meltzer, 1933; Richardson, 1918)" (p. 1146). His reference list spans 75 years, suggesting stability of the anger experience as well as the everyday frequency. Given these observations, it is no surprise that anger is a common reason that leads people to seek professional help.

As with most phenomena of scientific and clinical interest, a number of different perspectives exist. Some scientists and practitioners believe that anger and aggression are but two views of the same event, with similar elicitors and consequences. Others believe they are different, and that anger precipitates aggression. Congruent with each of these positions, we note that both anger and aggression are frequent in the workplace, in the home, and even in schools. More than 1,000 people are murdered on the job annually, more than 2 million suffer physical attacks, and more than 6 million are threatened (Toufexis, 1994). Even schools are not safe. In the 5-year period from 1986 to 1990, in anger-correlated or anger-caused events, more than 300 people were killed or seriously wounded in American schools, and an additional 242 were held hostage at gunpoint (Goldstein, 1994).

Within and across individuals, angry feelings vary in frequency, intensity, and duration, and they are associated with a number of maladaptive conditions, as mentioned earlier. Clearly, it is important to understand the causes, correlates, and outcomes of anger, with the goal of developing effective remediation programs when anger is excessive and disruptive. In this chapter, we place the study of anger within the historical backdrop of the study of feelings. We differentiate annoyance, anger, fury, rage, hostility, and the behaviors of aggression and violence. This is followed by a review of theory, including some developmental and cultural issues. Finally, we review approaches to the study of anger, with a focus on social constructivism. Other approaches are elaborated on in subsequent chapters.

THE STUDY OF FEELINGS

People who are "in touch" with their feelings can develop a fuller appreciation for the variations and nuances of everyday interpersonal encounters. At moderate levels, positive and negative feelings can add zest and passion to people's lives. However, when feelings are strong and negative, they can disrupt our behavioral, physiological, and thinking processes. When they are very strong and very negative, they can become highly disruptive and may even lead to (or become justifications for) crimes of passion committed while in an "insane" state. Because clients typically present with problems that involve negative feelings such as anger, anxiety, depression, and guilt, it is important for clinicians to have a full understanding of these common negative feeling states.

Regrettably, despite the obvious importance of feelings, psychologists and other social scientists have not given them consistent respect, either as causal variables for other human maladaptive behaviors and/or as phenomenological experiences worthy of study in their own right. Indeed, as Lewis and Haviland (1993) noted, "No one would deny the proposition that in order to understand human behavior, one must understand feelings . . . (and) the interest in emotions has been enduring: however, within the discipline of psychology at least, the study of feeling and emotions has been somewhat less than respectable" (p. ix).

This seems strange to the clinical practitioner because feelings are the subject of many psychotherapy sessions.

Of course, some clinical theories and intervention programs have focused on negative feelings. However, as shown in Figure 1.1, the primary interest during the past 25 years (based on keywords in PsycINFO) has been on anxiety and depression. Anger has been relatively ignored by scientists, thus little empirical help has been provided for practitioners.

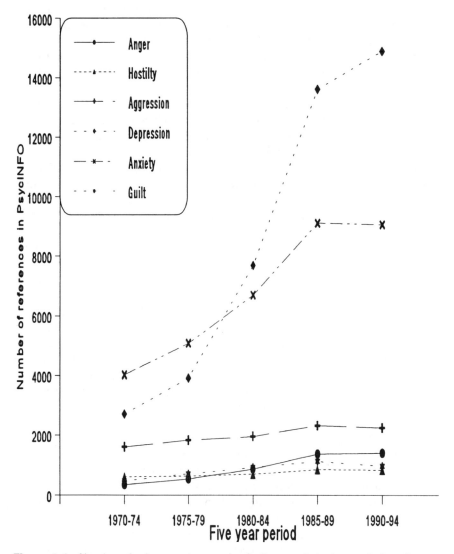

Figure 1.1 Number of references to negative feeling words in the psychology litera-ture (PsycINFO, 1970–1994).

The neglect of anger (and, it seems, guilt) as a phenomenon of interest is probably related to our attachment to the logico-empirical, positivist model. Scholars focused on the measurement of observables and minimized the scientific importance of phenomena available primarily through self-report. Within this tradition, it was relatively easy to study learning, worker productivity, aggression, and so on because the dependent variable could be reliably counted, weighed, or otherwise measured. *Anxiety* could be tackled if it were defined as "behavioral avoidance" or "physiological reactivity," and *depression* was generally seen as a pattern of slow responding or low-frequency responding. In contrast, *anger* was seen as an epiphenomenon—one that is a part of the "mind" and, thus, not part of science. Figure 1.1 also shows that the number of studies referenced under *aggression* (a measurable and observable behavior) is uniformly higher than those referenced under anger. The keyword *hostility* was referenced the fewest number of times.

While scientists were avoiding talking to people about their phenomenological experiences, clinical practitioners were using self-reports (as well as in-the-office behavioral observations) to assess affective states. For practitioners, everyday language such as "I felt angry this week" has always been an acceptable and important part of clinical data. Their scientist colleagues' unwillingness to use verbal reports to examine phenomena such as anger always seemed strange to clinicians. This is one likely reason that practitioners have rejected (or, at least, have not frequently read) the scientific literature as a source of practical guidance.

Well-trained clinicians do know, of course, that language (and, perhaps, thought) is an operant that is at least partially under environmental control. If, when clients are talking about their anger, practitioners say "uh-huh" or "I see" in a supportive tone, the probability is increased (at least for a while) that they will talk even more about their anger. If psychotherapists provide direct encouragement and reinforcement for getting anger "out" by screaming and beating a pillow, their clients will likely be even more angry in the future because they have actually practiced a social role known as the "anger script." However, clinical experience shows that if clinicians simply ignore client verbalizations about anger, clients do not report that their anger disappears. Instead, the clients are likely to disappear from the office and report to others that their practitioners were "unsympathetic" and wouldn't talk with them about their "real problem."

Nevertheless, anger can be approached from a pure learning theory perspective. Indeed, although methodological behaviorists resist entering the "black box" of the mind, radical behaviorists (e.g., Salzinger, chap. 4, this volume) can explain much about internal phenomena such as anger and have contributions to make to clinical practice. For example, simply reinforcing the client for acting "as if" he or she is calm and relaxed (not angry) is likely to lead to improvement. However, to consider anger as simply an operant verbalization may be to equate humans to parrots. With enough seeds (incentives and reinforcements), one can shape a parrot to say, "I feel angry" or "I feel better now!" However, few clinicians would find it acceptable to help a person solely by shaping a verbal response such as, "I feel OK. My anger is now gone." Such an approach does not reflect the full spectrum of the human experience, especially the internal experience.

Most clinicians and scientists believe that humans are proactive and creative creatures, and that anger is a complex gestalt that is more than the simple product of reinforcements or punishments. Feelings such as anger are produced by active processes, including remembrances of the past, expectations of the future, awareness of current behavioral and physiological responses, comparisons of actual to desired behaviors, judgments of what others are thinking, and so on. Because these are reflected in the language clinicians and scientists use, and are shaped by their cultures (see Tanaka-Matsumi, chap. 5, this volume) and subcultures (see Tsytsarev & Grodnitzky, chap. 6, this volume), scientists and clinicians would both be wise to study and use verbal reports.

None of this is meant to deny the observation that people often say what is socially desirable. Verbal reports by psychotherapy clients may not be objectively true because of pressure to conform to social expectations. Also, sometimes, even if it is desired, clients may not be able to report accurately on what is happening internally (Nisbett & Wilson, 1977). However, as Averill (1983) pointed out, social desirability is a confound only if it interferes with self-report. If social expectations, cultural norms, and accepted behavioral scripts are the focus of interest, as they often are when we study feelings such as anger, they are most likely to be reflected in self-reports. Thus, for example, when clients tell clinicians about their anger over discovering that their spouse is having an extramarital affair, the anger shows their social expectations and their desired marital state. A client's language about feelings indicates how he or she appraises a situation, how he or she constructs the emotional experience, and how it is displayed. Averill's (1983) argument is that ". . .we have tended to downgrade the great stock of knowledge that is embedded in ordinary language . . . (and) . . . psychologists should not impose a form of prior censorship on themselves by excluding from consideration a whole class of data and type of methodology, all in the name of science" (p. 1155).

As Averill (1983) noted, research findings can lead to situational and/or theoretical generalizations. Theoretical generalizations involve the significance of findings to explain underlying mechanisms. Thus, it might be shown reliably and consistently in the laboratory that subjects report feeling very angry when someone intentionally criticizes the shape of their nose while they are in a competitive situation with a member of the opposite sex. But how often does such an experience actually occur? Rather infrequently, and therefore this result has low situational generalizability. If clinicians wish to learn about the environmental or interpersonal situations that their clients are likely to be in, and the kinds of feelings they are likely to have in those situations, they would be wise to use self-report methods. There is much to be learned about the human anger experience from studying self-reports. We, however, are certainly not arguing against theories about anger based on lawful relationships and causal effects demonstrated in the laboratory. Instead, we believe the best way to understand angry feelings (and many other human phenomena) is to recognize that all kinds of data have assets and liabilities, and to use each class of data to its fullest.

FEELINGS AND EMOTION

According to Izard (1977), emotions take into account the conscious experience (i.e., the feeling), brain and nervous system processes, and observable expressive patterns (e.g., furrowed brow, clenched teeth, etc.), particularly on the face. In general, we use the term *feelings* to refer to the language-based, self-perceived, phenomenological state. In contrast, the term *emotion* refers to the complex of self-perceived feeling states, physiological reaction patterns, and associated behaviors.

Ortony and his social psychology colleagues (Clore, Ortony, & Foss, 1987; Ortony, Clore, & Collins, 1988) agreed that emotions have different facets. However, they started with the assumption that, through language, people conceptualize potentially emotion-eliciting experiences in a particular way and, thus, they do or do not experience particular feelings. The authors' perspective (i.e., that people's language-based perceptions of the world—their broad construals and more narrow appraisal of specific events—cause them to experience certain feelings) is congruent with conceptions of the cognitive–behavioral therapies such as Ellis' (1962, 1973) rational-emotive behavior therapy and Beck's (1976) cognitive therapy. Indeed, Ortony, Clore, and Collins (1988) noted that there is an "abundance of psychological evidence that cognitions can influence and be influenced by emotions (e.g., Bower, 1981; Isen, Shalker, Clark, & Karp, 1978; Johnson & Tversky, 1983; Ortony, Turner, & Antos, 1983; Schwarz & Clore, 1983)" (p. 5). Further, they stated, "We think that emotions arise as a result of certain kinds of cognitions and we wish to explore what these cognitions might be" (p. 2). To do this, they distinguished which words refer to emotions and which to cognitions; their work has opened the door for exciting new research studies.

Using a social constructivist position, which begins with data (and definitions) from the common person, the authors asked university students to judge which words (from a pool of 585 possibilities) represent emotions (or what we call *feelings*) when the words were presented in the being state (e.g., I *am* abandoned; I *am* angry) versus the feeling state (e.g., I *feel* abandoned; I *feel* angry). Their hypothesis was that words judged to represent emotions would be so judged in both states, and would fit into a cluster of words that refers to internal, mental, and affective conditions. From this analysis, the following list of words of interest to us (i.e., anger-oriented words) represented emotions: *aggravated, aggrieved, anger, angry, annoyed, bitchy, frustrated, fury, furious, hostile, hostility, incensed, irate, irked, irritated, mad, malice, malicious, outraged, peeved, pissed-off, rage, spiteful, vengeful,* and *violent.* In contrast, the following words did not refer to emotions: *abused, aggressive, antagonistic, awful, arrogant, cruelty, cynical, horrible, obstinate, rotten, sarcastic, stubborn, terrible, unpleasant,* and *willful*. *Aggressive* was (as expected) judged to be an external condition, and thus is not an emotion according to the conception that emotions are internal events. *Awful, terrible, horrible,* and the milder *unpleasant* were judged to be in the external, not the emotion, category. These points are important because the cognitive therapies are typically based on the hypothesis that we can shift levels of disruptive emotionality (e.g., reduce intense anger to milder annoyance) by reevaluating whether the events are cognitively appraised as "absolutely awful" or "simply unpleasant."

DEFINITION OF ANGER

We define *anger* as a *negative, phenomenological (or internal) feeling state associated with specific cognitive and perceptual distortions and deficiencies (e.g., misappraisals, errors, and attributions of blame, injustice, preventability, and/or intentionality), subjective labeling, physiological changes, and action tendencies to engage in socially constructed and reinforced organized behavioral scripts.*

Anger varies in frequency. Some people report feeling angry almost all of the time, whereas others rarely feel angry. Anger varies in intensity, from mild (typically labeled as *agitation* or *annoyance*) to strong (typically labeled as *fury* or *rage*). Anger also varies in duration, from transient to long term (i.e., holding a grudge). However, people express their anger experiences differently, thus many different behaviors (e.g., sulking, yelling, glaring, avoiding eye contact, leaving, making snide comments, etc.) are associated with the internal experience. It is the totality of specific cognitive and phenomenological experiences that differentiates anger from other feelings such as anxiety, sadness, and so on.

Our definition focuses on the phenomenology of the experience, but also recognizes that the behavioral display of anger plays a central role. It is congruent with Averill's (1983) position that an "anger display" is a socially defined transitory behavioral role that is based on behavior patterns developed and reinforced in a person's culture (see Tanaka-Matsumi, chap. 5, this volume). Anger is a reaction of the whole person, wherein the "correct" way to think and act is determined by modeling and reinforcement as the person develops. We do not deny the sometimes important role played by biophysical factors such as brain tumors, insulin reactions, and so on, and therapists would be wise to be alert to the possibility of such problems with their angry clients. However, we believe that, as psychologists and psychotherapists, it is wiser to focus on patterns learned from other family members, television, school, religious teachings, and so on. To better understand anger, we first discuss aggression as it provides a contrast to the focus of this book—anger. Although there is an obvious and important relationship between anger and aggression, anger is an independent (or at least semi-independent) and neglected phenomenon worthy of study in its own right.

AGGRESSION (WITH COMMENTS ABOUT ANGER)

According to Berkowitz (1993), aggression has to do with motor behavior that has a deliberate intent—to harm, hurt, or injure another person or object. Aggression is thus goal directed. However, some forceful goal-directed behaviors are not instances of aggression even if some harm occurs because there is no intent to harm. Forcefully pushing a child out of the way of an oncoming car may lead to pain and bruising or bleeding of the child. However, the intent was to help, and thus the behavior is not aggressive. We agree with this position; for example, helpful anxiety-evoking behavioral psychotherapy techniques (such as flooding) are not instances of aggression because their intent is to help the client.

In contrast, Bandura (1973) stayed close to the behavioral perspective, which tries to avoid internal concepts such as *intention*. Thus, he considered aggression harmful behavior that violates social roles. A criminal who stabs a victim with a knife is aggressive, but a surgeon or dentist who uses a scalpel is not, and neither is the butcher who cuts the meat that people eat. However, social roles are seen differently from different perspectives. Professionals generally consider spanking children to be wrong because it is aggressive. But some parents believe they are giving "needed discipline" to help children develop into well-socialized citizens.

A more problematic class of behaviors are those that seem to be aggressive, although the intent is actually physically noninjurious. For example, within closed social environments, such as classrooms or prisons, "aggressors" may yell, verbally threaten, push, or shove to build up their self-worth, coerce and control other people, manipulate what others think of them (i.e., impression management), or preserve dominance and power in a hierarchy (Patterson, 1979; Tedeschi, 1983). These goals may be achieved through verbal and/or motor behavior. Given that the intent of such behaviors is physically noninjurious, they may be instances of neither "real" anger nor "real" aggression. Rather, they can be seen as hybrid behaviors driven by a desire to arrange the environment in a comfortable way; displays of "true" aggression would occur as escalations only if there is noncompliance. For example, the classroom bully is often neither angry nor aggressive initially. Rather, his or her goal is to show others how important he or she is by his or her threats, profanity, and noncompliance with teacher requests. If others act scared, the bully will typically stop. However, if defied, he or she may become quite angry and escalate his or her behavior into aggression. Likewise, some young men (and women) enter marriages with a variety of controlling behaviors that emerge not from anger, but from a drive to maintain the "manly" (or "womanly") impression of leadership and dominance. Regrettably, these desires for dominance or control sometimes result in cases of spouse/ parent/child abuse, and there is no clear agreement as to when attempts at coercion become aggressive. It is not clear whether verbal behavior alone is included in the definition of *aggression* proposed by Berkowitz (1993). This is important because, if a person's behavior is limited to a loud voice with aversive content, we have to decide if it is an instance of anger or so-called "verbal aggression." For us, displays limited to verbal behavior are best seen as instances of anger, and correspond to the *anger-out* concept described by Spielberger (see chap. 3, this volume). *Aggression* is best defined as motor behavior with the goal of contact (e.g., hitting, pushing, shoving, throwing an object, etc.) and the intent to harm. Behaviorists (see Salzinger, chap. 4, this volume) see little reason to make the anger (cognitive-verbal) versus aggression (contact-motor) distinction because they believe the elicitors and consequences of both are the same. In contrast, social constructivists such as Averill (1982, 1983) and appraisal theorists such as Lazarus (1991) saw important differences, which we delineate in a later section of this chapter. The cognitive constructivist position holds that we can develop a variety of different ideas about, and responses to, verbal inputs (even to rather aversive verbal inputs such as, "You're a jerk!"). However, we do not often reinterpret the effects of an aversive physical input (a punch, a knife wound, etc.). Even here, however, we note that some gang members will submit to having cuts made on their bodies until they bleed and will interpret this positively as a sign of brotherhood.

Psychotherapies such as Ellis' (1962, 1973) rational-emotive behavior therapy, Beck's (1976) cognitive therapy, Kelly's (1955) personal construct psychotherapy, Frankl's (1955) logotherapy, and so on focus on helping patients reinterpret, reappraise, and reconstruct aversive life events so they will feel less upset. For example, Ellis postulated four specific core beliefs that are hypothesized to lead to anger, and four rational alternatives that are likely to lead to a less intense feeling, such as annoyance. Specifically, anger-engendering beliefs are: (a) *awfulizing/catastrophizing/horriblizing* ("It's absolutely awful that my child failed his test"), (b) *no frustration tolerance or "I can't stand it-itis"* ("I can't tolerate the fact that he failed the test"), (c) *shoulds and oughts, or musturbation* ("He ought to have studied and he should have passed"), and (d) *global self- or other rating* ("He's really a total jerk!"). Rational alternate beliefs that would hypothetically yield milder feelings of annoyance would be: (a) "It's *unfortunate* he failed," (b) "I *don't like* this outcome," (c) "It *would have been better or preferable* if he had studied and passed," and (d) "He is a *fallible mistake-making child* who does some things very well and other things poorly."

Likewise, Beck postulated five specific cognitive errors that are thought to cause emotional distress, including personalizations, polarized thinking, selective abstraction, arbitrary inference, and overgeneralizations. The literature behind such approaches is quite large, and hence a review is beyond the scope of this chapter. However, as but one example, a recent study by Eckhardt and Kassinove (1995) demonstrated support for both of these theories of the etiology of emotional disturbance. Using a technique known as "articulated thoughts in simulated situations" (Davison, Robins, & Johnson, 1983), they showed that violent, maritally dissatisfied men emitted higher levels of irrational verbalizations and cognitive errors, compared with happily married men, when exposed to overheard conversations designed to be inflammatory. Thus, to achieve reduced anger, it is recommended that such men reconstruct their evaluations of overheard inflammatory statements.

As noted, it is obviously possible and easier to reconceptualize an aversive verbal stimulus (e.g., "You're just plain stupid"), compared with an aversive motor stimulus (a punch or a knife). Nevertheless, aversive verbal stimuli can have learned or conditioned effects, but they are not directly harmful. No child develops a poor self-image or becomes angry or suicidal if a parent says, "Ti Durak!" every single day, unless the child has learned that it means "You are a fool" in Russian. In contrast, motor behavior such as having a knife thrown at one's body can have both unlearned and learned effects, and is directly harmful by the tissue damage it causes. One cannot learn to be physically unaffected if stabbed in the heart.

Because we are also interested in the relationship between anger and aggression, we note that aggressive acts can be either instrumental or emotional. *Instrumental aggression* is defined as behavior carried out for an extrinsic purpose. Aggression carried out to earn money or as part of a job (e.g., a professional "hit" man, a physician who delivers the lethal injection as part of the death penalty on behalf of the state, or a veterinarian who euthanizes a terminally ill dog) is instrumental, and can presumably occur without anger. Some acts (e.g., making threats) are best seen as cases of instrumental anger because they involve only verbal attempts to achieve power. An adolescent boy was brought to one of us for psychotherapy because he was making verbal threats against his parents and himself to coerce them into buying rock concert tickets for him. Given the middleclass, nonviolent history of his family and his conscious awareness of the reasons for his actions at the time he made the threats, this was clearly instrumental anger.

In contrast, *emotional* or *hostile aggression* (Feshbach, 1964) derives from an urge to attack someone when one feels bad (perhaps angry), even though one may not profit from it and one may even pay a price for the aggression. This type of aggression may occur in response to some perceived injustice (e.g., "You shouldn't have taken my special parking space! Now I am angry and I will spray paint your car"). Others become aggressive when bored or when they want a thrill. Farley's (1986) Type T (thrill and adventure-seeking) personality represents a recognition that some people seek stimulation (in the form of aggression) in the absence of anger. As an example, consider the New York City Central Park jogger case, which is popularly called a case of *wilding*. Seemingly, the gang members went wild "just for the hell of it" and beat a female jogger into a coma.

Berkowitz (1993) further categorized aggression as physical or verbal, and direct or indirect. Physical and direct would be shown when someone hits another person in reaction to an insult. Physical and indirect would be shown by placing water and sugar in the gasoline tank of someone who insulted you. The last two categories are more problematic for those who study anger. Verbal and direct would be shown when a person yells or screams at another person who delivered an insult. Verbal and indirect would be to spread rumors and/or gossip about someone who insulted you. We define the last two categories as *anger* (not aggression) because they focus on verbal behavior. Although verbal behavior is often under the same controlling conditions as motor behavior, we believe it is important to recognize that society typically sees physical abuse/aggression as different from verbal abuse/anger. Even our legal system generally protects free speech but punishes wrongdoers for behavioral actions. In addition, many practitioners and parents teach that "Sticks and stones can break our bones but names can never harm us," and advise children to "turn the other cheek" (i.e., ignore) when they are verbally insulted.

In summary, *aggression* refers to motor behavior carried out with the intent to hurt someone through physical contact. It can be instrumental, emotional, or done in the absence of any goal or anger. It can be directed at the source of the problem or it can be expressed indirectly. We differentiate behavioral (aggressive) actions with the goal of bodily harm (which produces direct results) from verbal (angry) actions, which are more likely to be the preservation of a reputation or status in a hierarchy as the goal and which produce learned or conditioned outcomes. The learned effects of aversive verbal stimuli have the potential to be modified by clinical practitioners; the unlearned effects of aversive motor assaults cannot be modified and usually require medical intervention.

ANGER (WITH COMMENTS ABOUT AGGRESSION)

The previous material on aggression is presented as a backdrop against which we can better understand anger. As noted, *anger* refers to a label given to a constellation of specific uncomfortable subjective experiences and associated cognitions (i.e., thoughts, beliefs, images, etc.) that have various associated verbal, facial, bodily, and autonomic reactions. It is a transient state, in that it eventually passes, and it is a social role, in that our culture or subculture allows for the display of certain kinds of behaviors associated with the internal experience, but punishes others. Thus, anger is felt in people's conscious awareness and is communicated through verbalizations and bodily reactions. Some of the bodily reactions (e.g., flushing of the face, standing up, leaning forward, etc.) can be observed by others. Others (e.g., an increased heart rate, pupillary changes, sweating, etc.) typically are not.

Berkowitz (1993) stated that anger may not have a particular goal. According to the author, angry feelings stem from an unpleasant occurrence that yields internal physiological reactions, *involuntary motor reactions* (clenched fist, postural changes, etc.), facial changes (muscle-induced changes that yield dilated nostrils, frowning brow, etc.), and thoughts and memories that arise at the time of the unpleasant occurrence. He thought of anger as the experienced combination of these inputs, and believed it is not aimed at achieving any particular goal and does not serve any useful purpose for the person.

However, we would emphasize that anger often is goal directed. It has its origins in the social environment and it is aimed at the correction of an appraised wrongdoing. For example, a person might become angry at his or her spouse when he or she perceives and believes that an avoidable, intentional, and/or wrongful act has occurred (e.g., wasting hard-earned money, not checking the oil in the car, thus causing the need for a major repair, drinking while driving). The anger represents an attempt (albeit a poor one) to change the probability of the act in the future, and to maintain dominance. The anger also represents the person's attempt to have his or her spouse, or someone else, uphold sociocultural or personal standards (of spending money, caring for the car, or drinking), and the person's anger reflects his or her belief that the spouse must comply. If the person "allowed" the spouse to spend wildly (i.e., if he or she told him- or herself that wild spending was merely *unfortunate*, but not *awful*) and didn't have the *must*, there would be less anger. In addition, because anger (yelling, debating, forcefully attempting to modify attitudes and behavior) is often successful (Averill, 1982, 1983), it certainly does have a goal, and it certainly does serve a useful purpose. Even if a person does not know why he or she is angry at the moment of anger (Nisbett & Wilson, 1977), the often reinforcing consequences of the anger makes it "useful."

DOES ANGER CAUSE AGGRESSION?

Berkowitz (1993) noted that, "anger, as an experience, does not directly instigate aggression but usually only accompanies the inclination to attack a target. . . . I wouldn't say that the man hits his wife *because* he is angry with her. I would hold, instead, that the husband's attack results from an instigation to aggression that was generated by an unpleasant event. The man might or might not have an anger experience at this time, but if he does, this experience only goes along with his aggressive inclination and does directly create it" (p. 20). Averill (1993) took the relationship between anger and aggression one step further. He wrote that, ". . . anger can be likened to an architect's blueprint. The availability of a blueprint does not cause a building to be constructed, but it does make construction easier. In fact, without a blueprint, there might not be any construction at all. . ." (p. 188). Psychotherapists and clients alike have often confused correlation with causation, and have typically believed that anger directly causes aggression. Neither Berkowitz nor Averill nor we would agree. In fact, as noted by Kassinove and Eckhardt (chap. 11, this volume), and in keeping with the view of Salzinger (chap. 4, this volume), anger and aggression actually overlap each other quite significantly, and in some respects are the same. Thus, rather than asking whether anger causes aggression, we prefer Averill's conception. Like an architect's blueprint is to building a house, anger makes aggression a lot easier.

Not everyone agrees that anger and aggression are only loosely related or are only parallel processes. Rubin (1986) defined *anger* as ". . . the elicitation of one or more aggressive plans by the combination of threat appraisal and coping processes" (p. 116). He noted that aggressive plans can occur without other aspects of an emotion, such as physiological arousal. However, a process of threat appraisal is always operating in people who are in conflict, such as those likely to apply for psychotherapeutic treatment. Threat appraisal, in turn, varies along a scale of magnitude. When the magnitude of the threat is judged to be low (e.g., a mother suggests to an agoraphobic daughter that the family will have to move to another state in 12 months), a class of plans enters the daughter's consciousness that feels like considerations, opinions, beliefs, and attitudes (e.g., "I just won't go"). However, as the magnitude of the appraised threat increases (e.g., the mother tells the daughter that their house has already been sold and they are moving in 1 week), the calmness becomes mild anger, then strong anger, then fury, and then rage (e.g., the daughter yells, argues, and throws a plant at the mother). Coping plans are aggressive in nature and are accompanied by a feeling of anger when the level of judged threat is high.

Rubin's position has an important differentiating feature. He stated that, when people experience an aversive situation and appraise it as a threat but do not take an overt action, they take covert actions (i.e., have imagined angry plans). Threat appraisal, not general arousal, is central for him. He noted that people can be aroused and aggressive without feeling angry, which is why we believe that intent must be considered in any act. For example, children often get aroused about a competitive game they are playing, and they engage in aggressive roughhousing with each other. Yet they are not angry, and they quickly return to a state of calm behavior when the game is over. In contrast, if they appraise a threat and have a fight, they then feel angry and may dwell on the incident with aggressive fantasies for a long time.

Hostility must also be considered. According to Berkowitz (1993), hostility is a "decidedly negative attitude" toward one or more people. It is reflected in people's negative judgments about others, and the verbal behavior associated with hostility is certainly a marker for anger. This is seen in common phrases emitted during anger displays, such as, "I hope she drops dead tomorrow," "I hope he rots in hell," and so on. A hostile person (i.e., high on the trait of hostility) is quick to indicate negative evaluations of others, and shows a dislike for many people.

Obviously not every angry or hostile person is aggressive. However, some authors (e.g., Spielberger, 1988) see hostility as a complex set of feelings and attitudes, including anger, that motivates aggressive and vindictive behavior. The task for the clinician, then, is to evaluate the likelihood that the angry and hostile client will act on his or her inclination or blueprint. This is the old and perplexing problem of predicting motor behavior (aggression/violence) from verbal behavior (anger); as any professional clinician can report, it is not easily done. If, based on verbal anger, a therapist alerts the State Protective Services Agency or the police because he or she wrongly judges that a client will harm another, the professional runs the risk of damaging the therapeutic relationship with the client. However, if he or she wrongly failed to alert protective services or the police and the client injures or kills another person then we have clearly acted unwisely. Unfortunately, one's ability to make accurate judgments about aggression, although better than chance alone, is poor. We advise clinicians to use the best scientific information available today, which is that the best predictor of aggression is previous aggression, not clinical judgment (Mossman, 1994; Olweus, 1979).

At the same time, we recognize that all aggression must start somewhere. Therefore, in the absence of prior aggression, other clues to consider include hostile attitudes and imagined plans, aggression modeled by others (such as an aggressive father or older sibling), and reinforcements for successive approximations to serious aggression (such as pushing and shoving) that have been reinforced in the past. Aggression cues, such as the presence of a gun, can also elicit aggressive behavior in angry people, and general negative affect caused by an aversive situation can lead to aggression. Thus, people who are exposed to aversive stimuli (electric shocks, high temperatures, foul odors, etc.) respond with negative affect and then tend to become aggressive (Berkowitz, 1993). As noted in the earlier allusion to "wilding" and the Type T reaction, aggression can occur even when it is clear that the aggression cannot lessen the aversive situation. Thus, although anger and hostility sometimes lead to aggression, some anger just accompanies the aggression.

THEORIES OF EMOTION/
THEORIES OF ANGER

To fully understand contemporary perspectives on the cause and treatment of anger, it is worthwhile to review some early, but lingering, issues. Plato, Aristotle, Seneca, Descartes, James, Dewey, and others certainly had much to say about feelings; however, we begin with the early debate of American psychologist William James and Danish physiologist Carl Lange (Lange & James, 1922), who were at odds with American physiologists Walter Cannon (1929) and Philip Bard (1935). The James–Lange theory of emotions runs contrary to the everyday notion (held by almost every client we have ever seen in psychotherapy) that feelings such as anger come before bodily reactions. Instead, James and Lange said that the body has specific physiological responses to aversive stimuli, and that feelings are actually perceptions of the body's reaction. From their perspective, when parents notice that their young child is putting soft, creamy fudge bars into the new and expensive VCR, they have a specific physiological reaction (e.g., an increased heart rate, an increase in perspiration, tightness in the stomach, changes in the facial musculature, etc.) and then they feel angry. The angry feeling follows the specific bodily reaction.

Cannon and Bard saw this chain of events as wrong because it did not seem likely that the body had physiological reactions specific to each emotion. After all, like most people, they knew that hearts race and people perspire when they have a number of different feelings, such as anger, fear, guilt, and love. They also questioned the likelihood that there are specific facial muscle changes that become manifest for each feeling, such as for anger. Alternatively, they proposed that the physiological arousal of the body is general in nature, and that this general arousal and the feeling occur simultaneously. Thus, as parents see their child putting the soft fudge bar into the new and expensive VCR, their heart rates increase, their facial muscles tense, they begin to sweat, and they feel angry—all at the same time.

For many years, there was no evidence that the body reacted differently when it experienced different feelings, and thus many scholars dismissed the James–Lange theory. However, current evidence has given renewed support to their proposal. For example, Rajita, Lovalo, and Parsons (1992) produced emotion-specific blood pressure responses (anger vs. sadness vs. fear) in response to imagined situations. Also, when Laird (1974, 1984) and Laird, Cuniff, Sheehan, Shulman, and Strum (1989) induced students to frown by telling them to contract certain facial muscles and to pull their eyebrows together, the students reported feeling more angry. However, when the students were induced to smile, they reported being happier and they found cartoons to be more humorous. This perceived change in feelings has been explained by changes in cerebral blood flow and cerebral temperature caused by muscle changes in the face. In turn, the blood flow and temperature changes may cause release or blocking of emotion-linked neurotransmitters (Zajonc, 1985; Zajonc, Murphy, & Inglehart, 1989). This evidence is congruent with the James–Lange hypothesis that people interpret their musculature, and with the early writing of Darwin (1872/1965) who noted that, "He who gives way to violent gestures will increase his rage."

PUT ON A HAPPY FACE

If making an angry face induces one to feel angry, should psychotherapists work with their clients to practice putting on a "happy face" and act happy? Yes, indeed. The now famous Russian Stanislavsky method for training actors and actresses does just that. Performers are trained to think and behave "as if" they were angry. This leads to the most convincing performances because the actors really feel the emotions when they act—"as if" they are experiencing them. We believe that psychotherapists have much to learn from the Stanislavsky method. When it was fashionable for therapists to tell their angry clients to beat a pillow and scream (Casriel, 1974; Janov, 1970), or to hit someone or something with a soft foam bat, these therapists were actually (and inadvertently) teaching their clients to become more angry. Good anger-reduction programs would be wise to incorporate happiness exercises or relaxation training into their curriculum (see Deffenbacher, chap. 9, this volume; Feindler, chap. 10, this volume). In fact, good therapist training programs (and we say this only half facetiously) might be wise to incorporate some Stanislavsky classes into their curricula. We may even discover that teaching clients emotion contrasts by first having them talk calmly (slowly, glancing around, relaxed muscles, etc.) and then angrily (fast, eyes focused on the target, tense muscles, etc.) may be a fine way to reduce anger.

THINKING ALSO MAKES IT HAPPEN

This recommendation does not mean that anger always occurs without cognitive activity. There is little doubt that appraisals, memories, perceptions, and interpretations of events (i.e., cognitive processes) affect people's level of anger. In Schacter and Singer's (1962) two-factor theory, and in various scientific and clinical appraisal theories (e.g., Ellis, 1973; Lazarus, 1991), anger has been hypothesized to come from people's interpretations of an event. An aversive occurrence (e.g., soft fudge in the VCR) may indeed lead to generalized physiological arousal, as proposed by Canon and Bard. However, the emotion may not occur simultaneously, as they proposed. Rather, it seems likely that cognitions determine the specific feeling experienced by the person. Thus, if one's spouse (whom one loves) screams a profanity ("You are a damned jerk!"), it is likely to lead to arousal. If this outburst occurs at the dinner table, in front of important family members or business guests, one is likely to feel very angry. However, what if a person's spouse was in an auto accident and was in a coma for 3 weeks? Each day the spouse has no movement or response. In a somber tone, the neurologist states that if it lasts much longer there is almost no chance the spouse will come out of it. Then, one day, as the person is sitting next to the bed in a highly dejected state, the spouse sits up and suddenly says, "You are a damned jerk!" Well the person is likely to take this as a very good sign, and feel quite happy. The arousal is combined with an interpretation or appraisal of the event, and it is the appraisal that determines which emotion is felt.

Appraisal-based theories have clear treatment implications for anger reduction. Techniques that center on reorienting attributions or reframing (e.g., Telling a highly religious client that, "Calmly accepting and forgiving that insult by your spouse shows your willingness to be tested by God") may lead to reductions in anger. Alternatively, if clients can be led to believe that their physiological arousal is not caused by an aversive verbal stimulus (such as an insult), but instead is caused by caffeine (too much coffee or cola), then they may become less angry.

As an alternate to appraisal theory, a basic question to consider is this: Do emotions occur in the absence of cognitive activity? This question has been hotly debated by Zajonc (1984) and Lazarus (1984), among others. Zajonc, who focused on animal and brain physiology evidence, noted that some emotional reactions involve no thinking processes. Indeed, there is physiological evidence (e.g., LeDoux, 1986) to show the existence of neural pathways that bypass cortical areas involved in thinking and that involve emotions such as anger and aggression. However, Lazarus strongly disagreed with this analysis. He recognized that people process vast amounts of environmental and bodily stimuli, and that some emotional responses occur without conscious cognitive activity. However, he thought there must be some kind of cognitive activity that goes beyond simple sensation (at least perception) or people would not know what they were responding to. We agree.

DEVELOPMENTAL AND SOCIALIZATION ISSUES

It seems likely that Zajonc and Lazarus were considering different dependent variables in their analyses. Some basic "emotional" reactions, such as simple avoidance or attraction, or attack reactions, can indeed be studied in lower animals, and they may be totally a function of neural activity in the absence of "cognition." However, complex feeling reactions—which humans label as *annoyance, anger, hostility, bitterness, churning, fuming, holding a grudge, seething,* and so on—surely involve higher cognitive processes such as ideas, beliefs, attitudes, appraisals, and so on. It is true, of course, that clinical practitioners can learn some things about anger from examining animal data. However, as we pass from animals to infants and children, and then to adolescents and adults, we are likely to find that cognition plays an increasingly important role in anger reactions. In fact, we might say that primitive emotional responses (such as aggression) develop into sophisticated feelings (such as anger and indignation) as organisms move up the phylogenetic and ontogenetic scales, and as organisms become more cognitive.

Lewis (1993) proposed a model of emotional development that spans the first 3 years of life. He noted that most adult emotions develop during this period, although anger experiences cannot yet be measured because of the absence of complex language skills. Instead, the focus during this period is on the expression of emotion based on behavioral observation. This differentiation of the experience and expression of feelings is reflected in Spielberger's (1988) State–Trait Anger Expression Inventory, which is discussed fully in chapter 3. From birth to 6 months, Lewis suggested a tripartite division using the simple dimensions of pleasure, distress, and interest. The assumption is that anger is an adaptive response designed to overcome an obstacle. Using a methodology wherein a learned instrumental act is removed, he and his colleagues demonstrated the expression of anger in 2-month-old infants (Lewis, Alessandrini, & Sullivan, 1990). This is the earliest time that anger expression has been shown, although we must question whether such a reaction truly reflects the adult experience of anger in terms of frequency, intensity, duration, attribution of cause, desired responses, and so on. In addition, the "understanding" of means–ends relationships was defined as crucial in discriminating between general distress and anger. Because the expression of anger requires understanding that one can act intentionally to cause harm, it suggests knowledge acquisition in very young children.

The emergence of self-awareness during the second half of the second year marks another hallmark for emotional development. Once people become aware of themselves, they develop self-conscious and complex emotions, such as envy and embarrassment. At this point in development, the observation of emotions involves measuring facial expressions and vocal and bodily behaviors. Another milestone in emotional development proposed by Lewis is a child's cognitive ability, emerging in the second year, to evaluate his or her behavior against a standard. Based on this ability, by the age of 3, emotions begin to become highly differentiated, and a wide range is present. Writing about anger, Lemerise and Dodge (1993) noted that Goodenough (1931) found that "angry outbursts reach their peak in frequency during the second year and decline thereafter" (p. 540). The most frequent elicitors were interactions with the mother in the context of caregiving (e.g., objecting to food) or play (e.g., removal of play objects), which accounted for 80% of anger events. Boys showed more anger than girls, and as all children got older they used less (behaviorally) violent expressions and more symbolic forms of anger. Language development, of course, renders possible the use of self-report methodologies; Miller and Sperry (1987) indicated that, by the age of 2½, children have a variety of verbal resources for communicating their anger and aggression. Thus, at that age, one begins to understand anger as a phenomenological experience of the organism.

Averill (1982) described anger as an interpersonal, socially constructed emotion with three levels: biological, psychological, and sociocultural. He suggested that "the child is socialized into the emotional life of his or her culture through paradigm scenarios" (p. 335). Paradigm scenarios represent any kind of significant event or learning experience that results in new emotional knowledge and behavior. Further, because it is the parents and then peers who act as the major socializers during the early years, it is assumed that socialization starts with the first visual contact of a newborn with his or her mother, and continues throughout life. Thus, children learn scripts about how and when to become angry, and what alternatives to anger are possible. As they get older and play with others outside of the home, they become socialized by peers. If they display anger incorrectly, they suffer rejection. When these normal socialization forces fail, the development of deviant, extreme anger and aggression is seen.

Research often focuses on the individual components of emotions, and different authors have distinguished different numbers of possible components. However, the socialization of display rules for anger is a topic of great interest. Malatesta and Haviland (1982) suggested that acquisition of "display rules" for anger can be observed in the first year of life. Although there is variation, parents generally encourage and reinforce positive emotions and discourage negative feelings such as anger.

Radke-Yarrow and Kochanska (1990) addressed the socialization of anger in 1½- to 5-year-old "normal" children. They were interested in learning how mothers react to their children's expression of anger. Using observational methods, it was found that, "the older the child, the less likely is the child's anger to result in the mother's affection and support. With increasing age, children are increasingly commanded to stop expressing anger" (p. 304). Consistent with our cultural stereotypes, they found that greater maternal attention is paid to boys' anger, whereas girls' anger displays are more often ignored. Such early attention (i.e., reinforcement) may partially account for the higher level of anger seen by teachers, parents, and psychotherapists in older male children.

Other methodologies have been used successfully to study anger. Miller and Sperry (1987) inferred from an ethnographic study of an urban working-class community that the expression of anger in children was accepted as "justified" under conditions of self-defense, but was considered "unjustified" under conditions of self-indulgence. In addition, anger displays were encouraged toward provoking peers but not toward adults, even if the adults' behavior was defiant. By the age of 2½, children had a number of verbal resources to express anger, and they were beginning to be able to justify it. This supports the idea that the expression of feelings such as anger develops early in life.

Display rules can be viewed as guidelines for the genuine expression of an actually experienced emotion, or as a series of rules for controlling or masking emotional expression. Thus, Underwood, Coie, and Herbsman (1992) studied rules for the masking of anger in third-, fifth-, and seventh-grade children. Using a methodology wherein children gave responses to videotapes with anger-provoking vignettes, they found that children tend to mask the expression of anger (as noted by reduced facial expression and actions) with teachers more than in interaction with peers. Masking of anger toward teachers increased with age, and girls masked their anger more than boys did. These findings again fit our stereotypes and demonstrate that, in normal children, the display of anger toward authority figures, such as parents and teachers, is successfully extinguished by means of socialization at a relatively early age. In contrast, the expression of anger toward peers tends to provoke similar reactions in return, and does not diminish with age. However, peers also have the means to reduce the expression of anger. This was shown by Lemerise and Dodge (1993), whose work indicated that, in the long term, angry and aggressive behavior leads to peer rejection.

Anger and aggression in children and adolescents is not only a function of *socialization*, if this process is defined only as the reinforcement, punishment, or extinction of behavior by peers, parents, teachers, and others. A large body of evidence (e.g., Crick & Dodge, 1994; Dodge & Coie, 1987) has shown that aggressive children have distorted and deficient social information-processing mechanisms. They have hostile attributional biases and cue-detection deficits that lead them to experience anger in situations wherein nonaggressive children simply "see" the situation differently. Thus, as can be seen in the work of Feindler (see chap. 10, this volume), many child and adolescent anger-reduction programs focus on improving social information-processing skills.

Most studies on the socialization of anger and social information-processing deficits deal with factors within the individual. For example, life experience with anger and violence, caregivers' childrearing ideology, and childrearing practice affect children's experience and expression of anger. At the same time, social and cultural forces also have an important influence on the socialization of emotions in general and anger in particular. Broadly speaking, the socialization of anger involves children's incorporation of rules about what to feel angry about, under what circumstances to feel angry, and to whom to show the anger. The social constructivist approach to feelings and emotions suggests that these rules are culture-specific, and are formed and accumulated by a group of people sharing a particular lifestyle. For example, Nisbett (1993) provided data on the difference in attitudes toward violence, acceptability of violence in childrearing, and responses to an insult between people living in the northern and southern regions of the United States. He concluded that southerners are more sensitive to a provocation, think of spanking as more justified as a means of discipline, and are more inclined to endorse violence both for protection and in response to insult. Given our mobile culture, clinicians would be wise to inquire about the region in which their clients were raised.

As discussed in detail by Tanaka-Matsumi (chap. 5, this volume), different cultures ascribe different social roles to the emotion of anger, and thus determine how anger is expressed and, possibly, how it is experienced by individuals. Again, this has obvious implications for clinical practitioners working in a multicultural society. Levy (1984) distinguished between hypercognized emotions, for which society possesses much knowledge and experience, and hypocognized emotions, for which society has little knowledge and experience. The significance of a particular emotion within a given culture can be illustrated by the level of development of linguistic tools, words and concepts, for this emotion. For examples, Tahitian has 46 separate terms for different types of anger (*riri*), which indicates that it is hypercognized in that culture. An interpretation by Solomon (1976) of Briggs' (1970) "Never in Anger," an ethnographic study of the Utku society, indicates that the Utku neither express nor experience anger. Other authors (e.g., Oatley, 1993; Russell, 1994; Stearns & Stearns 1986) suggested that the Utku Eskimos suppress interpersonal manifestations of anger, but they experience it inside and express it indirectly, such as when sulking or beating their dogs.

When faced with the need to translate the word *anger* into Russian, we have a number of words to choose from because we conceptualize anger in differing ways. Roughly speaking, *zlost* refers to the subjective experience of anger that is not justified from the standpoint of social rules and is always negative. It can refer to a state (*zol*) or a trait (*zloi*). A person in a state of *zlost* is said to be bad tempered, childish, and immature. Sometimes people do not admit that they have this feeling. On the other hand, although *gnev* is also negative, it can have the connotation of a socially approved emotional state. *Gnev*, in addition, never refers to a trait. When wronged or mistreated, or when fighting for one's country, one has the right to feel *gnev*. *Gnev* refers to a more intense state than *zlost*, but still refers to anger rather than rage, which is called *yarost*. Also, the milder word *zlost* does not refer to the milder English word *annoyance*. Annoyance is *razdrazhenie*. These examples point out that people from different cultural backgrounds construct the anger experience differently, and thus the practitioner would be wise to inquire about, be sensitive to, and understand the language and culture within which the client developed (see chap. 5, this volume, for further discussion of cross-cultural differences).

MULTIPLE PERSPECTIVES

At this point, it is clear that there are a number of ways in which the scientist and practitioner can conceptualize and deal with anger. A psychometric approach allows for the reliable assessment of specific facets of the anger experience, as well as modes of expression. This approach is typified by the model developed by Spielberger (1988), which suggests that clinicians can measure anger as a momentary state of the client, or as a trait (i.e., a propensity to frequently experience the state of anger in a variety of situations). Further, anger can be held in (anger-in), or it can be expressed (anger-out), or it can be controlled. Control in this case refers to the healthy elimination of anger by cognitive reframing, relaxation, and so on. A behavior-analytic approach uses learning and conditioning principles to develop lawful relationships among the antecedents (triggers) and consequences (outcomes) of anger. It suggests that practitioners look to the contingencies of the immediate environment to change anger behaviors. From this perspective, anger reduction is unlikely to occur through talking to a therapist in an office. Rather, the therapist has to work to shift the contingencies in the family, or at work, at play, and so on. A developmental perspective recognizes that the shaping forces are likely to change in different periods of life, and that the person has different physical and psychological capabilities at different times of life. A cultural perspective examines those larger forces embedded in society that shape anger scripts, and suggests that clinicians be alert to the cultural environment in which the client was reared. A similar model is useful to examine anger in specific subcultures, such as those of criminal populations. Each of these can help the practitioner who wants to develop a therapeutic relationship with angry clients and deliver "ideal" treatment packages. Some of these models are presented in some detail in later chapters.

At this point, we present a model based on the hypothesis that anger is a socially constructed experience, and thus can be best understood from an analysis of the verbal behavior of the clients we see in treatment. It represents the first step in understanding anger—that is, how clients "see" the world around them. If the anger that is constructed by the client is excessive or disruptive, an anger-management program is needed to either shift the construction of the experience to "acceptance" rather than mere "understanding," or to teach skills that reduce attributional biases leading to anger, or to attempt to change the objective elicitors and consequences.

A SOCIAL CONSTRUCTIVIST PERSPECTIVE

Constructivism refers to the imposition of meaning or structure on events. This meaning can develop during perception of the events or, later, based on memory of the events. This imposed meaning or structure can come from social, cultural, or biological forces. However, the social constructivist position suggests that feelings are more social than biological constructions, and thus this model is helpful to social scientists and psychotherapists.

According to Neimeyer and Lyddon (1993), constructivism is often contrasted with objectivism (and the logical positivist school). Objectivists believe in a free-standing truth (i.e., a stable and external reality). In contrast, constructivists believe that the primary source of knowledge is the human capacity for creative and imaginative thought (i.e., an invented reality). Objectivists focus on the accuracy of knowledge as it copies objective reality. In contrast, constructivists view all knowledge as inherently fallible, and measure the value of knowledge in terms of its current utility or viability. A central difference (Wessler, 1992) is in epistemology, or the theory of knowing, that each adopts. Wessler said,

> Like Zen Buddhism, the constructivist position maintains that human beings construct a private reality and that objective reality is unknowable if it exists at all. The rationalist position assumes that humans are more or less accurate perceivers of an objective reality. The constructivist position implies that a person's version of reality cannot be tested by objective criteria, for there are none; instead a criterion of utility is applied: is the person's version of reality useful in living in the world. (p. 620)

Ellis (1962, 1973) and Beck (1976) both quoted a number of Stoics, including Epictetus, who said, "People are not disturbed by events, but by the views and opinions they have of those events." In this sense, rational-emotive behavior therapy and cognitive therapy are constructivistic forms of intervention. They proposed that nothing in and of itself (e.g., seeing one's child cheat on a school examination or place the soft fudge bar in the VCR, or learning that one's spouse has been having a sexual interlude with someone else) can *make* one angry because anger responses are not hard wired. Instead, one constructs a reality about the behavior. So, if one believes one's spouse *must* be monogamous—that lack of monogamy is *awful* and that one *can't stand* one's spouse's behavior—one invents one kind of reality and has one kind of emotional reaction—anger. However, if one is an Eskimo and believes in sexual sharing as a sign of hospitality, then one invents another reality and has a different emotional reaction—perhaps happiness.

Social constructivism makes a number of assumptions about the human experience (Averill, 1983). First, emotions are responses of the whole person and cannot be defined in terms of subclasses of responses (i.e., physiological changes, expressive reactions of the face, cognitive appraisals, specific acts, or subjective experiences). Thus, anger can exist with or without motor behavior, with or without yelling and screaming, and with or without images and fantasies. Second, the rules that govern the organization of the elements (of anger) are social in origin. This suggests the importance of studying anger episodes in the natural environment, as they freely occur, as well as considering cultural influences on the anger state (i.e., the transitory social role people play, to which they say, "I am angry"). Third, emotions serve a function within the social system or, at the very least, are correlated with other behaviors that have a social function. Thus, anger is unlikely to be aimless. Instead, the anger role exists because it fulfills some purpose for the client (e.g., it leads to reinforcement). For us, anger serves to give an impression to others; to keep the social order in classrooms, prisons, and within families; to coerce, control, and preserve dominance; and so on. External, anger-out behaviors (governed by display rules or scripts) are likely to exist because they succeed; that is, they are reinforced by behavior change in others.

In summary, the constructivist perspective suggests that, although we accept the role of genetics and biology, the traditional search for the meaning of emotions in biological evolution (e.g., Plutchik, 1980) as opposed to social evolution is misguided, as is any attempt to define emotions solely in physiological, cognitive, or behavioral terms. Given the importance of social forces, appraisals and misappraisals of objective reality are central in the creation of a personal reality and feelings. This has been shown repeatedly in studies with youths. These have shown that aggressive children and adolescents construct ambiguous situations differently, have a tendency to see intentional wrongdoing where none exists, feel more angry, and want to "get even" (Graham, Hudley, & Williams, 1992).

In college students and adults, Averill (1982, 1983) examined natural episodes of anger, the perceived/appraised (i.e., constructed) perceptions of the triggers, and the consequences. He used the controlled diary method, which requires subjects to complete written descriptive accounts of their anger episodes to answer some basic questions about anger. We turn to these now.

How often do people become angry? Most people reported becoming mildly to moderately angry from several times a day to several times a week. When asked to keep daily records of their feelings, the subjects reported an average of 7.3 incidents of anger per week and 23.5 incidents of annoyance per week. Obviously, from the perspective of self-perception, we are dealing with a high-frequency phenomenon.

What is the connection between anger and aggression? The conventional answer, still held by almost all clients in psychotherapy and probably most psychologists, is that anger is the drive behind aggression. However, the most frequent responses reported during anger episodes were nonaggressive (60% were calming activities and 59% were talking the incident over). When aggression did occur, it typically was not motoric. Instead, the aggression was primarily (49%) verbal or symbolic. According to our definition, *direct physical aggression*, wherein one person acted against another, occurred in only 10% of the episodes. Surprisingly, mollifying reactions, such as trying to be especially friendly, were about twice as frequent. When physical action was reported, it often was an event such as the spanking of a child as a socializing response; that is, with the aim of deterring an unwanted behavior. Given a definition that includes intent as central to the demarcation of aggression, we might not have coded these as instances of aggression because the primary aim was not to harm others. In short, in Averill's samples, self-reported episodes of anger were not very aggressive. Of course, when he asked about "impulses felt," aggressive tendencies did become more apparent. Impulses toward verbal aggression (perhaps we would have called these anger-out, verbal reactions) were at 82% and toward physical aggression were at 40%, still not very high. As we noted earlier, the hypothesis that there is a strong, basic causal connection between anger and aggression may simply be wrong. Anger may be a blueprint, or even an instigator, for aggression, but it does not seem to be a direct cause (see Kassinove & Eckhardt, chap. 11, this volume).

What is a typical anger episode like? Based on the reports from Averill's subjects, it was not possible to describe a "typical" incident. All kinds of behaviors were considered (constructed) as causes and manifestations of anger: puns, withdrawal of affection, sulking, and so on. Even being quiet could be seen as a sign of strong anger! This variation suggests that clinicians not make global judgments about their clients' anger, and not use single signs to determine if they are angry. This evidence led us to note in our definition that a variety of behaviors are associated with anger, but none is necessary or sufficient.

At whom do people typically become angry? We might expect that people get angry at people whom they dislike. However, the data did not support that assumption. Over 75% of the anger episodes involved a loved one, someone who was well known and liked, or an acquaintance. In only 8% was the target well known and disliked. In 13%, the target was a stranger. Thus, anger seems to be an interpersonal emotion, which cannot be understood apart from the social context in which it occurs. That context is typically a close affectional relationship between the angry person and the target of the anger. This is congruent with clinical experience, wherein anger is almost always directed at spouses, lovers, children, co-workers, and the like.

What are the causes of anger? Many possibilities were reported to this fundamental question, including frustration (e.g., the interruption of a planned activity), loss of pride, loss of self-esteem, and so on. But the major issue for Averill's subjects was the perceived justification of the instigator's behavior. Anger, for them, was an accusation. Over 85% of the acts that led to anger were considered to be voluntary and unjustified, or potentially avoidable. In short, anger is an accusatory response to some perceived misdeed. The typical instigation to anger is a value judgment; it is an attribution of blame. Thus, as noted by the constructivists, people do not behave independently of the way they conceptualize their interpersonal relationships.

As scientist practitioners, then, we would be wise to learn how people form their conceptualizations of how their friends, family members, colleagues, and others "should act." Scientists such as Graham et al. (1992) called anger a "moral emotion often associated with judgments of 'ought,' 'should have,' or 'could have'" (p. 732), and practitioners such as Ellis (1962, 1994) and Horney (1950) both wrote extensively of the "tyrany of the shoulds." Practitioners would be wise to heed their advice.

What are the consequences of anger? We might expect that anger has largely negative consequences. If anger is a negative emotion in terms of subjective evaluation (i.e., people say it feels bad) and social evaluation (i.e., we don't like to be with angry people, and we often tell them so), why is it so frequent? The answer, given by Plutchik (1980) and others, is that anger is part of people's biological past and has a protective function. Thus, it continues as a function of natural selection. In contrast, the constructive position is that anger is a socially constructed syndrome that is maintained today because of (not despite) its consequences; that is, it works. Averill's studies supported this. The ratio of reported beneficial:harmful consequences was 3:1 for angry persons. It was even 2.5:1 for the target of anger. Of course, the incidents were perceived to be unpleasant, but the consequences of most incidents were considered to be positive. Because angry persons might be likely to rationalize their own behavior, the evaluations of the targets are especially important. In 76% of the cases, targets said that the anger of the other person made them realize their own faults. Also, the target's relationship with the angry person was more often strengthened rather than weakened (48% vs. 35% of the episodes) following the anger episode. The target more often gained, rather than lost, respect for the angry person (44% vs. 29%). Thus, the everyday experience of anger seems to be sufficiently reinforced to explain its high incidence in our current society. In this analysis, there is little need to refer to biology to explain the level of anger extant in society.

A caveat, however, is in order. In an early study, Meltzer (1933) also used the controlled diary method in a college student sample. In contrast to Averill, he reported, "Almost two-thirds of the anger responses are followed by unfavorable after-effects symptomatic of a dissociative trend. In only 15% of the cases does the after-effect indicate an improved self-feeling symptomatic of an integrative trend" (p. 305). Meltzer seemed more interested in the level of personality integration following the anger, rather than the specific interpersonal effect. Nevertheless, a replication of Averill's work would be welcome.

How does anger differ from annoyance? This question is important because many therapists see anger as generally bad, and, using a unidimensional conception, their goal is to reduce anger to annoyance. In fact, Averill's subjects did report anger to be more intense than annoyance. Also (boding well for the goal of Ellis' rational-emotive behavior therapy [REBT] and other cognitive therapies), subjects were able to distinguish annoying from angering events. When asked to keep daily records of anger, annoyance, or uncertain event categories for 1 week, 1,536 events were recorded. Of these, 73% were labeled *annoyance*, 23% *anger*, and only 4% *uncertain*. However, although subjects did construct anger as more intense, we have to inquire about the meaning of *intensity*. Psychologists think in terms of greater physiological arousal. For Averill's college student and community subjects, *seriousness* or *importance* seemed a better word. For example, his subjects reported being angry over the killing of baby seals, but only annoyed over loud gum chewing. At the same time, although it is less serious, the gum chewing might be more immediately upsetting. Anger (in keeping with the conclusion of Graham et al., 1992) also seemed to have a moral connotation, whereas annoyance did not. Finally, anger seemed to demand expression, whereas people who were annoyed often tried to hide their feelings. If a person who is angry (i.e., believes that something morally wrong occurred and should not have occurred) does not act, he or she is considered to be shallow and unassertive. Thus, according to Averill's analysis, anger also represents a commitment to action. In summary, the difference between anger and annoyance seems to be both quantitative and qualitative.

Are women less able then men to experience and express anger? Women reported becoming angry as often as men, for the same reasons, and they expressed their anger with equal frequency. Women, however, reported crying about four times as often as men. Because anger does not involve direct physical aggression, and our social norms do not suggest sex differences in reactions to provocation, social constructivism does not postulate sex differences. However, a cautionary note is again in order because Meltzer (1933) found sex differences. Men in his sample experienced anger six times per week, as compared with four episodes for women; and men were more likely to have an impulse to do bodily harm.

Although Averill is recognized as a constructivist pioneer, he is a social psychologist who has worked with normal subjects (college students and unselected community residents). For the practitioner who works with people in distress, this brings up the issue of representativeness and generalization. Practitioners will want evidence that the knowledge gained by scientists is applicable to persons with disruptive, real-life anger problems. Thus, although we strongly believe that practitioners have much to learn from Averill's findings, we also believe that further studies on the construction of anger in clinical samples will yield important fruits for the practitioner. Learning about the kinds of constructions that distressed adults make will likely lead to efficient and effective therapies for change.

SUMMARY

Anger is a frequent and neglected experience that deserves more attention. It is defined as a negative phenomenological feeling state associated with specific cognitive distortions (e.g., misappraisals, errors, attributions of blame, injustice, preventability, and intentionality), physiological changes, and subjective labeling. The display of anger is socially constructed by cultures and subcultures, and is maintained by reinforcement. It varies in frequency, intensity, and duration. People express their anger experiences differently, and thus no single behavior pattern is characteristic of anger. Anger can been seen in infants, and as people develop they learn and refine the rules for its display. It is only loosely related to aggression, which has its own set of rules. Anger can be studied from the psychometric, developmental, behavior-analytic, cultural, sociological, or constructivist traditions. All have scientific merit, and all are likely to be helpful to the practitioner who deals with disruptive anger.

Chapter 2

Diagnosis of Anger Disorders

Christopher I. Eckhardt
University of North Carolina at Wilmington

Jerry L. Deffenbacher
Colorado State University

Despite the significant advances that have occurred in the understanding and treatment of human emotional disturbances over the last century, clinical psychology has yet to focus its research energies on the intense and powerful emotion of anger. If one were asked what the most important research areas have been in clinical psychology and psychiatry over the last century, the answer certainly would be anxiety and depression. From Freud's (1920) early case studies and theoretical formulations on the manifestations of unconscious psychic energy (anxiety), to Barlow's (1988) important contributions on the treatment of anxiety and panic disorders, and from Beck's (1963) early research on the nature of depressogenic affect and cognition, to the recent multimillion dollar National Institute of Mental Health (NIMH)-sponsored collaborative treatment research project on depression (Imber et al., 1989), it seems clear that these two affective disturbances has received the bulk of scientific attention from the clinical research community. Although few would question the enormous advancements that have occurred in the assessment and treatment of anxiety and depression as a result of this attention, there has been at least one unfortunate side effect. The clinical research community, including funding agencies and clinical investigators, has neglected the study of anger and hostility. This neglect was clearly demonstrated in chapter 1 of this volume, where Kassinove and Sukhodolsky showed the large gap in citations for anger compared with depression and anxiety.

But is there sufficient cause for shifting research attention toward the anger construct? We believe so. In addition to the maladaptive social consequences that emerge from angry interactions, at least three serious social and medical problems affecting our society seem to be anger related and warrant increased attention. First, the United States has the highest homicide rate of any Western industrialized country, and homicide is the second leading cause of death among 15- to 24-year-olds (Novello, Shosky, & Froehlke, 1992). The lay public, at least, is a strong believer in the relationship between anger and aggression (Tavris, 1989). Does such a relationship exist? If so, how can assessment efforts be constructed to facilitate the identification of persons at risk for engaging in such acts?

Second, 40% of all women murdered in the United States die at the hand of their husbands (Sigler, 1989), and at least 2 million women are battered by their husbands or intimate acquaintances each year (Straus & Gelles, 1986). Anger has been found to be a distinguishing characteristic of maritally violent men (Maiuro, Cahn, Vitaliano, Wagner, & Zegree, 1988), and is also a distinguishing factor of violent and nonviolent couples during laboratory husband–wife interactions (Margolin, John, & Gleberman, 1988). In addition, some form of anger-management training is typically included in the treatment of maritally violent men (e.g., Rosenbaum & O'Leary, 1986), further soldering the link between anger and aggression. Thus, the assessment of anger in at-risk couples becomes a critical factor in battering prevention.

Third, the number one cause of death of Americans—coronary heart disease (CHD)—is related to anger. The conclusion among most researchers in this field (e.g., Suarez & Williams, 1989) is that individuals with high levels of anger and hostility are at high risk for CHD, even when controlling for traditional biomedical indices (e.g., family history, blood pressure, and serum cholesterol levels). Although the exact pathway between excessive anger and CHD is disputed (Smith, 1992), evidence suggests that intense and chronic anger not only submits the body to a high degree of sustained autonomic arousal, but also perpetuates chronic disruptive environmental stressors, which lead to repeated anger arousal. The identification of such individuals early in life may assist in displacing this killer from the top of the mortality list.

Obviously, there are compelling reasons to engage in more focused clinical research on anger. This chapter confines itself to reviewing the cornerstone of basic anger research—clinical assessment. The chapter has three primary goals. First, we offer a comprehensive theoretical framework of clinically intense anger to serve as a basis for the concept of an *anger disorder*. Second, we review the current status of the diagnostic assessment of anger, focusing especially on the surprising lack of official diagnostic attention given to anger problems. Third, we offer a new approach to clinical research on anger and hostility by presenting three Axis I-type diagnoses, with anger as a core defining feature derived from our working model of anger. We close by outlining major unresolved research issues that could benefit from the model of anger presented in this chapter.

DEFINING THE CONSTRUCTS

It seems self-evident that the first step in the development of clinical assessment techniques for a concept such as anger is to provide a working definition of the construct. Considerable confusion has existed regarding how to define *anger*, notably in terms of how it differs from similar constructs such as hostility, annoyance, and aggression. As indicated in chapter 1, despite the recognition that anger has long been acknowledged as a significant emotional excess, there has been little systematic progress in laying a basic framework of anger theory, research, and application. Because of this, the first step toward such a framework is to provide clear definitions of the constructs under investigation. Without accepted definitions, the ability to adequately measure the construct is hampered, and the demonstration of construct validity is severely limited, both of which prevent valuable research findings from being integrated into a viable theory (Chesney, 1985).

CLARIFYING CONSTRUCTS AND A WORKING MODEL OF ANGER

Delineating meaningful, clinical anger disorders is confounded by the long-established tendency to use related concepts interchangeably (Spielberger, 1988; Spielberger, Jacobs, Russell, & Crane, 1983). This conceptual confusion may be reduced if terms and concepts are anchored in one or more of three dimensions. First, a concept may be defined in terms of the response system(s) involved. That is, human experience may be broken down into four correlated, yet distinct response dimensions: cognitive, affective (phenomenological), physiological, and behavioral. The cognitive element refers to encoding and information-processing styles, and includes concepts such as *attention and scanning, attributions, attitudes, concept accessibility and memory, emotional scripts, self-talk, imagery,* and the like. The affective component refers to the phenomenological, subjective experience of specific feelings that one actively labels and identifies. The physiological component refers to changes in skeletofacial muscle tone, autonomic arousal, and adrenal and other endocrine changes. The behavioral dimension encompasses overt motor behavior and verbal forms of expression. Different anger-related constructs often refer more to one response parameter than another. Second, constructs can be defined in terms of their dispositional or momentary referent. A term may refer to the way an individual habitually tends to think, feel, and behave (a dispositional or trait referent), or to how a person is thinking, feeling, and behaving at a given moment or over a short period of time (a momentary or state referent). Third, although it may be somewhat artificial in some cases, reactions (and the concepts describing them) can be described in terms of how situation- or context-bound they are. Some reactions appear to be relatively situation-specific and occur primarily in the presence of specific environmental cues or conditions. Other reactions seem more generalized and cut across a wide range of situations; the individual simply seems more prone to anger and irritability (i.e., high on a trait of General Anger). This does not indicate that the individual is angry all the time, but only that the anger experiences have generalized across many situations and are experienced more intensely for a longer duration.

In describing a specific anger episode (state anger), the outcome emerges from complex interactions among: (a) one or more prompting conditions; (b) the individual's pre-anger state, including momentary and enduring characteristics; and (c) appraisal processes (Deffenbacher, in press). In this sense, anger is one type of an internal experience or response. It consists of physiological, cognitive, and phenomenological components that rapidly interact and influence each other, and that generally appear in a simultaneous manner such that the individual experiences them together as anger. This experience of anger, however, is not synonymous with how the individual behaves. Likewise, so-called "angry behaviors," such as verbal or physical aggression, are neither necessary nor sufficient conditions for the presence of an angry emotional state. The individual may do a wide variety of things when angry, and these behaviors should be conceptually and clinically distinguished from related constructs.

Anger Prompts

Anger is often elicited by one or more of three classes of stimuli. Occasionally, anger appears to be triggered by an identifiable event, such as being cut off in traffic, a flip retort from an adolescent, an object such as a computer that malfunctions, or a personal characteristic such as being clumsy. A second source is the anger-laden memories and internal images that are triggered by external cues. For example, an adult may overreact with anger in response to a supervisor's comment because it redintegrated memories of being verbally abused as a child, or anger when teased may be due to the triggering of memories of being ridiculed as a child. Other anger experiences appear to be elicited by different types of internal stimuli—namely, other cognitions and emotions. For example, a person may respond to feelings such as rejection, hurt, anxiety, or humiliation with anger. In this case, anger is secondary to the experience of the other emotions. Anger may also stem from ruminating and brooding about a past or future event, such as thoughts of a partner's infidelity or an unfair performance review at work. In such cases, the individual is experiencing anger, but the actual events are far removed in time and space. Moreover, people may vary in their awareness of the prompts of anger, especially the latter two types of prompts, and may experience anger but not know why or be unable to attribute it to the right source.

Pre-Anger Characteristics

The person's state prior to the elicitation of anger consists of two parts: enduring person characteristics, and momentary cognitive–emotional–physical state. Enduring characteristics might be subsumed under Lazarus' (1991) concept of *ego identity*, or Beck's (1976) concept of *personal domain* (i.e., those things central about and to the person, and those beliefs, values, people, causes, and things about which the individual cares, values, and holds dear). Anger is elicited when the individual perceives a blameful or shameful attack on the individual's ego identity (Lazarus, 1991), a trespass on the personal domain (Beck, 1976), or a violation of personally defined rules for behavior or events (Beck, 1988; Dryden, 1990; Ellis, 1977). Intense or otherwise dysfunctional anger often develops from rigid and highly extended boundaries to the personal domain. Preferences are no longer personal and flexible guidelines for behavior, but become dictatorial commandments of self and others. Values and commitments become imperatives, rather than things about which the person deeply cares, but in which shortcomings can be tolerated. Agreements and expectations become inviolate decrees, rather than meaningful but tentative contracts and promises. Things with which the individual is identified or involved become sanctified and off limits to negative events, rather than experiences that naturally, although undesirably, are occasionally difficult or bothersome. The individual views goals as ends unto themselves, rather than as desired outcomes. Goals must not be blocked or stymied, and the person has little tolerance for frustrating, goal-blocking events. Anger eventuates when any of these rigidly, and often arbitrarily, defined parameters are violated.

The probability and intensity of anger is also influenced by the immediate physical–emotional–mental state of the individual. All other things being equal, a negative internal state increases the probability of anger (Berkowitz, 1993). The level of anger at the time of provocation, even if it is unrelated to the current provocation, seems to transfer and increase the probability, intensity, and sometimes the duration of anger arousal (Zillman, 1971; Zillman & Bryant, 1974). The influence of negative affective states is not, however, limited to anger and frustration. A series of studies by Berkowitz and his colleagues (cf. Berkowitz, 1989, 1990) have shown that a wide variety of aversive states, including fatigue, illness, stress or anxiety, hunger, extreme cold or heat, and the like, increase the likelihood of an anger response. Such aversive conditions seem to increase the presence of aversive images, memories, and feelings that lower the threshold for anger.

Thus, although transitory affective states may increase the likelihood of an anger response, the individual's enduring traits and characteristics may dictate the nature of a particular anger episode, a theme discussed over 30 years ago by

Ellis (1962). He wrote, "Thus, almost anyone will respond immediately with some degree of anger to an insult or an injury, because almost all humans will appraise such a stimulus as being bad *to them*. But those individuals with a bellicose, when-you-say-that-partner-smile!, philosophy of life will tend to remain angry much longer, and to do more about their anger, than those with a meekshall-inherit-the-earth philosophy" (p. 46; italics original).

Appraisal Processes

Anger is not an automatic reaction. Potential provocations are appraised through dispositional tendencies, temporary physical–emotional–cognitive states, and temporary characteristics of the situation. Primary appraisal (Lazarus, 1991) involves an evaluation of an event and its context in terms of its potential relevance and threat or harm value. Anger is unlikely if the event is appraised as either irrelevant or benign or positive. However, anger becomes more likely to the extent that the event is appraised as relevant and as a trespass on the personal domain, a violation of expectations or freedoms, and/or an interference with goal-directed behavior. In other words, from the individual's perspective, something has happened (or may happen) that "should not" happen. Moreover, certain collateral judgments or appraisals tend to escalate anger. Specifically, anger increases with attributions of *injustice* (i.e., the source is unwarranted and unfair as judged against the individual's sense of values, justice, and equality), *preventability* (i.e., the source could have and should have been controlled to prevent or minimize the effects of the event), *intentionality* (i.e., someone or something purposefully made the event happen to the person), and/or *blameworthiness* (i.e., the source responsible for the event should be made to pay or suffer for its occurrence).

Secondary appraisal processes involve a judgment about the person's coping capacities, rather than the precipitating condition. Anger is not likely to eventuate if the individual perceives him- or herself as possessing adequate coping skills. However, even when the individual has adequate coping skills, anger is likely if he or she engages a secondary appraisal style labeled as "I-can't-stand-it-itis," or low frustration tolerance by rational-emotive theorists (Dryden, 1990; Ellis, 1977). Specifically, the person arbitrarily judges that he or she should not have to be exposed to or tolerate the frustrating event, and that the accompanying discomfort is more than he or she can bear. Anger is also likely to increase when aggression is the preferred mode of coping, and when the individual has positive outcome and efficacy expectancies for attack (Lazarus, 1991).

Anger

Using the appraisals described previously, the internal experience of anger may result. Anger is composed of cognitive, affective, and physiological elements. Much of the cognitive component of state anger is an extension of the prior appraisal processes (i.e., the individual continues to recycle demanding, critical, and denigrating thoughts and appraisals). Additionally, cognitive processes include attention to and labeling of the feelings as angry ones, often using such feelings as justification for current thoughts, feeling, and behavior, which then may escalate and solidify anger. Moreover, the individual often tends to elaborate cognitive biases, such as selective attention to negative or aversive elements, overgeneralized and inflammatory labeling, and additional demanding and blaming. Physiologically, anger is characterized by activation of the sympathetic nervous system, dumping of adrenal hormones, and increased tension in the skeletal and facial muscles.

The affective phenomenological component of anger has been the subject of much theoretical and empirical debate. The original Yerkes–Dodson Law (1908) suggests that anger is experienced along a continuum from mild frustration, annoyance, and irritation through more moderate levels such as feeling angry, to more extreme states of fury, rage, and being "mad as hell." Spielberger's research team (Spielberger, 1988; Spielberger et al., 1983) espoused this single-continuum theory of anger arousal as well. Ellis (1977; Ellis & Dryden, 1987), however, has long maintained that all emotions, including anger, are best understood along dual continua. "Appropriate" emotions exist on the first continuum, which, in regard to anger, corresponds to feelings of annoyance and irritation. Any intensity of annoyance and irritation is deemed appropriate, ranging from feeling mildly annoyed to very irritated. However, the second or "inappropriate" continuum consists of the qualitatively different emotions of anger and rage. Any experience of these inappropriate emotions, including feeling mildly angry to very enraged, is viewed by Ellis as being associated with an irrational thinking style and leading to the obstruction of goal achievement. Thus, according to Ellis, the therapeutic goal is to shift the individual from inappropriate emotional experiences to any intensity of appropriate emotionality. Using a self-report controlled diary methodology, Averill's (1982) community sample viewed anger as a qualitatively different kind of experience than annoyance, providing evidence for Ellis' view. The difference appears to be an attribution of seriousness of the activating event, with annoyance being the result of less serious life events and anger the result of more serious offenses. Experimental investigations have failed to confirm Ellis' dual-continua theory, however. Cramer (1985) and Cramer and Fong (1991) found no evidence to support the quality distinction, and noted that "since the appropriateness of a feeling cannot be identified independently of its beliefs, it seems unnecessary to attempt to use the type of emotion as a basis for determining its appropriateness" (Cramer & Fong, 1991, p. 32). Similarly, Kassinove, Eckhardt, and Endes (1993) found that, although a student sample consistently judged the "inappropriate" emotion to be stronger than its appropriate counterpart, the simple addition of a modifier such as *very* or *mildly* resulted in appropriate emotion words (e.g., *very annoyed*) being judged as significantly more intense than inappropriate emotion words (e.g., *mildly angry*). Thus, the question remains as to what our patients are referring to when they say "I feel a little angry" versus "I feel so very annoyed."

Even though the cognitive, physiological, and phenomenological components of anger are separated here, it should be noted that for many individuals they are at least moderately correlated, and they tend to cycle rapidly and complement each other. Nevertheless, the salience and magnitude of each response system's contribution to the experience of anger may vary considerably from person to person.

Anger-Expression Style

When angered, people express themselves in different ways, both within individuals over time as well as across people within the same situation. Anger does not predestine aggression. Certainly some angry individuals are outwardly and negatively expressive (i.e., anger-out style). For example, these individuals may verbally or physically attack others, objects, or themselves. Sometimes the behavior is less overt, but still outwardly expressive in negative ways, such as people who sulk and pout, or who make indirect and subtle cutting remarks. Others experience anger, but tend to withhold, suppress, or repress anger (i.e., anger-in style). They may show little external expression, but experience considerable internal turmoil and stress. In still other cases, they may show little awareness of their anger, but reflect it physically through ailments like headaches and gastric distress. Some of these individuals may also withdraw from the situation inappropriately, and others may employ neurotic defenses such as intellectualization or denial. Other individuals, when angered, engage in a variety of calming and palliative coping skills that lower their arousal and allow them to endure and deal more calmly with a provocative situation (anger-control style). Yet another angered individual may engage in a variety of appropriate approach, problem-solving, limit-setting, and assertive expression and negotiation skills (i.e., an anger-prosocial, active style). The general point is that, when angered, people respond in a variety of adaptive and maladaptive ways. These behaviors can be separated, conceptually and diagnostically, from the experience of anger. To the extent that anger expressive styles or behaviors are problematic, they can be conceptualized and treated as problems related to, but not synonymous, with anger.

The working model outlined in the previous paragraphs describes a set of input, internal, and output variables associated with an episode of state anger. *Anger* can also be described as a trait (Spielberger, 1988), defined as the propensity to experience state anger more frequently and intensely. Although Spielberger described *trait anger* as a general personality trait, the concept may be narrowed to refer to situational reactions (i.e., the propensity to experience anger more intensely when exposed to a given situation or cluster of related situations). *Hostility*, another term often confused with anger, is also a more traitlike term referring to appraisal and cognitive processes through which the individual tends to code others' actions as harmful and unjustified attacks, which prime aggressive counterresponses. Hostility involves an attitudinal or cognitive set of ill will, enmity, discounting or denigration of others, and blame and punishment of the provocation. Hostile attitudes often elicit anger, but the relationship is not linear. For example, one could respond with cold detachment or develop a plan to harm another severely without the experience of much affective or physiological arousal.

Aggression is another term often confused with anger. Aggression refers to overt behavior, either physical or sometimes verbal, that does or could bring harm to another person, object, or system. As outlined earlier, aggression is but one class of behavior in response to anger. Aggression typically occurs in the context of an anger-out response style. Moreover, two different types of aggressive behavior have been distinguished (Buss, 1961; Feshbach, 1964; Spielberger et al., 1983). Hostile aggression is intended to bring about harm, pain, or destruction. Anger often accompanies hostile aggression and may be quite intense, with accompanying self-statements and/or images of harm and destruction. Instrumental aggression is behavior that can bring about damage, but may be enacted without either hostile intent or angry affect. The goal or motive in instrumental aggression may be to remove an obstacle blocking goal-directed behavior. For example, a football player may throw an aggressive block that damages an opposing player, but the goal was not to harm the opponent; instead, the goal was to open a lane for a runner. More often, however, anger varies in relationship to instrumental aggression, with anger existing at a moderate level without the associated hostile verbalizations and imagery components.

THE DIAGNOSIS OF ANGER

The working model presented in the previous section outlines basic factors involved in the onset, experience, and expression of anger. The next step is to describe how anger can be assessed in clinical contexts. Despite the significant advances that have occurred in the assessment of major affective and personality disorders in the last half century, little progress has been evidenced in the assessment of anger in what is the most common form of clinical measurement—diagnosis. The most obvious indication that contemporary psychology and psychiatry have neglected anger as a clinically relevant problem is the absence of a diagnostic category with anger as the central and defining feature. As a frame of reference, there are currently 11 potential Axis I disorders for anxiety-related problems and nine Axis I disorders for depression/bipolar-related disorders in *DSM-IV* (American Psychiatric Association, 1994). For example, diagnoses are available for chronic, moderate depression (dysthymia) and chronic, moderate anxiety and unrealistic worry (generalized anxiety disorder), but not for a parallel condition of chronic, moderate, and pervasive anger. Categories exist for situational anxiety reactions (phobias), but not for a situational anger reaction such as intense anger that occurs primarily in the presence of a spouse's criticism or in response to other automobile drivers on the road. It seems likely that substantial advancements in the assessment and treatment of anxiety and depression have occurred partly as a result of being officially recognized as serious and pervasive disorders. With clearly defined diagnostic criteria, relevant subject samples can be identified and clinical research can progress. Novaco (1985) argued that a major reason for the dearth of basic clinical anger research is the lack of accepted diagnostic criteria to identify clinical subjects. Several other authors have commented on the lack of such a diagnosis (Deffenbacher, 1994; DiGiuseppe, Eckhardt, & Tafrate, 1993; O'Leary & Murphy, 1992; Tavris, 1989).

There are disorders where anger contributes to a diagnosis, such as dysthymia and posttraumatic stress disorder (PTSD) on Axis I, paranoid and borderline personality disorders on Axis II, and high blood pressure and coronary artery disease (CAD) on Axis III. However, there are no disorders where anger is a primary diagnostic criterion. The absence of specific anger disorders in our current nosology, however, does not mean that people do not suffer from anger-based emotional disorders, or that such disorders are not worthy of conceptual delineation, empirical research, and focused treatment. In this section, we first review some conceptual issues relating to the absence of anger in available diagnostic criteria, and later combine dimensions of the working model of anger presented earlier in this chapter to address this diagnostic oversight. We then outline several proposed anger disorders defined by the presence and predominance of anger.

Anger, Anxiety, and Depression

From a clinical assessment perspective, it appears that individuals who present with intense and problematic anger are captured diagnostically by depressive and anxiety-based disorders. What is unclear, however, is whether this classification bias is due to the historical preference of viewing anxiety and depression as the core affective disorders, or whether anger is considered a variation or subcomponent of anxiety and depression. The traditional psychoanalytic notion, of course, was that depression was the result of self-directed anger; however, this hypothesis has received little empirical support (e.g., Beck, 1963). Although it is often the case that individuals experience anger and depression simultaneously, it is an oversimplification to assume a linear relationship between such complex emotional experiences. In a review of this research, Tavris (1989) concluded that "sometimes depression is 'anger turned inward,' but sometimes it is only depression, which is bad enough. . . . Just as there are different kinds and causes of anger, there are different depressions, and different relationships between the two emotions" (p. 108).

Fava, Anderson, and Rosenbaum (1990) described several cases of patients presenting with what they termed *anger attacks*. These patients reported brief, episodic occurrences of high levels of autonomic arousal, sweating, tachycardia, and feeling out of control. However, they reported anger and the desire to attack others as more salient components than anxious or panic feelings, and they responded well to medication typically used for panic disorder. These patients did not meet the criteria for any Axis II disorder, suggesting that the phenomenological experience and outward expression of anger manifested clinical syndromelike features. The authors characterized these cases as variants of either panic disorder or "an atypical presentation of depressive disorder." Thus, despite the importance of identifying a subset of patients who experience intense and dysfunctional anger as the core diagnostic feature, these patients' idiosyncratic affective style and personality functioning were unfortunately discarded in favor of traditional diagnostic nosology.

More recent investigations (Fava et al., 1993; Rosenbaum et al., 1993) have deemphasized the link between anger attacks and panic disorder, and have highlighted the association between anger attacks and depressive disorders. These studies revealed that 44% of outpatients meet *DSM-III-R* criteria for major depression, and 21% of an unselected sample also reported the presence of anger attacks. Presence of anger attacks was determined by the authors' Anger Attacks Questionnaire (Fava et al., 1991), a 15-item self-report scale that does not directly assess the subjective experience of anger but, instead, assesses autonomic arousal and aggressive behavior. Subjects classified as having anger attacks scored significantly higher on the Cook–Medley Hostility Inventory than nonanger attack subjects, and the sample was diagnostically heterogeneous on Axis II, with a high percentage of anger attack patients receiving the entire array of personality diagnoses. Anger attack subjects experienced significant reductions in hostility after 8-week fluoxetine treatment.

Although the notion of an *anger attack* is a useful clinical descriptor, this assessment is made without directly assessing the subjective element of anger; perhaps the descriptor should have been termed *aggression attack* until a more direct assessment of anger is made. Although these investigators have provided important new information on patients whose primary affective disturbance is anger, and have suggested that approximately 20% of unselected adults and 40% of depressed outpatients may experience such episodes, by following traditional psychiatric nosology that largely omits the anger construct, they have explained away the patients' anger in favor of other affective disorders and personality disorders. That anger is associated with depression and anxiety is undisputed, but the continued practice of categorizing anger problems with other emotional disorders will do little except thwart anger research and inhibit the understanding of a powerful and costly emotion.

Anger and Intermittent Explosive Disorder

Standard diagnostic documents address anger in several largely indirect ways. The Axis I disorder in *DSM-IV* most frequently used for patients with dysfunctional anger is intermittent explosive disorder (IED). The criteria for this disorder are largely expressive-destructive in nature, with affirmative diagnoses noted when there are "discrete episodes of failure to resist aggressive impulses that result in serious assaultive acts or destruction of property" (American Psychiatric Association, 1994, pp. 609–610). Although there may be signs of generalized impulsivity or aggressiveness between explosive episodes, the authors of *DSM-*

IV suggest that an underlying personality disorder is the cause. This category appears in the "Impulse Control Disorders Not Elsewhere Classified" section of *DSM-IV*, and no prevalence or course of onset information is provided with the exception of the following cryptic statement: "Reliable information is lacking, but Intermittent Explosive Disorder is apparently rare" (p. 611).

Thus, the hallmark of the disorder is the "aggressive impulses" that presumably cause the individual to destroy property and attack others, but only occasionally. The notion that the destructive behaviors are a result of the "failure to resist aggressive impulses" implies that such impulses are inherent in all people, and that most manage to stifle such drives. This age-old, psychoanalytically based idea is, if nothing else, controversial (Peele, 1989), and is most likely empirically untenable (Geen, 1990). McElroy, Hudson, Pope, Keck, and Aisley (1992) reviewed the status of impulse control disorders, including IED, and concluded that these diagnoses ". . . remain a mysterious group of conditions. Even their diagnostic validity, individually and as a category, remains in question" (p. 323). These authors noted that, because IED is associated with a variety of affective disorders, and because there are few well-designed studies supporting the diagnostic inclusiveness of IED, it would be more profitable if it were reformulated to address affective features. In addition, this review suggests that the focus on overt behavior and irresistible impulses in the absence of a thorough phenomenological assessment provides an incomplete clinical picture.

From a theoretical perspective, IED is insufficient for chronically angry patients because it fails to address the relationship between anger and aggression. Aggressive behaviors are the only required feature. Thus, individuals who experience intense and chronic anger and have impaired functioning as a result would meet the criteria for this disorder only if they also engage in occasional acts of destruction or interpersonal aggression. Given that Averill (1982) found that 90% of anger episodes occur in the absence of aggressive behavior, requiring aggressive behavior but not angry affect reflects a diagnostic scale balanced in the wrong direction.

Anger and Personality Disorders

The second inclusion of anger in *DSM-IV* is as a symptom of Axis II personality disorders, in which anger is viewed as only a small part of a larger personality pattern. Anger is addressed in the following personality disorders: borderline ("inappropriate, intense anger or difficulty controlling anger. . ."), antisocial ("irritability and aggressiveness, as indicated by repeated physical fights or assaults"), and paranoid (". . . is quick to react angrily or to counterattack"). The presence of anger as a symptom in such a variety of personality disorders, but virtually absent as a feature of major clinical syndromes (anger is a criterion for PTSD on Axis I), suggests that anger is important in the assessment of disordered personality. However, none of these personality disorders seems particularly accurate in describing many patients whose primary clinical problem is anger.

One reason that anger is viewed as a symptom of a personality disorder (rather than a clinical syndrome) is the well-documented stability of aggressive behavior (Olweus, 1979; Patterson, 1986). Given that anger and aggression are often regarded as inextricably linked, it is understandable that anger has been viewed as a stable trait as well. This hypothesis has at least been indirectly confirmed by Larsen and colleagues (Larsen & Diener, 1987; Larsen, Diener, & Cropanzano, 1987), who have gathered data suggesting that negative emotion intensity and the quality of emotion-induced cognitive appraisals are stable personality dimensions. Similar findings have emerged from researchers investigating the five-factor model of personality (cf. Costa & Widiger, 1994). These authors noted that the trait of Neuroticism, the factor on which measures of anger load, is highly stable over time.

Even if certain expressions of anger are relatively stable, a certain degree of diagnostic complexity still exists. For example, Suarez and Williams (1989) divided subjects into high- and low-hostile groups based on Cook–Medley Hostility Inventory scores, and subjected both groups to an anger-arousing laboratory manipulation, during which they obtained various physiological measures. Interestingly, they found that high hostiles did not differ from low hostiles in physiological reactivity at rest; autonomic differences between the two groups were only revealed during the stressful task. Thus, individuals high in hostility (a personality predisposition) are not in a state of perpetual anger and hostility; the heightened emotional response (Axis I clinical syndrome) is only evident during stressful, anger-provoking environmental events. Similarly, because *DSM-IV* does not make this empirical distinction, angry patients may be relegated to an Axis II dimension that does not sufficiently describe the intense and potentially harmful nature of their affective responding. Therefore, it would be best for a diagnostic system to include a primary Axis I clinical syndrome that describes patients with chronic and dysfunctional anger and hostility.

The notion of anger and hostility being more akin to a disorder of personality is based on the assumption that Axis I and Axis II disorders are fundamentally different categories of disturbance, with little comorbidity. However, available evidence suggests that Axis I and Axis II disorders share a similar etiology, combining biogenetic and psychosocial precursors (Livesley, Schroeder, Jackson, & Jang, 1994). In addition, the stability criterion commonly associated with personality disorders is frequently found in Axis I disorders. "Dysthymic disorder, schizophrenia, and some cases of delusional disorder can be as stable as many personality disorders. The exacerbations that characterize the course of these disorders are often superimposed on more chronic symptoms" (Livesley et al., 1994, p. 14). Empirically, there is considerable diagnostic overlap between the two axes (Docherty, Feister, & Shea, 1986; Trull & McCrae, 1994). Given the high rate of Axis I–Axis II comorbidity, it is plausible to theorize that the hostility trait so often discussed in behavioral medicine research (cf. Smith, 1992) may be the personality dimension (Axis II) underlying individuals who experience episodes of intense and problematic anger (Axis I).

With regard to Axis I–Axis II comorbidity, it is interesting to note that borderline personality disorder (BDL) was most frequently associated with a concurrent affective disorder, with prevalence rates of BDL and comorbid affective disorders ranging between 25%–60%. BDL is perhaps the most likely diagnosis for intensely angry clients (especially those who are female). It is also the most frequently diagnosed personality disorder (Widiger & Trull, 1993). A very high number (75%) of the Fava et al. (1993) anger attack patients met the criteria for BDL, suggesting that angry displays play a large role in the diagnosis of BDL. However, Trull and McCrae (1994) noted that if one considers the diagnostic criteria for BDL given in *DSM-IV*, "there are literally 93 ways to be a borderline." Thus, the disorder is extremely heterogeneous, with some clients characterized by intense anger/affective arousal, and others having little problem with anger expression, but demonstrating serious impulsivity and parasuicidality. This heterogeneity suggests that the concepts of *anger* and *hostility* be more formally addressed by a unique diagnostic category or combination of categories.

It appears that intensely angry clients are underserved by current nosological models. Despite evidence by Fava et al. (1991) that dysfunctional anger takes the form of a "clinical syndrome," there are currently no available diagnostic categories that capture this affective and behavioral symptom cluster. Likewise, confining anger as an indirect feature of several personality disorders is incongruent with current conceptualizations of anger experience and expression, and fails to account for the overlap evidenced between Axis I and Axis II disorders.

ANGER-BASED DIAGNOSTIC MODELS

In this section, dimensions of the working model of anger introduced at the beginning of the chapter are combined to address this diagnostic oversight and outline anger disorders defined by the presence and predominance of anger. In making any of the proposed diagnoses, significant angry affect (i.e., feelings of being angry, furious, mad, livid, enraged, very frustrated, pissed off, etc.) are necessary for a positive diagnosis, and several indices of physiological arousal and anger-laden cognitive processes are also necessary, even though the exact configuration of these varies from case to case. Physiological responses include: (a) increased heart rate, (b) increased general muscle tension or increased tension in specific muscles such as clenched hands or jaws, (c) trembling or shaky feelings, (d) sweaty or clammy hands, (e) rapid breathing, (f) reddening of the skin or hot sensations, (g) restlessness or agitation, (h) jumpiness or exaggerated startle reactions, (i) feeling hyperaroused, keyed up, or on edge, or (j) stomach pain or nausea. Cognitive indices include: (a) a strong belief that one has been treated unfairly, trespassed on, or violated in some way; (b) rigid demands that others or events should be as he or she desires; (c) demanding that he or she should not be or have been exposed to or have to endure the provocation; (d) blaming of others or outside events for the extent of problems, angry feelings, and/or reactions; (e) inflammatory labeling (e.g., cursing) of people or events involved; (f) a belief that anger or aggression is justified because of the nature of outside events; (g) thoughts and/or images of harm to, revenge on, or retaliation against the source of the provocation; (h) brooding or angry ruminations about the provocation; and (i) racing thoughts or concentration difficulties. Problematic anger reactions may appear in relatively circumscribed situations (situational anger) or be more general and pervasive (generalized anger).

Employing these dimensions, we propose the following three anger disorders: (a) Adjustment Disorder with Angry Mood, (b) Situational Anger Disorder, and (c) General Anger Disorder. The latter two categories can appear with or without aggressive behavior, yielding a total of five proposed disorders. To make the diagnoses of Situational Anger Disorder with Aggression and General Anger Disorder with Aggression, significant aggressive behavior must also be present in addition to meeting the other diagnostic criteria for Situational Anger Disorder and General Anger Disorder. Verbally and physically aggressive behaviors include: (a) engaging in loud verbal outbursts, yelling, and screaming; (b) becoming verbally threatening, insulting, intimidating, or highly argumentative; (c) engaging in repeated sarcasm, cutting verbal remarks, or hostile humor; (d) acting in a physically threatening or intimidating manner; (e) engaging in physically assaultive behavior toward others (e.g., hitting, kicking, slapping, punching, grabbing, shoving, throwing things, etc.); (f) engaging in physically assaultive or destructive behavior against property (e.g., throwing, slamming, banging on, pounding on, breaking, etc.); (g) actively seeking out or provoking a verbally aggressive confrontation; (h) engaging in belligerent or stubborn refusal to cooperate with reasonable requests in dealing with provocation or difficulties; and (i) engaging in sullen or sulky withdrawal (e.g., pouting, icy stares, etc.).

Adjustment Disorder with Angry Mood

According to *DSM-IV*, adjustment disorders are maladaptive reactions to identifiable psychosocial stressors that occur within 3 months after onset of the stressor, and have persisted for no longer than 6 months. In *DSM-IV*, several adjustment disorders are characterized by their emotional or mood elements (i.e., Adjustment Disorder with Anxiety, Depression, or Mixed Emotional Features). None, however, is characterized by anger alone. For anger to be included as part of a diagnosis, it must be mixed with other emotional elements, problems of conduct, or significant disruption of normal work or school activities.

The lack of an adjustment disorder category defined primarily by angry mood overlooks a number of individuals who have suffered significant stress and who are experiencing a great deal of anger, but who are not experiencing other strong negative emotions and who are not acting in a significantly disruptive manner. For example, there are no clear diagnostic schema currently available for the following common clinical examples.

- An individual going through a divorce often experiences periods of anger and irritability seemingly without cause, and is very angry at his or her ex-spouse such that the sight of, thought of, mention of, or any interaction with the ex-spouse leads to intense feelings of anger. Yet this individual does not seem significantly anxious or depressed, and does not act aggressively (with the probable exception of a few angry words over the phone or in an interpersonal encounter).
- A child or adolescent is sullen, argumentative, irritable, and angry with his or her parents for moving away from established friends, school, and neighborhood. However, the youngster is not experiencing other negative emotions to the degree that anger is being experienced, and is not doing such things as running away, skipping school, getting drunk or high, or showing significant decreases in academic performance.
- A marital partner is angry, irritable, touchy, and argumentative after a diagnosis of infertility. Once again, other emotions are not strong, work performance is not disrupted significantly, and there is not a disturbance in usual deportment beyond some minor argumentativeness.

In all of these cases, angry emotionality is central to the adjustment disorder, and criteria for other adjustment disorders do not apply.

To address these clinical examples, it is suggested that a new adjustment disorder, Adjustment Disorder with Angry Mood, be added to the diagnostic lexicon. It would parallel the criteria for Adjustment Disorder with Anxiety or Depression, except that the defining characteristics would be a predominant manifestation of anger, such as periods of angry affect and irritability, sullenness, anger outbursts, or behavioral displays not sufficient to fit conduct problems, such as irritable complaining and "pickiness," "snappiness," making but not acting on verbal or physical threats, slamming objects, or throwing things.

A major diagnostic concern is the discrimination between this adjustment disorder and other adjustment disorders. Specifically, Adjustment Disorder with Mixed Emotional Features would be appropriate where anger is observed along with other emotional excesses, but is not the primary manifestation of the stress reaction. The proposed diagnosis would also have to be distinguished from Adjustment Disorder with Disturbance of Conduct and Mixed Disturbance of Emotions and Conduct if aggressive, antisocial behaviors are sufficiently strong enough to abridge the rights of others and/or violate age-appropriate norms. If interference with work or school performance is a prime manifestation, then either the diagnoses of Adjustment Disorder with Work (or Academic) Inhibition or Adjustment Disorder Not Otherwise Specified would be considered first, depending on the degree of anger present. Finally, these proposed diagnostic categories do not include an Adjustment Disorder with Anger and Aggression because, at least within the framework of *DSM-III-R*, aggressive behaviors are adequately included under Adjustment Disorders with Disturbances of Conduct.

Situational Anger Disorder Without Aggression

This anger disorder describes a persistent (present 6 months or more), consistent, and intense anger reaction to a circumscribed situation (e.g., in response to a critical supervisor or discourteous drivers) or to a cluster of situations that share a common theme (e.g., being insulted or having one's authority challenged). Anger in this disorder is relatively delimited and is not experienced as a chronic mood state or pervasive response pattern. Although the individual becomes demonstrably angry, he or she does not show significant aggressive behavior (i.e., does not meet criteria for Situational Anger Disorder with Aggression outlined in the next section). When angered, the person experiences anger arousal, but either engages in appropriate behavior or in minimal (in both frequency and severity) aggressive behavior. Positive examples of this disorder would be an individual who is angry primarily in traffic situations, even after relatively minor driving hassles, but only curses internally at the offense; or a parent who becomes very angry when undone chores are encountered, but does not yell at or act aggressively toward the child. At the same time, the situational anger reaction disrupts the person's typical social, work, or school activities, impairs relationships, and/or causes the person significant distress.

In summary, the individual experiences significantly elevated anger in response to certain types of situations, but does not respond aggressively. This anger interferes significantly with the person's life in terms of more frequent interpersonal disruptions and personal distress. Specifically, for a diagnosis of Situational Anger Disorder Without Aggression to be made, it must be determined that the anger is not part of a diagnosable psychotic condition, borderline or antisocial personality disorders, or posttraumatic stress disorder, or is only present when drugs or alcohol are ingested. Presence of such elements would suggest either that the anger is best considered part of these conditions or that a dual diagnosis should be considered.

Situational Anger Disorder with Aggression

This disorder involves both elevated anger and aggressive behavior in response to specific situations. For example, the individual not only becomes angry in traffic when cut off, but also does things such as drives menacingly up behind the other driver, shouts a string of epithets, makes visible obscene gestures, or forces the offending driver off the road. Other examples include an employee who, when beeped repeatedly without an opportunity to return the calls, becomes highly angry and has thrown several beepers against the wall or floor; or a parent who becomes livid and yells at his or her child whenever undone chores are encountered. Although these are but a few examples, they show that an individual routinely employs a consistent pattern of physically and verbally aggressive behaviors in concert with intense angry affect when encountering a specific provocative situation. Also, the anger and aggression are disruptive to the individual's normal activities, relationships, and vocational or educational performance, and/or causes significant personal distress. Finally, Situational Anger Disorder Without Aggression must also be ruled out to confirm Situational Anger Disorder with Aggression.

General Anger Disorder Without Aggression

Whereas the situational anger disorders are more circumscribed, this disorder describes the individual who is chronically and pervasively angry, but not highly aggressive. That is, the person experiences anger as a fairly chronic mood state or is angered frequently in a wide range of situations, such that elevated anger is a near daily experience. Anger may be elicited by a wide range of external situations that do not appear thematic in nature by either internal psychological states (e.g., disappointment or perceptions of being rejected, memories of past mistreatment, ruminations about past injustices and failures, etc.) and/or aversive physiological states (fatigue, physical pain, chronic stress, etc.). The chronic, pervasive nature of this pattern of anger experience is described in two ways. First, this type of anger must be present, more days than not, for at least one calendar year. Second, the individual has not been without the frequent anger reactions or periods of angry/irritable mood for more than 1 month. It is not suggested that such individuals are never happy or are perpetually irate and angry. To the contrary, although they may experience many positive feelings, they are frequently angered as well. In addition, the individual may occasionally behave aggressively, either verbally or against objects (e.g., make sharp verbal comments, pout or sulk, slam doors); however, these behaviors tend to be relatively infrequent when compared with the high frequency of anger experienced, and moderate in severity such that the individual does not meet the criteria for General Anger Disorder with Aggression (see next section). As with the situational anger disorders, there is a sense of personal distress or cost. That is, the general anger level interferes with normal routines, social activities, relationships, and school or occupational functioning, and/or causes the individual significant personal distress. Finally, other diagnostic concerns must be ruled out. Specifically, the chronic or frequent anger should not be part of a diagnosable psychotic reaction, posttraumatic stress disorder, dysthymia, antisocial or borderline personality disorders, organic disorders, or occur only during alcohol or drug intoxication.

General Anger Disorder with Aggression

This disorder involves both frequent periods of generalized anger and frequent aggressive behavior. This disorder describes an individual who is frequently in an angry mood, but also does things such as engage in sarcasm, put others down, make verbal threats, or elevate discussions to loud arguments and yelling matches. For another individual, the mode of anger expression may be more physical than verbal. For example, the person might withdraw into an angry sullenness marked by terse communications and the tendency to throw or slam things around, or may frequently use an anger-out mode of anger expression involving pushing, grabbing, shoving, or slapping others, as well as more severe forms of physical aggression against others, such as closed-fist blows or choking. Put differently, the individual displays either a specific habitual pattern of aggressive behaviors or a significant frequency of a number of different aggressive behaviors. Finally, for a positive diagnosis, interference or disruption of the person's life must be established and other conditions (e.g., General Anger Disorder Without Aggression) must be ruled out.

DIAGNOSIS OF ANGER DISORDERS: FUTURE RESEARCH

As has been stated on numerous occasions in this chapter, a relatively scarce amount of data exists on anger and the nature of the anger construct largely because of the scientific neglect and conceptual confusion that has defined the study of anger in this century. This is extremely important because it points to a serious, yet unanswered, empirical question about the actual incidence and prevalence of individuals with major affective disorders, with anger and hostility as core defining features. Unfortunately, this is difficult to answer because there are no formal diagnostic categories to aid in the conceptualization of clinically relevant anger disorders. Without such schematic assistance, identifying clinically angry populations is largely a hit-or-miss ordeal; we do not know the answer to many crucial questions because the objective assessment and diagnosis of anger have not been priorities for the majority of clinical researchers. Individuals with anger problems no doubt exist (ask any independent practitioner), but are neglected diagnostically and schematically during clinical assessment.

The road toward validation and eventual acceptance of the previously discussed diagnostic categories is a particularly long one. Blashfield, Sprock, and Fuller (1990) offered a useful set of guidelines to govern the acceptance of any diagnostic category in future editions of *DSM*. In their view, categories worthy of inclusion should have: (a) a clear set of criteria from which self-report, rating scale, and structured interview assessment instruments can be constructed; (b) a minimum of 50 articles in support of the category, half of which should be empirical; (c) empirical demonstrations of interclinician reliability with $K > .70$; (d) unequivocal evidence that the symptoms cooccur as a syndrome; and (e) evidence that the proposed category can be differentiated from other diagnoses. Therefore, the anger disorders that we have suggested in this chapter exist as clinical hypotheses, and are preliminary models open for empirical scrutiny.

Construction and validation of a self-report scale and structured interview based on these diagnostic criteria have begun (Eckhardt, 1993; Eckhardt, DiGiuseppe, & Tafrate, 1994; Robin & Eckhardt, 1993). A 35-item Anger

Response Scale (ARS) was developed to assess the experience and expression of clinically intense anger. The ARS was given, along with a variety of self-report instruments, to numerous criterion groups, including outpatient adults, male prisoners, wife-abusing men, and college students. Results indicate that the ARS reliably assessed a form of anger distinct from that assessed by Spielberger's (1988) State-Trait Anger Expression Inventory (STAXI), as evidenced by separate loadings of ARS and STAXI subscales. Although the STAXI is an excellent measure of anger (particularly as a personality dimension), the ARS appears to assess a clinically relevant, intense form of anger likely to appear in angry outpatients. Additionally, a Structured Interview for Anger Disorders has been developed (Eckhardt, 1994) and is currently in the validation stage.

A careful epidemiological investigation of the prevalence of anger and anger disorders in the general population and the incidence of anger disorders in outpatient–inpatient samples would greatly enhance anger research. It is precisely this most basic form of descriptive data that anger research desperately needs. To formally address whether anger is indeed secondary or componential to other disorders, basic comorbidity data using the diagnostic models presented earlier would shed some objective light on this dilemma.

Current conceptualizations of diagnosis consider the notion of categorical, Kraeplinean diagnoses as an empirically untenable and outdated form of diagnostic assessment (e.g., Livesley et al., 1994). Thus, it would be wise for future research to examine the covariation of anger and anger disorders with the five-factor model (FFM) of personality. The FFM considers diagnosis from a dimensional, rather than a categorical, framework by considering two dimensions: scores on measures of normal personality traits (the "Big Five" dimensions of Neuroticism, Extroversion, Openness to Experience, Conscientiousness, and Agreeableness) and the degree of maladaptivity. Perhaps there are some individuals who are chronically angry and hostile (extreme scores on personality trait), but who experience little dysfunction. There are other individuals who experience heightened anger only during a specific stimulus event (e.g., a couple's infertility), and experience maladaptivity (argumentativeness, yelling, abuse) as a result. By utilizing FFM scales, such as Costa and McCrae's (1992) NEO-Personality Inventory–Revised (NEO PI–R), along with measures of anger and anger disorders, valuable information on the covariation of specific anger disorders with personality functioning can be integrated into treatment planning and existing diagnostic schema.

These are merely a few of the prominent but unresolved issues in anger research that serve to make this area of research so promising and exciting. Such basic research areas as the assessment and description of anger disorders remain empirically sparse areas of investigation, primarily because of the lack of a thorough conceptual framework to guide clinical research. It has been our goal to indicate how our model of anger and the diagnostic models derived from it can be usefully applied in the study of chronic and intense anger.

SUMMARY

In this chapter, we have suggested that anger refers to an internal, cognitive-affective/phenomenological-physiological condition that varies in intensity, duration, pervasiveness, and chronicity. Like other normally distributed emotional variables, such as anxiety and depression, anger can also present in severe and extreme forms. The probability of dysfunctionality increases as anger increases in frequency, intensity, or duration; when it involves more response dimensions (cognitive, affective, and physiological); and when it leads to more frequent and severe consequences (Deffenbacher, in press; Novaco, 1979). It was also noted that current diagnostic schemata neglect anger as a primary affective disruption. It was suggested that dysfunctional anger, much like depressive and anxiety disorders, can be described primarily in terms of its emotional and experiential qualities. Three such anger disorders—Adjustment Disorder with Angry Mood, Situational Anger Disorder Without Aggression, and General Anger Disorder Without Aggression—were proposed as preliminary categories to begin to fill this diagnostic gap and to aid conceptualization and research in the area. It was also noted that anger is related to, but distinct from, behavior that it may prompt. Therefore, two additional anger disorders—Situational Anger Disorder with Aggression and General Anger Disorder with Aggression—were proposed to capture both the dysfunctional anger and problematic aggressive acts of some individuals' reactions. It is hoped that these diagnostic descriptions further the understanding of dysfunctional anger and bring anger problems more into the mainstream as understandable, assessable, and treatable clusters of human experience.

Chapter 3

Measuring the Experience, Expression, and Control of Anger

Charles D. Spielberger, Eric C. Reheiser, and Sumner J. Sydeman

University of South Florida, Tampa

The biological bases of fear (anxiety) and rage (anger) were recognized by Darwin (1872/1965) more than a century ago. These emotions were regarded as adaptive for both humans and animals, having evolved over countless generations through a process of natural selection. Darwin also observed that both fear and rage vary in intensity. Fear increases from mild apprehension or surprise to an extreme "agony of terror" (Darwin, 1872/1965, p. 291). Anger and rage, he wrote, are "states of mind" that differ ". . . only in degree, and there is no marked distinction in their characteristic signs" (p. 244).

Emphasizing the profound psychobiological changes that occur as the intensity of anger increases, Darwin (1872/1965) observed that: "Under moderate anger the action of the heart is a little increased, the colour heightened. . . respiration is likewise a little hurried. . ." (p. 244). Similar, although much more intense, physiological and behavioral changes were noted in describing the characteristic manifestations of rage: "Under this powerful emotion the action of the heart is much accelerated. . . . The face reddens or it becomes purple . . . respiration is laboured, the chest heaves, and the dilated nostrils quiver. . . . The teeth are clenched or ground together, and the muscular system is commonly stimulated to violent, almost frantic action" (Darwin, 1872/1965, p. 74).

Like Darwin, Freud (1924, 1927) considered fear (anxiety) and aggression (anger) inherent characteristics of human behavior. However, Freud (1924) emphasized the feelings associated with these emotions, defining *anxiety* as "something felt," a specific unpleasant state or condition that included physiological and behavioral components. In his early writings, Freud considered aggression as an innate reaction to the thwarting of pleasure-seeking or pain-avoiding responses. Observing the carnage of World War I, Freud (1933/1959) conceptualized aggressive impulses as resulting from a biological instinct that motivates people to destroy themselves (i.e., the "Death Instinct"). This self-destructive behavior was inhibited, however, by a life instinct (libido), which turned the aggressive energy toward the outer world and away from the self. Aggression that could not be vented against external objects was turned back into the self, resulting in pathological symptoms such as depression, headaches, or other psychosomatic manifestations (Alexander & French, 1948; Freud, 1936).

Recent evidence supports an association between anger, hostility, and aggressive behavior and heart disease. Williams, Barefoot, and Shekelle (1985) found that hostility and cynicism were related to the presence and severity of coronary atherosclerosis. In addition, Dembroski, MacDougall, Williams, and Haney (1984) reported that potential for hostility was associated with coronary artery disease (CAD) for patients who suppressed their anger (anger-in), highlighting the importance of assessing the control of anger/hostility, in addition to measuring the experience and expression of angry feelings. Thus, qualities attributed to anger and aggression by Darwin and Freud have been incorporated into contemporary psychological theories, and there have been intensive efforts to measure constructs such as anger and hostility.

In this chapter, evolving conceptions of the nature of anger as a psychobiological emotional state are considered in historical perspective, and the relation of anger to aggression and hostility is examined. Advances in the measurement of anger and hostility are then briefly reviewed, and the construction of instruments to assess the experience and expression of anger is described in some detail. Gender differences in the experience and expression of anger are also noted. The chapter concludes with a discussion of anger control and the construction of a new scale to assess the reduction of angry feelings.

ANGER, HOSTILITY, AND AGGRESSION: THE AHA! SYNDROME

Early psychological studies of emotions focused on the qualitative feelings associated with these internal states. From an analysis of the introspective reports of trained observers, researchers endeavored to discover the "mental elements" of which different emotions were comprised (Titchener, 1897; Wundt, 1896). Unfortunately, this phenomenological approach generated findings that were unrelated to other behaviors, and resulted in a discouraging degree of conceptual ambiguity and empirical inconsistency (Plutchik, 1962; Young, 1943).

With the advent of behaviorism shortly after the turn of the century, psychological research shifted from the investigation of subjective internal feelings associated with emotional states, to the environmental antecedents, physiological manifestations, and objective behavioral consequences of emotion. The frustration-aggression hypothesis (Dollard, Doob, Miller, Mowrer, & Sears, 1939) became the predominant psychological theory pertaining to aggressive behavior in the 1940s and 1950s. Proponents of this theory rejected instinctual models of aggression (Freud, 1933/1959; McDougall, 1908), proposing instead that frustration provoked and stimulated an internal drive that motivated aggressive behavior. Although stated in behavioral terms, the frustration-aggression hypothesis was quite consistent with Freud's (1927) early writings, in which aggression was viewed as the primary reaction to interference with pleasure-seeking or pain-avoiding behavior. This theory is also quite compatible with the views of contemporary psychodynamic theorists, who regard aggression as a behavioral reaction to provocation (e.g., Hartmann, Kris, & Loewenstein, 1949; Storr, 1968).

During the 1950s, psychological research continued to focus on aggression; internal states such as anger, which might intervene between frustrating circumstances and aggressive acts, were generally ignored. This neglect of emotion was criticized by Berkowitz (1962, 1964), who argued that negative affective states such as anger and anxiety mediated the effects of frustration on fight-or-flight behavior. Berkowitz (1962) suggested that ". . . it might be helpful to think of the thwarting-generated instigation to aggression as 'anger' "(p. 68). However, he now seems to prefer to conceptualize anger "as a perceptual experience that typically parallels the negative affect-produced inclination to aggression" (1989, p. 68).

In his recent reformulation of the frustration-aggression hypothesis, Berkowitz (1989) theorized that: ". . . frustrations generate aggressive inclinations to the degree that they arouse negative affect" (p. 59), and that this negative affect ". . . gives rise automatically to a variety of expressive-motor reactions, feelings, thoughts, and memories that are associated with both flight and fight tendencies, that is, with inclinations to escape/avoid and to attack" (p. 69). In linking frustration to Cannon's (1914) concept of fight-or-flight behavioral reactions, Berkowitz (1989) concluded that: ". . . the frustration-aggression relationship is basically only a special case of a more general connection between aversive stimulation and aggressive inclinations" (p. 60).

Although it is generally agreed that frustration arouses anger and provokes aggression (e.g., Averill, 1977; Berkowitz, 1962, 1989), *anger* and *aggression*, along with *hostility*, have been defined in numerous ways by different investigators, and in some cases these terms are used interchangeably (Spielberger et al., 1985). Anger is most often conceptualized as an emotional state that varies in intensity, but different aspects of this emotion are emphasized in various definitions. For example, Moyer (1976) defined *anger* exclusively in terms of physiological variables, whereas Feshbach (1964) conceptualized anger as a "mediating affective response" with expressive components.

Schachter (1971) and Novaco (1975) called attention to both the cognitive and physiological aspects of anger, and Kaufmann (1970) included physiological arousal, anger-related cognitions, and intentionality in defining anger as: ". . . an emotion that involves a physiological arousal state coexisting with fantasized or intended acts culminating in harmful effects on another person" (p. 12). Although affective, physiological, and behavioral aspects of anger are emphasized in most definitions, and cognitive elements are given increasing attention, the unique quality of the feelings experienced during anger states has been relatively neglected. Recognizing this, Kassinove and Sukhodolsky (chap. 1, this volume) focused their definition around the negative phenomenological feelings and associated cognitions, which are labeled as *anger*.

Berkowitz (1962) and Moyer (1976) equated hostility with aggressive behavior. Buss (1961) defined *hostility* as an attitude that involves disliking others and evaluating them negatively, and *aggression* as a "response that delivers noxious stimuli to another organism" (p. 1). Although most authorities seem to agree that aggression involves potential injury to another person (Bandura, 1973; Berkowitz, 1962, 1964; Feshbach, 1970; Kaufmann, 1970; Moyer, 1976), the omission of intent in Buss' definition of aggression appears to be problematic. Behavior that results in accidental injury would be classified as *aggressive* by Buss, whereas behavior intended to injure, but failing to achieve this goal, would not be considered aggressive. Therefore, as noted by Kassinove and Sukhodolsky (chap. 1, this volume), most theorists consider intent as an essential element in definitions of aggression (Feshbach, 1964; Kaufmann, 1970; Moyer, 1976).

From the preceding review, it seems apparent that definitions of *anger*, *hostility*, and *aggression* are often inconsistent and ambiguous. Consequently, there is little agreement on how these constructs should be measured. Given the substantial overlap in the prevailing conceptual definitions of anger, hostility, and aggression, we have collectively referred to these constructs as the "AHA! Syndrome" (Spielberger et al., 1985). The following working definitions of the constructs comprising the AHA! Syndrome have been proposed:

> Anger usually refers to an emotional state that consists of feelings that vary in intensity, from mild irritation or annoyance to intense fury and rage. Although hostility usually involves angry feelings, this concept has the connotation of a complex set of attitudes that motivate aggressive behaviors directed toward destroying objects or injuring other people. . . . While anger and hostility refer to feelings and attitudes, the concept of aggression generally implies destructive or punitive behavior directed towards other persons or objects. (Spielberger, Jacobs, Russell, & Crane, 1983, p. 16)

Anger is clearly at the core of the AHA! Syndrome; different aspects of this emotion are typically emphasized in various definitions of hostility and aggression. Because *aggression* and *hostility* are often used interchangeably in the research literature, a useful convention for distinguishing between them is to take anger into account in considering the intention of an aggressor. *Hostile aggression* refers to aggressive behavior motivated by anger; *instrumental aggression* refers to behavior directed toward removing or circumventing an obstacle that stands between an aggressor and a goal, when such behavior is not motivated by angry feelings. This conception and differentiation have been discussed in detail by Kassinove and Sukhodolsky (chap. 1, this volume).

MEASURING ANGER, HOSTILITY, AND AGGRESSION

The earliest efforts to assess anger and hostility were based on clinical interviews, behavioral observations, and projective techniques, such as the Rorschach Inkblot Test and the Thematic Apperception Test (e.g., Rosenzweig, 1976, 1978). Physiological and behavioral correlates of anger and hostility, as well as various manifestations of aggression, have also been investigated in numerous studies. In contrast, the phenomenology (experience) of anger (i.e., angry feelings) has been relatively neglected in psychological research. Moreover, in most psychometric measures of anger and hostility, angry feelings that vary in intensity are confounded with the mode and direction of anger expression.

Beginning in the mid-1950s, a number of self-report psychometric scales were developed to measure hostility (e.g., Buss & Durkee, 1957; Caine, Foulds, & Hope, 1967; Cook & Medley, 1954; Schultz, 1954; Siegel, 1956). The Buss–Durkee Hostility Inventory (BDHI), consisting of 75 true–false items, is generally regarded as the most carefully designed psychometric measure of hostility. In the development of this inventory, hostility was conceptualized as multidimensional, and BDHI subscales were constructed to assess seven hypothesized components of hostility: Assault, Indirect, Irritable, Negativism, Resentment, Suspicion, and Verbal. There is also a subscale to measure Guilt. The orthogonality and meaningfulness of the BDHI subscales have been investigated in studies in which responses to the individual BDHI items were factor analyzed. In contrast to the seven dimensions of hostility hypothesized by Buss, Bendig (1962) found only two major underlying factors, which he labeled Overt and Covert Hostility. Russell (1981) identified three meaningful BDHI factors: (a) Neuroticism, (b) General Hostility, and (c) Expression of Anger.

The BDHI was recently revised by Buss and Perry (1992) to form the Buss–Perry Aggression Questionnaire (BPAQ), which was designed to assess four different components of aggression: Physical, Verbal, Anger, and Hostility. Responding to the 29 BPAQ items (e.g., If somebody hits me, I hit back), subjects rate themselves on a 5-point scale, with anchor points ranging from *extremely uncharacteristic of me* to *extremely characteristic of me* (Buss & Perry, 1992). Given this rating format, the content of the individual items and, importantly, the high test–retest stability of the scale, the BPAQ appears to be a trait measure of individual differences in the disposition to engage in various forms of aggressive behavior.

The need to distinguish between anger and hostility was explicitly recognized in the early 1970s with the appearance of three anger measures in the psychological literature: The Reaction Inventory (RI), the Anger Inventory (AI), and the Anger Self-Report (ASR). The RI was developed by Evans and Stangeland (1971) to assess the degree to which anger was evoked in a number of specific situations (e.g., People pushing into line). Similar in conception and format to the RI, Novaco's (1975) AI consists of 90 statements that describe anger-provoking incidents (e.g., Being called a liar, Someone spits at you). In responding to the RI and AI, subjects rate the degree to which they believe each situation or incident would anger or provoke them. Finally, the ASR was designed by Zelin, Adler, and Myerson (1972) to assess both "awareness of anger" and different modes of anger expression.

Over a 2-week interval, the test–retest correlation of the AI was only .17 (Biaggio, Supplee, & Curtis, 1981), indicating that this inventory is unstable as a trait measure, and that it may assess anger as a transitory emotional state. In validating the ASR, psychiatric patients' scores were found to correlate significantly with psychiatrists' ratings of anger. Because the ASR and RI have been used in relatively few published studies over the past 20 years, the construct validity of these scales has yet to be established. Although the AI has been utilized in research more often than the other anger measures, Biaggio et al. (1981) found that this scale failed to correlate significantly with either self- or observer ratings of anger and hostility.

The phenomena assessed by the BDHI and the RI, AI, and ASR appear to be heterogeneous and complex. A common problem with these measures is that, in varying degrees, the experience and expression of anger are confounded with situational determinants of angry reactions. Furthermore, none of these measures explicitly takes the state–trait distinction into account. The ASR Awareness subscale comes closest to examining awareness of angry feelings (S-Anger), but does not assess the intensity of such feelings at a particular time. A number of BDHI items specifically inquire about how often anger is experienced or expressed (e.g., I *sometimes* show my anger; I *never* get mad enough to throw things, italics added); such items evaluate individual differences in anger proneness as a personality trait. However, the BDHI subscales and most BDHI items seem to assess hostile attitudes (e.g., Negativism, Resentment, Suspicion) or physical or verbally aggressive behaviors (e.g., If somebody hits me first, I let him have it; When people yell at me, I yell back).

In a series of studies, Biaggio (1980) and her colleagues (Biaggio et al., 1981) examined the reliability and concurrent and predictive validity of the BDHI and the three anger scales described previously. On the basis of their findings, Biaggio and Maiuro (1985) concluded that evidence for the construct validity of these measures was both fragmentary and limited. A coherent theoretical framework that distinguishes among anger, hostility, and aggression as psychological constructs, and that takes the state–trait distinction into account, would seem essential in constructing and validating psychometric measures of anger and hostility.

MEASURING STATE AND TRAIT ANGER

The concept of *anger*, as previously noted, refers to phenomena that are more fundamental and less complex than hostility and aggression. The State–Trait Anger Scale (STAS), which is analogous in conception and similar in format to the State–Trait Anxiety Inventory (STAI; Spielberger, 1983; Spielberger, Gorsuch, & Lushene, 1970), was constructed to measure anger as an emotional state that varies in intensity, and individual differences in anger proneness as a personality trait. Prior to the STAS, working definitions of *state anger* and *trait anger* were formulated.

State anger (*S-Anger*) was defined as a psychobiological state or condition consisting of subjective feelings that vary in intensity, from mild irritation or annoyance to intense fury and rage, with concomitant activation or arousal of the autonomic nervous system. It was assumed that S-Anger would fluctuate over time as a function of frustration, perceived affronts, injustice, or being verbally or physically attacked. *Trait anger* (*T-Anger*) was defined in terms of how often angry feelings were experienced over time. It was assumed that persons high in T-Anger perceive a wider range of situations as anger provoking (e.g., annoying, irritating, frustrating) than persons low in T-Anger, and that high T-Anger individuals would be more likely to experience more frequent and intense elevations in S-Anger whenever annoying or frustrating circumstances were encountered.

On the basis of these working definitions, a pool of items was generated to assess the intensity of angry feelings (S-Anger) and individual differences in anger proneness (T-Anger). In responding to the S-Anger items (e.g., I am furious; I feel irritated), subjects are instructed to report the intensity of their angry feelings at a particular moment by rating themselves on the following 4-point scale: *not at all, somewhat, moderately so,* and *very much so.* In responding to the T-Anger items (e.g., I am a hotheaded person; It makes me furious when I am criticized in front of others), subjects indicate how they generally feel by rating themselves on the following 4-point frequency scale: *almost never, sometimes, often,* and *almost always.*

Factor analyses of the STAS S-Anger items for a sample of 550 young adults, consisting of 280 undergraduate college students (95 males, 185 females) and 270 Navy recruits (198 males, 72 females), identified a single underlying S-anger factor for both males and females, indicating that the S-Anger scale measures a unitary emotional state that varies in intensity. In contrast, factor analyses of the T-Anger items identified two correlated factors, which were labeled *Angry Temperament* (*T-Anger/T*) and *Angry Reaction* (*T-Anger/R*). The T-Anger/T items describe individual differences in the disposition to experience anger, without specifying any provoking circumstance (e.g., I am a hotheaded person). The T-Anger/R items describe angry feelings in situations that involve frustration and/or negative evaluations (e.g., It makes me furious when I am criticized in front of others).

Evidence that the T-Anger subscales assess two different facets of trait anger was clearly reflected in a study by Crane (1981), in which the T-Anger scores of hypertensive patients were significantly higher than those of medical patients with normal blood pressure. This difference was due entirely to the substantially higher T-Anger/R scores of the hypertensives; no difference was found in the T-Anger/T scores of the hypertensive and control patients. Crane also reported that the S-Anger and S-Anxiety scores of hypertensives—while performing a mildly frustrating task—were significantly higher than those of control patients, and that the hypertensives had significantly higher trait anxiety scores than the controls.

In a study on the relation between anger and hostility, the STAS, the BDHI, and the Minnesota Multiphasic Personality Inventory (MMPI) Hostility (Ho; Cook & Medley, 1954) and Overt Hostility (Hv; Schultz, 1954) scales were administered to undergraduate university students and Navy recruits (Spielberger et al., 1983). Moderately high correlations of the STAS T-Anger scale with BDHI Total (.66–.73) and Ho scale (.43 to .59) scores were found for both males and females, providing evidence for a substantial relationship between T-Anger and the most widely used measures of Hostility. Correlations of Hv scores with the STAS T-Anger scale and the other two hostility measures were much lower, indicating that the Hv scale is not a good measure of either anger or hostility.

The relationship between anger and hostility was further explored in a study in which the 10 STAS T-Anger items, the BDHI, and the MMPI Ho and Hv scales were administered to university students (Westberry, 1980). To evaluate the discriminant validity of the Anger and Hostility measures, students also responded to the State–Trait Personality Inventory (STPI) T-Anxiety and T-Curiosity scales (Spielberger, 1980). Responses to the Anger, Anxiety, and Curiosity items were factored, with the BDHI Total and subscale scores, and scores on the MMPI Ho and Hv scales, as marker variables. The resulting three- and four-factor solutions were similar for both males and females, had the best simple structure, and were psychologically the most meaningful. In the three-factor solutions, the STAS T-Anger and BDHI Total scores had the highest loadings on the very strong first factor, which measured an Anger/Hostility dimension; the second and third factors in this solution were Anxiety and Curiosity (Spielberger et al., 1983). All 10 T-Anger items, the Ho and Hv scale scores, and all of the BDHI subscales except Guilt also had salient loadings on the first factor. The BDHI Guilt, Suspicion, and Resentment subscales had higher loadings on the Anxiety factor than on the Anger/Hostility factor.

Separate Anger and Hostility factors were identified in the four-factor solutions for both males and females, along with Anxiety and Curiosity factors that were essentially the same as those obtained in the three-factor solutions. The T-Anger scores and all but one of the T-Anger items had their highest loadings on the Anger factor. The Ho scale and the BDHI Total scores had their highest loadings on the Hostility factor, as did all of the BDHI subscales, except Guilt. Three of the BDHI subscales—Resentment, Irritability, Suspicion—also had salient secondary loadings on the Anger factor. Interestingly, the Ho scale and the BDHI Suspicion and Resentment subscales had higher secondary loadings on the Anxiety factor than on the Anger factor. Taken together, the findings in the three- and four-factor solutions indicated that the measures of Anger and Hostility assessed different but related constructs, and that the Ho scale and several BDHI subscales are associated more strongly with anxiety than with anger.

MEASURING THE EXPRESSION OF ANGER

As anger research has progressed, the critical importance of differentiating between angry feelings and how that anger is expressed has become increasingly apparent (Spielberger et al., 1985). In addition to distinguishing between the experience of anger as an emotional state and individual differences in anger proneness as a personality trait, it is essential to identify and measure the characteristic ways in which people express their anger. Expressing angry feelings in aggressive verbal or motor behavior directed toward other people or objects in the environment (anger-out) or suppressing those feelings and holding them in (anger-in) are the two modes of anger expression that have been the focus of most research.

In fact, the conceptual and empirical (operational) distinction between anger-in and anger-out has long been recognized in psychophysiological research. The effects of different modes of anger expression on the cardiovascular system was the focus of Funkenstein and his co-workers' research more than 40 years ago (Funkenstein, King, & Drolette, 1954). In these studies, healthy college students were exposed to anger-inducing laboratory conditions. Students who became angry and directed their anger toward the investigator or laboratory situation were classified as *anger-out*; those who suppressed their anger and/or directed it at themselves were classified as *anger-in*. The increase in pulse rate for students classified as anger-in was approximately three times greater than for the anger-out students.

Following the lead of Funkenstein et al., individuals who inhibit or suppress their anger are classified as anger-in expression types in anger-expression research (Averill, 1982; Tavris, 1982). When held in or suppressed, anger is subjectively experienced as an emotional state, S-Anger, which varies in intensity. However, the definition of *anger-in* as suppressed anger differs from the psychoanalytic conception of anger turned inward toward the ego or self (Alexander, 1939, 1948). In psychodynamic conceptions of anger-in, angry feelings as well as thoughts and memories associated with anger-provoking situations are not experienced because they have been repressed, resulting in guilt and depression (Alexander & French, 1948).

Anger directed outward, which involves both the experience of S-Anger and its manifestation in some form of aggressive behavior, is essentially equivalent to hostile aggression as previously defined. Anger-out may be expressed in physical or motor behavior acts such as slamming doors or assaulting other persons, or in verbal behavior in the form of criticisms, threats, insults, or extreme use of profanity. These physical and verbal manifestations of anger-out may be directed toward the source of provocation or frustration, or they may be expressed indirectly toward persons or objects associated with, or symbolic of, the provoking agent.

In a series of studies, Harburg and his associates (Harburg, Blakelock, & Roeper, 1979; Harburg, Erfurt, Hauenstein, Chape, Schull, & Schork, 1973; Harburg & Hauenstein, 1980; Harburg, Schull, Erfurt, & Schork, 1970) reported impressive evidence demonstrating that anger-in and anger-out have different effects on the cardiovascular system, and Gentry (1972) and his colleagues (Gentry, Chesney, Gary, Hall, & Harburg, 1982; Gentry, Chesney, Hall, & Harburg, 1981) subsequently corroborated and extended Harburg's findings. In classifying individuals as either anger-in or anger-out, *anger-expression* was implicitly defined by Funkenstein et al. (1954), Harburg et al. (1973), and Gentry et al. (1982) as comprising a single dimension, varying from the extreme suppression or inhibition of anger to the overt expression of anger in assaultive or destructive behavior.

In keeping with the conception of anger-expression as a unidimensional, bipolar variable, Spielberger et al. (1985) attempted to construct a scale to measure this dimension. Working definitions of anger-in and anger-out were formulated to guide the construction of this Anger-Expression (AX) scale. *Anger-in* was defined in terms of how often angry feelings were experienced but not expressed (suppressed). *Anger-out* was defined in terms of the frequency that angry feelings were expressed in verbally or physically aggressive behavior. The content of individual AX scale items included descriptions of the suppression of angry feelings (AX/In) or the expression of anger in aggressive behavior (AX/Out). The rating-scale format for the AX scale was the same as that used with the STAS T-Anger scale (Spielberger, 1980), but the instructions differed from those used in assessing T-Anger. Rather than asking respondents to indicate how they generally feel, they were instructed to report ". . . how often you generally react or behave in the manner described *when you feel angry or furious*" (italics added). The following are examples of AX/In and AX/Out items: I boil inside, but I don't show it; I strike out at whatever infuriates me.

Contrary to expectation, factor analyses indicated that the anger-expression items were tapping independent Anger-In and Anger-Out factors, rather than a unidimensional, bipolar variable. Therefore, loadings on these factors and item-remainder correlations were used to derive 8-item subscales to measure anger-in and anger-out. Pollans (1983) and Johnson (1984) found essentially zero correlations between the AX/In and AX/Out subscales for both males and females in large samples of high school and college students. Similar findings have also been reported for other populations (Knight, Chisholm, Paulin, & Waal-Manning, 1988; Spielberger, 1988). Thus, the AX/In and AX/Out subscales are empirically independent and factorially orthogonal. Clearly, these subscales assess two independent anger-expression dimensions.

Moderately high correlations of AX/Out with T-Anger/T, and smaller correlations of both AX/Out and AX/In with T-Anger/R (Spielberger, 1988), suggested that individuals who have an angry temperament are more likely to express their anger outwardly than suppress it, whereas those who frequently experience anger when they are frustrated or treated unfairly are equally likely to express or suppress their anger. Small, but significant, positive correlations of the AX/In and AX/Out scales with measures of trait anxiety suggest that individuals with high scores on these scales experience anxiety more often than individuals with low AX/In or AX/Out scores.

Harburg et al. (1973, 1979) and Gentry et al. (1981, 1982) reported that persons who suppress anger have higher systolic blood pressure (SBP) and diastolic blood pressure (DBP), as previously noted. Johnson (1984) administered the AX scale to 1,114 high school students, and obtained measures of SBP and DBP for these students during the same class period in which they responded to the psychological tests. Highly significant positive correlations were found between AX/In scores and both SBP and DBP for both males and females; there was also a slight tendency for students with higher AX/Out scores to have lower blood pressure. When the students were divided into five subgroups on the basis of their AX/In scores, both SBP and DBP were substantially higher for students of both sexes in the group with the highest Anger-In scores (Spielberger et al., 1985). This finding is incorporated into the anger model presented by Kassinove and Eckhardt in chapter 11.

MEASURING ANGER CONTROL

The need to control anger is an important characteristic of Type A individuals, who are at risk for developing heart disease. According to Glass (1977), Type A individuals endeavor to gain and maintain control over their environment. They also try to dominate others in interpersonal relationships, even after it becomes clear that a situation is unmanageable, as was documented by Burke (1982). To evaluate how Type A persons and others manage anger, a reliable and valid measure of individual differences in anger control is needed. The 134-item Anger Control Inventory, developed by Hoshmand and Austin (1985, 1987) to assess cognitive and behavioral anger-control problems in clinical settings, has promise for fulfilling this need. Unfortunately, the items comprising the Anger Control Inventory have not been published, and no research using this measure could be found other than the studies reported by Hoshmand and Austin (1987).

Research with the 20-item AX scale provided the impetus for developing a brief objective measure of individual differences in anger control as a personality trait. Three AX scale items (*control my temper*, *keep my cool*, and *calm down faster*) were included in the original item pool to assess the middle range of the hypothesized Anger-In/Anger-Out dimension. Because these items had substantial loadings on both the Anger-In and Anger-Out factors and relatively high item-remainder correlations, they were retained in the 20-item AX scale. However, when more than two factors were extracted, these items coalesced to form the nucleus of a small Anger-Control factor (Pollans, 1983). Therefore, in developing an AX Anger-Control subscale, the three original AX scale anger-control items served as a guide for writing 17 new anger-control (AX/Con) items. Dictionary and thesaurus definitions of *control* and idioms pertaining specifically to the control of anger were also consulted when writing these items.

The 17 new AX/Con items, along with the 3 original AX scale anger-control items, were administered to a large sample of undergraduate university students (Krasner, 1986). When responses to these 20 AX/Con items were factored, a strong Anger-Control (Anger/Con) factor was found for both males and females. The new AX/Con items with the largest loadings on this factor for both sexes were added to the three original AX/Con items to form an eight-item AX/Con subscale. Two of the three original AX scale anger-control items were among the items with the highest loadings on the Anger/Con factor. The third item, I calm down faster than most other people, was included in the AX/Con subscale to provide continuity with the original AX scale, even though the loadings of this item on the Anger/Con factor were somewhat lower than those of most of the new items.

To evaluate the independence of the Anger/Con factor and its relation to anger-in and anger-out, the eight-item AX/Con, AX/Out, and AX/In subscales were administered to another large sample ($N = 409$) of university students (Spielberger, Krasner, & Solomon, 1988). In factor analyses of the 24 AX scale items, the Anger/Con factor was the strongest to emerge for both males and females; all eight AX/Con items had their largest salient loadings on this factor. Well-defined Anger-In and Anger-Out factors were also found; all eight AX/In and AX/Out items had their largest salient loadings on the appropriate factor.

The AX/Con subscale correlated negatively with AX/Out ($r = -.59$ for males; $r = -.58$ for females). Correlations of the AX/In subscale with AX/Out and AX/Con were essentially zero for both sexes. The orthogonality of the AX/In and AX/Out subscales (Pollans, 1983; Spielberger et al., 1985) and moderately high negative correlations of AX/Con with AX/Out have been consistently found in subsequent research (Spielberger, 1988; Spielberger et al., 1988).

The AX/Con subscale assesses individual differences in how often individuals attempt to control the expression of angry feelings (Spielberger, 1988). Persons with high AX/Con scores are thought of as investing a great deal of energy in monitoring and preventing the expression of anger. Moderately high negative correlations of AX/Con with AX/Out suggest that such efforts are reasonably successful. Persons with high AX/Con scores and who are also high in T-Anger/Temperament may be strongly authoritarian and use anger to intimidate others (Spielberger & Sydeman, 1994). Although controlling anger is generally desirable, excessive overcontrol may result in passivity and withdrawal, and persons with high AX/Con and high trait anxiety scores are likely to experience depression. However, it may also be possible to conceptualize control of anger as the development of strategies to resolve the anger experience. Based on the work of Deffenbacher (chap. 9, this volume) and Feindler (chap. 10, this volume), Kassinove and Eckhardt incorporate this possibility into the model they present in chapter 11.

The STAS and the AX scale were recently combined to form the 44-item State–Trait Anger Expression Inventory (STAXI), which provides relatively brief, objectively scored measures of the experience, expression, and control of anger (Spielberger, 1988). The STAXI consists of five primary scales: State Anger, Trait Anger, Anger-In, Anger-Out, and Anger-Control. The STAXI T-Anger Scale has 2 four-item subscales: T-Anger/Temperament and T-Anger/Reaction. Although the AX/Con scale has only been available for a relatively brief period of time, the STAS and the AX/In and AX/Out scales, which were incorporated in the STAXI, have been used extensively in research on the relationship between anger and health (Brooks, Walfish, Stenmark, & Canger, 1981; Cavanaugh, Kanonchoff, & Bartels, 1987; Johnson & Broman, 1987; Johnson-Saylor, 1984; Schlosser, 1986; Vitaliano, 1984; Vitaliano et al., 1986).

Suppressed anger as assessed by the STAXI AX/In subscale has been consistently identified as an important factor in elevated BP and hypertension (Crane, 1981; Deshields, 1986; Gorkin, Appel, Holroyd, Saab, & Stauder, 1986; Hartfield, 1985; Johnson, 1984; Johnson, Spielberger, Worden, & Jacobs, 1987; Kearns, 1985; Schneider, Egan, & Johnson, 1986; van der Ploeg, van Buuren, & van Brummelen, 1988). The STAXI scales have also been used to examine relationships among hardiness, well-being, and coping with stress (Schlosser & Sheeley, 1985a, 1985b), to investigate the role of anger in Type A behavior (Booth-Kewley & Friedman, 1987; Croyle, Jemmott, & Carpenter, 1988; Goffaux, Wallston, Heim, & Shields, 1987; Herschberger, 1985; Janisse, Edguer, & Dyck, 1986; Krasner, 1986; Spielberger et al., 1988), and in a series of studies by Kinder and his colleagues on psychological factors that contribute to chronic pain (Curtis, Kinder, Kalichman, & Spana, 1988; Kinder, Curtis, & Kalichman, 1986).

GENDER DIFFERENCES IN THE EXPERIENCE AND EXPRESSION OF ANGER

Recent research by Thomas (1989, 1993) has called attention to the different ways men and women experience and express anger. Contrary to previous research with the Framingham Anger Scales (Haynes, Levine, Scotch, Feinleib, & Kannel, 1978), in which women were more likely to suppress anger than men, Thomas (1989) did not find any gender differences in either anger suppression (anger-in) or anger-expression (anger-out). However, she found that women were more likely to discuss their anger, women had more anger-related physical symptoms, and that trait anger, as measured by the State–Trait Anger Scale (STAS), was strongly related to perceived stress, especially vicarious stressors arising from women's concern about others and their drive to care for them.

In Thomas' (1989) study, correlations between the Framingham anger-in and anger-out measures were essentially zero for both males and females. This finding was consistent with that reported by Spielberger et al. (1985). Kopper and Epperson (1991) also failed to find any gender differences in trait anger, anger-in, anger-out, or anger-control. However, subjects of both sexes, with masculine sex-role identity as measured by the Bem (1981) Sex-Role Inventory, had higher STAXI T-Anger and AX/Out scores and lower AX/Con scores than those with feminine sexual identity.

To further evaluate gender differences in state and trait anger, and anger expression and control, we examined the STAXI scores for a heterogeneous sample of 1,010 young adults. The means, standard deviations, and alpha coefficients for the STAXI scales for the men and women in this sample are reported in Table 3.1. The resulting F ratios for gender differences evaluated by analyses of variance (ANOVA) are also presented in Table 3.1. Alpha coefficients for the STAXI scales were .74 or higher, except for the four-item T-Anger/Reaction subscale (.69 for females, .64 for males). Males scored significantly higher than females on the T-Anger scale, due primarily to their higher scores on the T-Anger/Temperament subscale. Men also scored significantly higher than women on the AX/In and AX/Out subscales. No gender differences were found in S-Anger, T-Anger/Reaction, or Anger-Control measures.

Significant gender differences on the individual items comprising the various STAXI scales suggest that interpreting the presence or absence of differences in mean scale scores at face value may be misleading. For example, although no difference was found between men and women on the T-Anger/Reaction subscale, highly significant differences ($p < .01$) were found for three of the four items comprising this scale. These differences were not reflected in the mean scale scores because males had higher scores on two items (I feel annoyed when not given recognition for good work; I get angry when I am slowed by others mistakes) and women scored significantly higher on one item (It makes me furious when I am criticized in front of others). The overall difference in T-Anger was due primarily to the much higher scores of men ($p < .01$) on two items that are not included in the subscales (When I get mad, I say nasty things; When I get frustrated, I feel like hitting someone). This point suggests a stronger disposition for men to express their angry feelings in physically or verbally aggressive behavior.

Table 3.1   Means, Standard Deviations, Alpha Coefficients, and Gender Differences for 1,010 Young Adults

Scales and Subscales	Females[a]			Males[b]			F value
	Mean	SD	Alpha	Mean	SD	Alpha	
State Anger (S-Anger)[c]	12.06	3.67	.91	12.46	4.44	.94	0.63
Trait Anger (T-Anger)	20.46	5.32	.83	21.46	5.72	.83	8.06**
T-Anger/Temperament	6.86	2.80	.89	7.23	3.05	.88	3.91*
T-Anger/Reaction	10.04	2.57	.69	10.22	2.54	.64	1.19
Anger Expression (AX)							
AX/In	17.04	4.39	.76	17.84	4.25	.74	5.41*
AX/Out	15.97	3.93	.75	16.91	4.31	.78	8.49**
AX/Con	22.26	4.88	.85	22.32	4.79	.83	0.02

[a]$n = 616$. [b]$n = 394$. [c]This scale was evaluated on a sample of 302 college students, females ($N = 209$) and males ($N = 93$).
**$p < .01$. *$p < .05$.

MEASURING THE CONTROL OF
SUPPRESSED ANGER

In the construction of the STAXI AX/Con scale, we recognized the importance of distinguishing between "keeping cool" to control the outward expression of anger and calming down to reduce the intensity of angry feelings that were suppressed and held in. Although the psychometric properties of one of the original AX anger-control items (I calm down faster than most other people) were not as good as several of the new items that were constructed to assess anger control, this item was retained in the AX/Con scale to serve as a possible bridge for developing a subscale to measure the control of suppressed anger.

The development of a scale to assess anger-in control was also influenced by Lakoff's (1987) psycholinguistic analysis of English metaphors for anger. According to Lakoff, the predominant metaphor for anger in American English is: "Anger is the heat of a liquid in a container" (p. 383). In his analysis of this metaphor, Lakoff observed that anger as an emotional state heats the blood, for which the body is the container. Examples of anger metaphors noted by Lakoff include: *You make my blood boil, Letting off steam, Doing a slow burn, Getting hot under the collar, Simmer down, Reached the boiling point, Seething with rage, All steamed up, Blowing off steam, Fuming, Anger bottled up inside, Blew a fuse, Blew my top, Breathing fire, Burned up.*

Lakoff's analysis of anger metaphors contributes to the theoretical framework for understanding the processes that underlay the experience, expression, and control of anger. The intensity of anger as an emotional state is analogous to the heat of the hot liquid (i.e., S-Anger increases in intensity as angry feelings rise, from mild irritation or annoyance to fury and rage). Feeling *burned up* and *boiling inside* indicates an extremely high level of intensity of suppressed anger; *blowing off steam* reflects the outward expression of angry feelings; *keeping the lid on* controls anger's outward expression.

Lakoff's anger metaphors also suggest that there are two distinct mechanisms for controlling anger—namely, keeping it bottled up and not letting it escape, and reducing the intensity of suppressed anger by cooling down inside. The implication of these anger metaphors highlights the need to develop separate scales to assess controlling the expression of anger in aggressive behavior (AX/Con-Out) and reducing the intensity of suppressed anger by calming down inside (AX/Con-In). On examining the content of the items comprising the original STAXI AX/Con subscale, it is apparent that most of these items were concerned primarily with controlling the outward expression of anger (i.e., *Keeping the lid on*).

In a recent study, Sydeman (1995) investigated the control of anger-in, which was conceptualized as cooling off and calming down to reduce the intensity of angry feelings that were experienced and suppressed. To measure anger-in control, AX/Con-In items were constructed in accordance with this definition, which had previously proved useful in developing the Dutch adaptation of the

STAXI (Spielberger & Maes, 1985–1986). Literal and idiomatic English translations of items from the Dutch AX/Con-In scale were written, and new items with similar meaning were constructed based on English idioms and synonyms found in a standard thesaurus.

Sydeman's (1995) original item pool, consisting of 45 AX/Con-In items, was reviewed by a heterogeneous group of native English speakers, including PhD psychologists and graduate and undergraduate psychology students. Ambiguous or similarly worded items, and those with content judged to be less closely related to the anger-in control construct, were eliminated to reduce the pool to 15 items. Three anger-out control items were constructed as possible replacements for the item that had been retained in the original eight-item AX/Con scale as a bridge for developing an AX/Con-In subscale.

The 15 remaining AX/Con-In items, the 3 AX/Con-Out replacement items, and the 8 items comprising the original AX/Con subscale were administered to 315 undergraduate students (218 females, 97 males) enrolled in psychology classes at a large urban university. In separate factor analyses for males and females of responses to the 26 AX/Con items, based on Eigenvalues greater than one and screen tests, it was determined that either two or three factors could be extracted. The two-factor solutions with oblique rotation had the best simple structure and were most meaningful in identifying clear AX/Con-In and AX/Con-Out factors for both sexes.

Based on a series of successive factor analyses, the items with the strongest loadings on the AX/Con-In and AX/Con-Out factors were selected to form the new AX/Con-In and AX/Con-Out subscales. The loadings of these items on the AX/Con-In and AX/Con-Out factors are reported in Table 3.2, in which it may be noted that the AX/Con-In factor was first to be extracted, and was much stronger for both sexes. Loadings of individual items on this factor were .54 or higher, with a median factor loading of .76. The loadings of individual items on the AX/Con-Out were also quite strong for both sexes, with a median loading of .65.

The items comprising the AX/Con-In scale all described calming down, cooling off, or relaxing in an effort to reduce the intensity of suppressed anger. The AX/Con-Out scale consisted of five of the original STAXI AX/Con items, plus all three replacement items. Although the content of these items is related to controlling the outward expression of angry feelings, this relationship is more explicit for some items than others.

The means and standard deviations for the AX/Con-In and AX/Con-Out subscales, and for the individual items comprising these scales, are reported for males and females in Table 3.3. Alpha coefficients, gender differences, and item-remainder correlations are also reported for the two subscales and for each item. Although males had slightly higher scores on the AX/Con-Out subscale, no significant gender differences were found in the scale scores. Males also had significantly higher scores on one AX/Con-Out item (I cool down as quickly as possible) and on one AX/Con-In item (I keep my cool). Interestingly, both of

Table 3.2 Loadings of Anger-Control Items for 302 University Students

Item Statements	AX/Con-In		AX/Con-Out	
	Female[a]	Male[b]	Female	Male
Do something soothing to calm down	.91	.64		
Do something relaxing to calm down	.85	.54		
Cool down as quickly as possible	.76	.80		
Cool off as soon as possible	.69	.90		
Try to relax	.68	.76		
Try to calm myself as soon as possible	.62	.84		
Try to simmer down	.60	.82		
Reduce my anger as soon as possible	.61	.80	.31	
Control my urge to express angry feelings			.76	.68
Control my behavior			.68	.68
Control my angry feelings			.67	.65
Stop myself from losing my temper			.59	.48
Keep my cool			.57	.57
Control my temper			.55	.85
Do not lash out at what angers me			.53	.67
Try not to express my anger			.45	.69
Eigenvalues	7.15	7.40	1.18	1.69

[a]$n = 209$. [b]$n = 93$.

these items involve cooling down or keeping cool, which may reflect a stronger tendency for men to be "cool" in controlling their angry feelings.

The reader will find that Kassinove and Eckhardt (chap. 11, this volume) believe that various cognitive-behavioral therapy techniques, such as are used in Ellis' rational-emotive behavior therapy (including cognitive reconstruction, reframing, negotiations, etc.), are valuable to control anger intensity.

SUMMARY AND CONCLUSIONS

Evolving conceptions of the nature of anger as an emotional state were reviewed in historical perspective. Substantial overlap in prevailing conceptual definitions of anger, hostility, and aggression were noted, the relation of anger to hostility and aggression was examined, and psychometric approaches to the measurement

Table 3.3 Means, Standard Deviations, Alpha Coefficients, and Gender Differences for 284 University Students

Anger-Control Scales and Items	Females[a]			Males[b]			F value
	Mean	SD	Alpha	Mean	SD	Alpha	
AX/Con-In Subscale	22.06	5.44	.91	22.48	5.50	.92	0.36
Do something soothing to calm down	2.73	0.91	.67	2.58	0.88	.67	1.71
Do something relaxing to calm down	2.65	0.91	.64	2.52	1.03	.65	1.20
Cool down as quickly as possible	2.68	0.91	.69	2.90	0.83	.71	3.89
Cool off as soon as possible	2.70	0.90	.83	2.83	0.90	.72	1.22
Try to relax	2.98	0.79	.75	2.89	0.83	.70	0.70
Try to calm myself as soon as possible	2.86	0.87	.80	2.94	0.89	.76	0.46
Try to simmer down	2.83	0.86	.77	2.86	0.83	.75	0.09
Reduce my anger as soon as possible	2.84	0.83	.76	2.89	0.81	.78	0.29
AX/Con-Out Subscale	20.92	4.74	.84	22.07	5.43	.88	3.22
Control urge to express angry feelings	2.48	0.89	.68	2.60	0.97	.67	1.23
Control my behavior	2.90	0.87	.69	3.00	0.83	.73	0.80
Control my angry feelings	2.63	0.88	.74	2.68	0.97	.73	0.16
Can stop myself from losing my temper	2.74	0.99	.51	2.80	0.93	.51	0.20
Keep my cool	2.74	0.85	.64	2.99	0.87	.69	5.41
Control my temper	2.98	0.78	.65	3.01	0.94	.76	0.11
Do not lash out at what angers me	2.49	0.90	.42	2.54	0.97	.58	0.18
Try not to express my anger	2.20	0.85	.32	2.40	0.97	.53	3.42

[a] n = 199. [b] n = 85.

of anger and hostility were briefly reviewed. The need for a coherent theoretical framework that distinguishes anger, hostility, and aggression as psychological constructs, and that takes the state–trait distinction into account, was considered an essential prerequisite to constructing and validating psychometric measures of anger and hostility.

The construction of the State–Trait Anger Scale (STAS) to measure the intensity of anger as an emotional state and individual differences in anger proneness as a personality trait was described in detail. Evidence of the convergent and divergent validity of the STAS, and research findings demonstrating that measures of anger and hostility assessed related but different constructs, were reported.

The critical importance of differentiating between angry feelings and how anger is expressed was noted, and the construction of the Anger-Expression (AX) scale to assess anger-in and anger-out as modes of anger expression was described. The need to differentiate between the control (reduction) of suppressed anger and the control of outward expression of anger towards other persons or objects in the environment was examined, and the construction of scales to assess anger-in control and anger-out control was described. Research findings on gender differences in the experience, expression, and control of anger were also reported.

Chapter 4

A Behavior-Analytic View of Anger and Aggression

Kurt Salzinger

Hofstra University, Hempstead, New York

The object of this chapter is to show that the behavior-analytic approach provides a useful way to study those behaviors known to the general public, and to nonbehavioral practitioners, as "anger" and "aggression." These behaviors are often viewed as two separate phenomena, according to which some kinds of aggression are said to be caused, or at least instigated, by anger (see reviews by Kassinove & Sukhodolsky, chap. 1, this volume; Berkowitz, 1993).

The chapter's approach consists of using basic behavioral classifications to gain an understanding of this set of disruptive behavior patterns. This approach, based on a method for modifying behavior, can then be used in treatment. The behavior-analytic approach posits that practitioners would be wise to look to the environment for causes of, and treatments for, disruptive anger and aggression. Clinical practitioners are likely to be most helpful if they examine *current environmental cues* within the family, school, workplace, and so on, and relate them to previously learned anger (aggression) responses in similar situations. This type of analysis guides a treatment program aimed at changing the control of discriminative stimuli over anger (aggression) responses, which have been previously reinforced.

CATEGORIZATION AND DESCRIPTION OF BEHAVIOR

Behavior can be classified into three general classes: operant, respondent, and hybrid. First, *operant* refers to behavior that acts on the environment and is controlled by its consequences. The following is an example of operant aggressive behavior: Richard pushes a smaller and shy child (Phil) in the school cafeteria and calls him a "jerk." Phil cries and Richard's friends, who observed the incident, inform Richard that he is "cool" because "Phil really is a jerk." Under these conditions, Richard's pushing response has two consequences: Phil cries and Richard's friends comment that Richard is "cool." This is a complicated situation because it is unclear whether either of the consequences is a positive reinforcer. For most members of society, causing somebody to cry is a punishing consequence and being praised is a positive reinforcer. Thus, although one might expect the first consequence to suppress Richard's behavior, one would expect the second to strengthen it. An additional complication is that if Richard's friends' favorable comments are strong positive reinforcers, the effect of having someone cry because of one's behavior might eventually become positively reinforcing because of its pairing with the praise positive reinforcer. Finally, if Richard is a psychopath, production of crying behavior in another person might constitute a positive reinforcer in the first place. The point is that consequences do not usually come singly, but in groups, and the analysis must be done carefully. Of course, watching Richard's behavior after the incident tells empirically what kinds of consequences occurred.

Second, *respondent* or *classical responses* refer to behavior that is elicited by the environment. Respondent behavior begins its course by being wired in the organism, so to speak. In the previous example, Phil's heart rate probably increased when he was pushed; hence, if pushed often enough by Richard, the latter's presence or his approach might become a stimulus for eliciting Phil's increased heart rate.

Third, *hybrid* behaviors are both operant and respondent, and are therefore controlled by both contingencies, sometimes simultaneously, sometimes sequentially. In the earlier example, Richard's behavior also might give rise to respondents; that is, his own heart rate might increase as he pushes Phil around. Phil might be the stimulus that elicits Richard's increased heart rate (respondent behavior) and be the occasion for the pushing (operant behavior).

Behavior is now described from a topographical perspective. To the extent that one can recognize anger behavior one can define it with the following components: (a) actions, such as hitting and hurting other people, destroying property, cursing, or insulting other people; (b) *subvocal actions*, such as talking to oneself; (c) *imaging* of the same kind (i.e., picturing particular scenes to oneself of pushing, yelling, etc.); and (d) various *physiological and biochemical reactions*, such as an increase in heart rate or a rush of adrenaline.

Many of these behaviors are recognizable because of the consequences to the "recognizer" of doing so: People take care to stay away from angry people, and/or they talk to them more carefully because of their experience (i.e., their conditioning history) with such people. These angry people tend to produce aversive stimuli (such as yelling, pushing, and hitting), which most others prefer to avoid. People also learn to "recognize" anger by the situations that evoke that kind of behavior, such as being thwarted, threatened, insulted, or frustrated.

Most people have observed people—both adults and children—engage in angry behavior without any warning. For example, people often curse (respondent behavior) when suddenly elbowed, regardless of whether the elbowing was intentional. Some anger/aggression is fully planned and rehearsed, such as when people prepare for a boxing match or when attorneys prepare for a meeting with adversaries. This is likely to be operant aggression. In the course of a fight, the victim of a planned attack hits back in a planful way (still operant aggression), but sometimes the aggressive behavior turns into the kind that seems almost automatic (respondent). So eventually the hybrid form of aggression is seen.

Of course, interspersed in all of the physical fighting behavior of the boxers, one may also observe some verbal behaviors, such as shouting and insulting. In other words, the behaviors are both physical and verbal. Verbal behavior is less likely to be automatic (i.e., respondent), although some of it clearly is (e.g., when people curse on sudden pain).

Whichever form anger takes, current approaches to the study of anger and aggression assume that people can and do report on their past behavior, and indeed are able to abstract it to report accurately that "I am a hotheaded person," to take an item from Spielberger's (1988) Anger scale. This also assumes that people have the insight to characterize their own behavior.

In this discussion, only environmental events have been implicated as causes, or at least initiators, of aggression. I have appealed to no internal sources of causation, and I have imbued verbal behavior with no special status in aggression. The implications for professional practitioners who work with angry and aggressive clients are clear. From the behavior-analytic perspective, it is important to look for stimuli in the family, work, and recreational environments for clues to the problem's source.

I now return to the status quo of research in this area, namely self-reports. Spielberger (1988) designed an anger questionnaire modeled after his successful anxiety inventory. The method is based on the simple notion that people can tell others how they feel. Indeed, the point is often made that verbal behavior is the gateway to understanding anger and aggression. Interestingly enough, this approach trusts what people have to say about themselves. Clinicians trust their clients or patients to be truthful and knowledgeable about their feelings, yet when the statistical analysis says differently, professionals disregard what they have to say. Spielberger (see Spielberger & Sydeman, 1993) omitted the following items from the trait portion of the anger questionnaire: I feel irritated; I feel angry. It seemed those items related better to anxiety (or, at least, to Spielberger's anxiety inventory) than to anger (i.e., his anger inventory). Hence, there is a mixture here of trusting and not trusting what people have to say. Obviously, if science is to guide practice, it needs to be clearer on this issue.

There is another assumption here, however—that is, there is a particular inner state (or trait) of the organism that constitutes anger, and it is that state that determines whether a person will be angry and/or aggressive. Thus, in contrast to the behavior-analytic model, which looks to the environment for causes, this paradigm posits a cause stemming from within the organism.

In addition, the questionnaire is more complicated because the statements the subjects endorse are reports about anger rather than the anger itself. For that reason, the behavior analyst would want to check whether the variables that control the verbal behavior constituting the report are the same as the ones that control the behavior or feeling referred to in the report. So, too, a finding relating self-report to, say, the probability of a heart attack must be checked by investigating the extent to which that relation is indebted to the reporting behavior, and the extent to which it relates to the behavior or feeling reported.

I now look at internal causes. First, people's behavior is determined by their current environment. Second, the way people respond to their current environment is partly a function of their previous responses to that environment (i.e., their conditioning history). That history makes people respond differently to the same stimulus at two different times. Thus, before going into psychotherapy, Mary might respond with verbal aggression ("You're a jerk!") to David's inadvertent slights ("Your report was not that bad"). Her more friendly response after therapy ("Thanks, I'm glad you liked it") can be attributed to the intervening reinforcement history. For example, the therapist could have changed her behavior through social skills training, in which she rehearsed behaving in a friendly way to the therapist (who takes David's place) expressing "slights." This kind of role-playing approach, which is often used in behavior therapy, represents an important part of the successful treatment in the case of Erica presented by Feindler (chap. 10, this volume).

HISTORY VERSUS INTERPRETATION

What is the difference between saying "history differentiates people from one another" and "people interpret that to which they are exposed"? History allows one to point to variables that can be examined. By way of contrast, interpretation is an ad hoc concept, dependent on the other responses made by the person at the same time. Thus, if an adolescent client (Adam) hits another boy (Bill), the assault may be interpreted by Adam (or by Adam's therapist) as caused by Adam's thinking that Bill will hit him unless he hits Bill first. Examination of the history of the client with Bill might reveal that the client had in fact been hit first by Bill in the past. That history would thus constitute a much better explanation of the aggressive behavior, and, more important, it would supply the therapist with the data needed to justify that conclusion. If the therapist found no such history, he or she would have to look for other causes of this behavior, and might find it in the client's hitting behavior having been reinforced in the past whenever people stared at him, to suggest but one alternative explanation.

The other problem with the interpretation model is that it posits that people often, if not always, think before they act—an assumption patently absurd to anybody but a visiting martian. When one designs a questionnaire to discover how people "interpret" various stimuli, and then one assumes that the interpretation is what determines how people respond to those stimuli, one is assuming (without any independent evidence) that people first interpret stimuli around them and then behave in particular ways.

PRIVATE EVENTS

A problem inherent in the consideration of anger and aggression is that of "inner cause." Interpretation is an example. The lay person, with the clinical practitioner in close pursuit, assumes that others are angry because of an "internal state" of anger that the angry person somehow owns. This is so despite what James (1891/1952) pointed out long ago in that famous James–Lange theory of emotion—that people are angry because they strike out, rather than vice versa. James asked whether one could imagine rage and "picture no ebullition in the chest, no flushing of the face, no dilatation of the nostrils, no clenching of the teeth, no impulse to vigorous action, but instead limp muscles, calm breathing and a placid face" (p. 744). It is these reactions, consisting of both visible and hidden (what Skinner [1945] called *private*) events, that constitute rage in James' mind and reveal to the angry person his or her feelings of anger.

James went on to say, "The internal shadings of emotional feeling, moreover, merge endlessly into each other. Language has discriminated some of them, as hatred, antipathy, animosity, dislike, aversion, malice, spite, vengefulness, abhorrence, etc.; but in the dictionaries of synonyms we find these feelings distinguished more by their severally appropriate objective stimuli than by their conscious or subjective tone" (p. 742). The resemblance of this manner of description to the behavioral one provided by Skinner is striking. Cognitive psychologists and cognitive-behavioral practitioners who increasingly see cognition as preceding any and all actions might do well to read James and his persuasive theory of emotions. In addition, Kassinove and Sukhodolsky (chap. 1, this volume) comment on new evidence in support of the James–Lange theory.

James' description also speaks of how unreliable verbal descriptions of emotions are. He described the literature of the emotions as tedious with subcategories that are either fictitious or unimportant, or that leave the reader to judge how closely this description applies to today's anger literature.

I now return to Spielberger's elimination of anger items for a trait scale such as: I feel angry. The point to consider here is that the lay person's definition of the emotions should not influence the thinking of how to classify them. If it is true that the previous item relates more closely (or, at least, as closely) to anxiety items as it does to other anger items, perhaps the better solution is to invent, or grudgingly admit to the existence of, a category of emotion something like *scared anger*, rather than arbitrarily keeping anger and anxiety separate but equal. This brings up consideration of how therapists can tell what a person "feels" when he or she tells them.

Back in 1945, Skinner presented a clear description of what he called *private events* (i.e., events to which only one organism is exposed). One's toothache is an important stimulus even though it clearly cannot be shared. Other private events of interest might include images of an embarrassing situation, thoughts of not being promoted at work because the boss prefers someone else who is less qualified, thoughts of friends disliking us and being the object of their jokes, and so on. Scientists and clinical practitioners must find ways to study such feelings, their relationship to anger/aggression behaviors, and the nature of that relationship.

The first step is to discover how to describe them. Children learn to describe objects accurately because the social community around them is exposed to the same stimuli. If a child calls a chair "plant," an adult can quickly and effectively show the child which object is the plant and which is the chair. Children spend a lot of time learning the names of things, sometimes generalizing to a greater extent than is warranted, as when they call all men "Daddy." They do, in fact, eventually learn to name objects and people accurately. The problem with private events is that the adult, who has to correct the incorrect naming behavior, is not privy to the stimulus to which the child is responding.

A personal story may help to explain this problem. I can still remember one of my children saying, "Daddy, my throat hurts," only to discover, on looking, that she was about to throw up. I was able to correct her incorrect verbal response for the next time because I could infer what she had been responding to when she complained of a throat ache. Similarly, one can recognize an accurate response when a child complains of a toothache because of various ancillary behaviors, such as crying, holding hand to cheek, and the dentist finding cavities by X-ray. Unfortunately, one cannot always be accurate in knowing if the child "feels" the toothache when saying "I have a toothache" because it has other possible consequences, such as avoiding school.

The problem becomes more complicated when one talks about feelings of anger, although there are some collateral responses that often (but certainly not always) accompany such feelings. These might include clenching of fists, raising of one's voice, and clenching of teeth. Some internal changes such as secretion of adrenaline cannot be observed by casual inspection, but even here there are some bothersome data. In a classic experiment, Schachter and Singer (1962) injected some subjects with adrenaline and others with a placebo, and then exposed them to a confederate who played the part of either a silly fool making merry or a man acting in an angry fashion. When they were uninformed or misinformed as to the effect of the drug, subjects who had received the adrenaline showed the emotion displayed and modeled for them by the confederate. The investigators concluded that the state of arousal was not enough for subjects to "know" what they were feeling; subjects needed a way to interpret their experience. A behaviorist would say that the conjunction of the physiological arousal and the environment of the acting confederate produced the feeling.

Regrettably, private events do not make reliable discriminative stimuli for human beings. When people respond with labels for their alleged feelings, a number of discriminative stimuli determine the responses they emit, especially when the purported stimulus has not acquired the discriminative control over their responses. Consider the following example. Suppose I showed you a dimly visible object surrounded by a clearly visible red ribbon, you called it "Schmatte," and I said, "That's right." The next time you saw the red ribbon, but you were not at all sure you saw the object, you still said "Schmatte" and I agreed with you, assuming that you knew a Schmatte when you saw one. Eventually, you might report "Schmatte" whenever you saw the red ribbon rather than the object. In this regard, Plutchik (1994) pointed out that autonomic nervous system responses are slower than people's introspections. His point raises the possibility that, when one talks about feelings, one might be responding to stimuli other than the so-called "internal" ones one is supposed to be reporting. The clinician who "listens for anger" (i.e., reinforces anger statements) in a psychotherapy session might be reinforcing verbal behavior under the control of stimuli other than the client's private events (feelings); the critical discriminative stimuli might be the clinician's verbal behavior. For example, when a therapist asks, "Were you angry with your wife this week?", this may be a stimulus that evokes a statement about anger, is reinforced, and possibly even evokes the emotion.

The literature contains some interesting and well-known data on how much influence private events (as discriminative stimuli) exert over their responses. In the classical autokinetic phenomenon experiment by Sherif (1935), subjects were exposed to a tiny stationary light in an otherwise completely dark room. The subjects were asked to make judgments about the distance the light traveled. This provides an example of a private event, the response to which can be easily modified. Sherif was, of course, interested in the social impact on such judgments, and showed that when you put together two individuals making judgments about the distance moved, they will each gradually alter their judgments until they are making the same judgments somewhere in the middle of the two distances originally estimated.

Subsequently, Mausner (1954) examined the effect of positive reinforcement and punishment on subjects' judgments about the size of lines in a completely dark room (thus, without any frame of reference). This is not quite as "private" as the autokinetic phenomenon experiment, but still without any surround, thus making the judgment almost as ambiguous. In fact, Mausner repeated the Sherif design, but added the reinforcement variable. Subjects' responses were either mostly positively reinforced or mostly punished when judging alone. Then he put the subjects with different reinforcement histories together, and had them judge the length of lines while alternating judgments with those of another person. He found, when pairing two subjects who had been positively reinforced for their judgments, that neither one altered his or her judgment when confronted with another person's differing judgments. However, when he paired two subjects, each of whom had been mostly punished for their judgments when in the alone condition, he found that the two would stumble over one another trying to judge the length of lines as much as possible as the partner was judging them. Again, we find that subjects will relatively easily alter their judgments about private stimuli, or at least ambiguous stimuli, in reaction to the response-produced stimuli (from other judges) supposedly unrelated to what they are judging.

Of course, many readers may recall the classic experiment of Asch (1955). He showed change of judgments in direct response to judgments made by other persons, where the stimuli to be judged were public and the responses quite obviously wrong. There seems to be no experiment that compared the judgments of different stimuli (ranging from completely private to completely public) to determine how easily judgments can be modified. However, responses to private stimuli are more modifiable than those made to public stimuli.

This early work was done with college students, which raises the question of applicability to clinically distressed people. The following studies demonstrate the use of reinforcement with schizophrenic and physically ill patients. My colleagues and I (Salzinger & Pisoni, 1958, 1960, 1961; Salzinger & Portnoy, 1964; Salzinger, Portnoy, & Feldman, 1964) conditioned what we called self-referred affect responses. Using interviews with schizophrenic patients, we asked a series of general questions during the first 10 minutes, without providing any reinforcement. This was followed by a 10-minute period of additional questions, wherein we reinforced self-referred affect statements. Then we reverted to the original pattern by not reinforcing any responses for the last 10 minutes. Statements about the feelings of schizophrenic patients turned out to be quite malleable, in that they increased when reinforced and decreased when not reinforced. This worked whether we conducted an interview, or simply had the patients speak in a monologue. Also, the same procedure worked for normal subjects who were physically ill. When we compared normal, but physically ill patients and schizophrenic patients, we found no difference in the amount of affect expressed by the two groups during their prereinforcement level or, for that matter, when we examined the conditioning levels. However, we did find that schizophrenic patients emitted a smaller number of self-referred affect statements than normals during extinction. The clinician's report that schizophrenic patients differ from normals in flatness of affect could be ascribed to their differential extinction rate of such responses. Thus, once again we find the malleability of responses to external stimuli determines the feelings expressed, rather than, or at least in conjunction with, whatever the private event it is that drives the verbal responses. As recently reported in a paper on private events (Salzinger, 1993), the tenuousness of people's reinforcement histories with private events makes them easily influenced by external stimuli.

A recent review of the study of private events (Lubinski & Thompson, 1993) is relevant here. The authors examined how human beings respond to private events, and how they communicate them to others, by setting up an animal model of such communication. The advantage of using an animal model is that one can manipulate the private event relatively easily, and that the interpretation is not ambiguous. This is accomplished by injecting an animal with a known drug on one occasion and injecting it with a known placebo (or a different drug) at another time. The animal is then trained to make one response when under the influence of Drug A and another when under the influence of Drug B, or placebo. The conditioning paradigm is the same as the one used when the discriminative stimulus is external. The experimenter then reinforces the appropriate response in the presence of the appropriate stimulus. When the pigeon is exposed to a green light, it must peck the green key; when exposed to a red light, it must peck the red key. Such discriminations can be trained in animals up and down the evolutionary scale, as we successfully did in goldfish (Salzinger, Fairhurst, Freimark, & Wolkoff, 1973), to give a rarely studied animal as an example.

Having established a discrimination based on internal stimulation, which is based on private events, the investigators went on to show how one can also train animals to communicate that state to another animal by making the reinforcement contingencies appropriate to that communication. Human beings do not get such systematic training, not with respect to public stimuli except in school, but certainly nowhere with respect to private stimuli. It might be that certain clients never have been trained even in the usual way, in which people all learn to discriminate how they feel and, therefore, what is often described as a problem in being able to express anger may be absent in the client. Furthermore, it may be that certain clients may have been trained not to communicate feelings, as is often said to be true of men in our society. The point is that the communication act has to be reinforced as well.

A question to be asked (now that we know how to establish a vocabulary, even in animals) is this: What can therapists do with this information in relation to the concepts of *anger* and *aggression*? They might begin by training people— maybe children, maybe retarded individuals, maybe adults who do not seem able to monitor their own emotions—to label emotions "correctly." That would allow clinicians to define emotions in the arbitrary ways that they, in fact, do define them in their various paper-and-pencil scales—the ones regularly administered to clients. It would force professionals to define the situations or stimuli that are supposed to elicit anger. It would then be possible to go one step further to do the same thing for anxiety. By training the vocabulary only for anger, therapists could determine whether trained verbal responses occur when they produce situations that, according to the theory of emotions, are the elicitors of anxiety or joy. Without the usual manner of interrogating their subjects, in which hand waving takes the place of precise experimental specification of conditions under which various responses are evoked, therapists would be in a much better position to find out how the various emotions (or the classes of private events that have been arbitrarily labeled to be particular emotions) actually arrange themselves.

Here is a concrete example. Set up an experimental situation in which anger is aroused. Reinforce some particular response, such as "I am angry," or a fresh response, such as "I am zuk." Then try out a series of other emotion-provoking situations and see the probability of obtaining the same response. Perhaps make it more complicated by also training the person to emit the response "kov" in response to a situation that is supposed to elicit "joy." Then observe which of the two responses just trained are evoked by a variety of other situations. One might find that "zuk" is evoked 100% of the time by frustration, 63% of the time by anxiety-provoking situations, and 7% by joy-eliciting situations. Certainly this might be a better way to determine what emotions constitute classes and which ones do not. All practitioners might have to learn an entirely new vocabulary, but perhaps it is time they gave up the lay dictionary. In an important sense, they already have, as witnessed by the exclusion of the item *I am angry* from a scale of anger.

ANGER *AND* AGGRESSION, ANGER *OR* AGGRESSION, ANGER *IS* AGGRESSION

Finally, what about the question about the relationship of anger and aggression? The intensity dimension might be the one to be explored. But before that is embraced, one should discover what the actual stimulus and response classes of emotion are. Then this problem can be addressed. If anger turns out to be a stimulus class produced by the response to frustration or a current insult, or one in the recent past, it might be a mediator along the route to actual verbal or physical aggression. This is, of course, one model accepted by many practitioners on the front lines with clients. Other practitioners are more extreme—that is, they view anger as the elicitor of aggression. I would put my money on viewing what we currently call *anger within*, as simply a reduced response of what we see when people actually attack someone. Thus, the evoking stimuli of anger and aggression (e.g., an insult or shove from someone) may be the same or similar, and the magnitude of the response (increase in blood pressure, muttering to oneself, yelling, pushing, hitting with a hand, murdering with a weapon) would be determined simply by the reinforcing and punishing contingencies of the environment. As noted by Tsytsarev and Grodnitzky (chap. 6, this volume), there are strong reinforcing contingencies in the world of the juvenile delinquent and the adult crime family member to use force and violence. Different contingencies are present in religious convents and, fortunately, in most families. Of course, when we talk about response classes, we must take into account both respondent and operant responses. Here the respondent is more likely to act as a private event that accompanies an operant that we gradually recognize as aggression.

SUMMARY

This chapter presented a behavior-analytic model of anger and aggression. It is easy to fall into the trap of using a lay person approach to the serious problem of anger and aggression, and to assume that the former causes the latter. Behavior analysis studies psychopathology—in this case anger and aggression—from a scientific perspective. Clear definitions of the variables in question and examination of the conditioning history of patients are likely to yield important clues to treatment. The cognitive approach to psychopathology assumes that people behave, therefore they think first (with apologies to Descartes). Thoughts can be viewed as behaviors in diminished magnitude. The behavior-analytic approach does not deny their existence. What it does do is view such responses in much the same way as the responses that can be more easily observed.

Not only can we not assume the old saw of post hoc ergo propter hoc (after this, therefore because of this), but, because we do not always know what the temporal relationship is between thought and action, we clearly cannot assume a causal relationship there. For all these reasons, it would be better to rely on changing environmental reinforcement contingencies to reduce and prevent both anger and aggression.

Chapter 5

Cross-Cultural Perspectives on Anger

Junko Tanaka-Matsumi

Hofstra University, Hempstead, New York

This chapter presents a cross-cultural perspective on anger, with a theme that anger is a social emotion. In cultures where anger is reported, it is described as a negative response predominantly to social events. An enactment of an angry role invariably has a consequence to social relations within a culture.

Ethnographic studies demonstrate that there are cross-cultural differences in the regulation and communication of anger. Cultures differ in the socialization of anger management and anger displays, and verbal and nonverbal cues used in the communication of anger have strong cultural messages. When individuals fail to use culturally appropriate methods of anger management, cultures have specific labels to describe those individuals.

Thus, culture plays a role at every step in the communication and regulation of emotions, and the potential is high for failure in effective intercultural communication and management of anger. The cross-cultural emotion literature has significant clinical implications for professionals working with clients from diverse cultural backgrounds. Lack of knowledge about this literature may lead to an incorrect assessment of the emotional state of the clients and their social interactions.

SUBJECTIVE CULTURE

As proposed by Herskovits (1948), *culture* can be concisely defined as "the man-made part of the human environment" (p. 17). For the study of emotions across cultures, it is particularly important to include the concept of *subjective culture* (Triandis, 1972, 1994), which addresses not only a denotative but also a connotative meaning of emotion words, categorization of emotional experiences, values, and norms for appropriate actions in emotionally charged situations (White, 1993). As emphasized by Sommers (1988) in her interdisciplinary approach to emotion studies, Bedford's (1957) early view is particularly relevant for cross-cultural studies of emotions: "Emotion concepts . . . presuppose concepts of social relationships and institutions, and concepts belonging to systems of judgments, moral, aesthetic and legal. In using emotion words we are able, therefore, to relate behavior to the complex background in which it is enacted and so to make human action intelligible" (p. 304).

CULTURE AND THE MANY WORDS FOR EXPRESSING ANGER: A PROTOTYPE VIEW

It is obvious that different languages have different words for emotions (e.g., Heider, 1991; Lutz, 1988; Russell, 1991; Wierzbicka, 1994), and one cannot assume that translations of the English word *anger* have equivalent cultural meanings. There are many words that cluster with *anger* in every language that has been empirically investigated, including English (Fehr & Russell, 1984; Shaver, Schwartz, Kirson, & O'Connor, 1987), Japanese (Tanaka-Matsumi & Boucher, 1978), Indonesian (Fontaine & Poortinga, 1994; Heider, 1991), and Chinese (Shaver, Wu, & Schwartz, 1992), among others.

Americans group the word *anger* with words like *rage, fury, wrath, hostility, resentment*, and so on (Shaver et al., 1987). Each word differs in its rated degree of membership in the anger cluster. In a field study conducted among three cultural groups of Indonesia, Heider (1991) developed "network mapping" of emotion words to depict interrelationships among words. Heider found that the three cultural groups in Indonesia differed in the number of word clusters expressing anger (*marah*). The number in the *marah* area ranged from one (in Minangkabau) to five (in Minagkabau Indonesian) clusters, each connected to the key word *marah*. The lexical categories of emotions are complex and subtle in their cultural meanings.

Investigating the emotion lexicon in the Ifaluk language of Micronesia in South Pacific, Lutz (1982, 1988) reported that the Ifaluk do not have a semantically equivalent word like *anger*, which tends to be used indiscriminatively in the West. Instead, the Ifaluk have the word *song*, which precisely means "justified anger." In fact, Lutz stated that the Ifaluk speak about many types of anger, but only *song*, or justifiable anger, is morally approved (Lutz, 1988). Lutz described the social conditions under which the word *song* is used among the Ifaluk: "(1) there is a rule or value violation, (2) it is pointed out by someone, (3) who simultaneously calls for the condemnation of the act, and (4) the perpetrator reacts in fear to that anger, (5) amending his or her ways" (p. 157). In short, *song* refers to a scene that involves the judgment about a violation of the culturally shared Ifaluk value system. One of their important values is sharing with others, therefore justifiable anger is culturally approved when someone violates this cultural code.

Two conclusions can be drawn from the emotion lexicon studies. First, the word *anger* is connected to a number of semantically similar words, each word differing in its degree of prototypicality (Fehr & Russell, 1984; Russell, 1991). Second, people define and organize emotion words according to cultural scripts. Subjective meanings associated with emotion words such as anger and their clusters reflect cultural values and norms (D'Andrade, 1984; Kostogiannis & Tanaka-Matsumi, 1994; Lutz, 1988; Russell, 1991; Tanaka-Matsumi & Marsella, 1976; Triandis, 1994). Thus, when clients say that they are angry, clinicians should assess cultural meanings of this word and try to obtain additional expressions. In that way, behaviors that are associated with particular forms of anger are more predictable and culturally valid.

ANGER AS A SOCIAL EMOTION: CULTURAL CONSTRUCTION OF ANGER

According to Wallbott and Scherer's (1986) cross-cultural survey, which used student subjects from seven European countries and Israel, over 80% of the self-reported antecedent events of anger involved interpersonal situations. Within the United States, Averill's (1982, 1983) survey of everyday experiences of anger by native-born American students and community residents indicated that 83% of the subjects reported becoming angry at least once or twice a week. When student subjects were specifically asked to keep daily records of each experience of anger and annoyance, they reported an average of approximately 7 incidents of anger and 24 incidents of annoyance each week. Clearly, anger is a frequently experienced emotion for Americans in various social situations.

Furthermore, Averill's (1982) data revealed that 88% of self-reports of anger-causing events involved at least one other person. Averill concluded that "anger is primarily an interpersonal emotion," an experience frequently involving a "loved one" (33% of the reported episodes) or "someone you know well and like" (21% of the reported episodes). Kassinove and Sukhodolsky (chap. 1, this volume) expanded on Averill's notion of anger occurring within close relationships. In a study investigating prototypes of "emotion knowledge" by American college students, Shaver and his colleagues (Shaver et al., 1987) reported similar findings. In summary, anger is social and unpleasant in nature, and frequently involves familiar people as targets.

Cross-Cultural Studies of Antecedent Events of Anger

What are the culturally shared elements of social situations that trigger anger? Are there cross-cultural similarities in anger-arousing events? Systematic research into the subjective experience of emotions began only recently (Kitayama & Markus, 1994; Mesquita & Frijda, 1992). Scherer and his colleagues (Scherer, Summerfield, & Wallbott, 1983; Scherer, Wallbott, Matsumoto,

& Kudoh, 1988; Scherer, Wallbott, & Summerfield, 1986) conducted the most extensive cross-cultural investigation into self-reported antecedents of prototypical emotions, including anger, sadness, fear, and happiness. Subjects initially included students from Europe (Belgium, France, Great Britain, Italy, Spain, Switzerland, and Germany) and Israel. Later, Scherer (1988) extended the International Study on Emotion Antecedents and Reactions (ISEAR) project to 30 countries on all five continents.

Subjects were presented with the words *anger, bad temper, rage*, and their translations. They were asked to write down their responses to the following questions: (a) What happened? (b) Who was present? (c) Where did it happen? and (d) How did you react? The investigators developed event codes to analyze the descriptive antecedent data. For anger antecedents, 11 specific categories of events were coded (Wallbott & Scherer, 1986): relationships, injustice, interactions with strangers, inconvenience, achievement, bad news, body–mind centered, social institutions, birth-death, temporary separation, and permanent separation. Wallbott and Scherer observed that, in various European countries, "personal relationships were by far the most important sources of anger" (p. 82), accounting for 37% of the self-reported situations. Being treated unjustly (18%) and strangers who did not behave well (18%) were the second most frequent anger-inducing situations. The violation of normative standards was a prominent anger antecedent.

In a Japanese–American comparison, Scherer et al. (1988) reported that 58% of the Japanese subjects described interactions with strangers as causing anger, whereas only 15% of the American subjects reported the same. Conversely, 58% of the Americans described relationships as causing anger, whereas only 29% of the Japanese reported the same. The Japanese self-reports of anger antecedents were described as radically different (Scherer, Wallbott, Matsumoto, & Kudoh, 1988) from the Europeans and Americans.

The Japanese–American differences in the proportion of situations involving strangers versus relationships may be explained by the existence of strict rules governing interpersonal behaviors for ingroup members in Japan. In a hierarchical society such as Japan (Nakane, 1970), role and status prescriptions govern ingroup social behaviors. Such a system may serve to reduce or prevent the frequencies of negative emotions such as *ikari* (the Japanese equivalent of anger) to maintain tight social networks (Markus & Kitayama, 1991, 1994).

In summary, research on antecedent events of anger shows that the theme of norm violation is associated with the subjective report of anger by people across Western and non-Western cultures. The level of categorization of the antecedent events, however, is quite abstract (Tanaka-Matsumi, Boucher, & Hasegawa, 1989). Because norms are inherently culture-specific, culture-relevant assessment of anger requires knowledge of normative behaviors in social situations. When it comes to specific events, Boucher and Brandt's (1981) American–Malay cross-cultural study indicated that subjects are accurate slightly more than 50%

of the time in recognizing specific antecedents of anger. Functional analyses are necessary to identify specific instances of offensive behaviors serving as cues for anger arousal, and clinicians will find that clients from different backgrounds become angry in response to unusual events from an American perspective.

FACIAL EXPRESSIONS COMMUNICATING ANGER: CROSS-CULTURAL JUDGMENT STUDIES

How does one know if someone is angry, and how do people express anger? The cross-cultural literature on the communication of anger and other prototypical emotions has predominantly focused on posed facial expressions (Ekman, 1973; Izard, 1980; Russell, 1994). Darwin (1872/1965) proposed an evolutionary view of facial expressions, stating that facial expressions are innate. Angry people can mobilize their energy and feel capable of "defending themselves with great vigor and strength" (Izard, 1977, p. 33). Ekman (1972) and Izard (1971, 1980) both postulated that the basic emotion called *anger* is universally expressed in the face.

Russell (1994) recently reanalyzed the recognition scores of the eight published methodologically similar, cross-cultural judgment studies of facial expressions. He found that there were significant effects of culture in the recognition of disgust, anger, and fear. The anger recognition scores of the Western subjects ($M = 79.1\%$) were significantly better than those of non-Western subjects ($M = 64.\%$). Further, in the Japanese–American comparison from six published cross-cultural studies, Russell found that, overall, Japanese subjects ($M = 64.8\%$) were significantly less effective than American subjects ($M = 87.3\%$) in recognizing posed photographs of angry facial expressions.

These cross-cultural differences in the recognition of angry facial expressions are important because all of the studies reviewed by Russell used the standard method: (a) subjects are typically exposed to a series of up to 100 photographs or slides of different and posed facial expressions, and (b) subjects are asked to identify each expression using a forced-choice response format by selecting one of the six or seven English emotion words or their translations (e.g., *angry, happy, sad, surprised, disgusted, fear, contempt*).

However, the consensual judgment about facial expressions changes when subjects are given a context. This has an important implication for cross-cultural communication of emotions because all emotions are expressed in context. In experimental judgment studies of facial expressions, context may be manipulated by providing one or more facial expressions prior to the judgment about a target face. Russell and Fehr (1987) found that the intensity and labeling of the target facial expression changed significantly depending on the context face. These same authors concluded that "the same facial expression will be seen as expressing different types and degrees of emotion, depending on what other faces are seen" (p. 223).

Russell and Fehr's findings were independently replicated in three experiments using White American subjects who viewed a target facial expression slide in different contexts consisting of a slide of another facial expression (Tanaka-Matsumi, Attivissimo, Nelson, & D'Urso, 1994). The authors obtained a recognition score of 41.7% for an anger expression when subjects were exposed to this slide alone without context. However, recognition scores of anger increased to 54.1% when it was preceded by a single happy expression, and to 57.9% and 66.7%, respectively, when it was preceded by a single surprised or sad expression.

In another study (Tanaka-Matsumi, Seiden, Xydas, & Lam, 1994) designed to compare the recognition scores of 42 randomly selected slides of facial expressions from Ekman and Friesen's (1976) *Pictures of Facial Affect*, the recognition scores were significantly lower for five of the six emotions (*angry, happy, sad, fear, surprised,* and *disgusted*) when subjects rated a single facial expression as opposed to rating an entire set of 42 facial expressions.

The results of the context studies suggest that, contrary to Ekman and O'Sullivan's (1988) position, perception of facial expressions are not accurate or absolute even within the same culture. Recognition scores of anger and other expressions change with the context. This suggests that recognition of a facial expression is relative, facilitated by the knowledge of the context (Russell, 1994; Thayer, 1980). According to Wallbott (1988), when contextual information that is concordant with person information (facial expression) is presented, judges use both sources of information in making emotion judgments. Experimental studies of context effects in facial affect recognition should be extended to the cross-cultural domain.

In addition to context effects, another possible source of variation in the consensus for recognition of facial expressions is language. When subjects were asked to freely label photographs of posed facial expressions by using one label, the percentages of judgments agreeing with the predicted angry face were 43% for Japanese subjects, 63% for Greek subjects, and 54% for English-speaking Canadian subjects (Russell, Suzuki, & Ishida, 1993). The word *angry* was used by 16% of Canadian subjects, *ikari* was used by 16% of Japanese subjects, and *thimos* (Greek equivalent of *anger*) was used by 22% of the Greek subjects. As Izard (1994) observed, "emotion recognition is a difficult task and that emotion labeling is much more difficult than emotion recognition" (p. 295). Furthermore, as suggested by the emotion lexicon studies (Heider, 1991; Lutz, 1988; Wierzbicka, 1986), it is extremely difficult to establish the semantic equivalence of even the prototypical word *anger* and its translations in different cultures.

Four conclusions can be drawn from facial expression judgment studies. First, posed prototypical facial expressions of basic emotions, including anger, can be recognized across cultures under certain methodological conditions. Second, cultures differ significantly in recognition scores. Western observers agree on angry facial expressions significantly more than non-Western observers. Potential sources of differences in the recognition scores between Western and non-Western observers for angry facial expressions need systematic investigation. Third, the context in which a particular facial expression is observed is an important determinant of emotion recognition and labeling. If a single photograph of a posed facial expression significantly alters the judgment about a target facial expression, what would be the effect of observing spontaneous facial expressions of anger in varying cultural contexts? Ecological validity of a context study should be enhanced by a dynamic presentation of situational context surrounding a spontaneous facial expression (Wallbott, 1988). Finally, clinicians would be unwise to assume that facial expressions are universal indicators of anger. A large degree of variability is expected, especially in cross-cultural therapist–client dyads. Facial expressions should be understood in context.

CULTURE AND ANGER MANAGEMENT

The communication and management of anger are subject to a variety of social constraints that vary across cultures. Cultures define norms for the verbal and nonverbal enactment of emotions (Ekman, 1972; Harré, 1986; Hochschild, 1979; Lutz & White, 1986; Stearns & Stearns, 1986; Thoits, 1989), and this seems particularly true of negative emotions. Only several empirical cross-cultural studies have examined specific cultural display rules (Ekman, 1972; Matsumoto, 1990, 1993).

Punishing Consequences of Anger Displays

The enactment of emotions has social consequences (Averill, 1982; Mesquita & Frijda, 1992). Anthropological studies have documented that enactment of anger is, in fact, strongly inhibited in certain non-Western and nonindustrial cultures. In her book *Never in Anger*, anthropologist Briggs (1970) reported that the Utku Eskimos believe that angry thoughts and acts are dangerous. Briggs wrote that her own display of temper and frustration were met with social isolation by the Utku Eskimos, with whom she had successfully interacted on a daily basis. She was "ostracized . . . for about three months" due to her display of anger. Although the Utkus are socialized to avoid angry interactions and confrontations, they are keenly aware of anger-provoking situational cues. Among the Utku Eskimos, losing control is regarded as extremely threatening to social cohesion, hence an angry person is actively avoided and isolated.

Similarly, anthropologist Levy (1973, 1984) reported that Tahitians are quick to see the cultural focality (Frijda & Mesquita, 1994) of anger-inducing events. Tahitians have many words to describe anger, which is translated as *riri*. Yet, they do not express anger overtly. According to Levy (1973), anger is a hypercognated emotion, defined by the existence of an extensive anger lexicon and cultural rules about anger. Anger is considered a bad thing, and the majority of Tahitians learn to express anger by using only words. Levy reported that there is virtually no physical violence among Tahitians, due to a variety of social arrangements that minimize interpersonal displays of anger. Thus, Levy reported that Tahitians discourage individual striving to avoid competition. They also learn to easily substitute a blocked goal with another goal. These cultural practices enhance interpersonal relations and help with anger management.

Individualistic Versus Collectivistic Cultures and Anger Displays: Toward Building a Cultural Hypothesis

In line with cultural relativism (Berry, Poortinga, Segall, & Dasen, 1992), anthropological studies have focused on one society at a time, without cross-cultural comparisons, because their goal is to describe each culture in its own right. As noted previously, however, Japan is one of the few non-Western countries included in a number of empirical cross-cultural studies of emotions including: facial expressions, emotion lexicons, antecedents of emotions, and display rules. This allows for comparisons with more individualistic cultures, such as the United States.

Japanese cultural tradition strongly inhibits public display of private emotions, particularly negative emotions. Japanese culture emphasizes conformity and homogeneity to maintain an interdependent network, rather than individualism and self-assertion (Johnson, 1993). Although the Japanese have an extensive and differentiated emotion lexicon, including an anger cluster, they avoid direct verbal expression of negative emotions in dealing with interpersonal conflicts (Lebra, 1984). Historically, Japanese culture has encouraged nonverbal and indirect communications (Benedict, 1946; Morsbach, 1973).

Several hypotheses can be advanced to account for cultural sanctions against the display of negative emotions, particularly anger. Cross-cultural differences in the emotion culture (Thoits, 1989) are explained by the cultural values of individualism versus collectivism (Hofstede, 1980; Triandis, 1994) and independent versus interdependent self-orientation (Markus & Kitayama, 1991). Utilizing the definitions of these cultural dimensions and self-orientations, Triandis (1994) and Markus and Kitayama (1994) hypothesized that different types of positive and negative emotions are reinforced in collectivistic versus individualistic societies. Negative emotions indicate disengagement of self from others. A public expression of anger, in particular, disrupts interdependent relationships among ingroup members. Therefore, ingroup members learn to be vigilant to cultural antecedents of anger to prevent confrontation. They avoid anger-related antecedents by developing specific role behaviors defined by the status within a social hierarchy (Nakane, 1970).

Using posed photographs of facial expressions as stimuli, Matsumoto (1990) examined Japanese–American similarities and differences in display rules according to cultural differences in individualism–collectivism and power status (Hofstede, 1980). He asked subjects if it were appropriate to display specific expressions, including angry facial expressions, in private (alone) and public situations involving ingroups (e.g., close friends, family members) and outgroups (e.g., casual acquaintances) from higher or lower status. The Japanese rated the display of angry facial expressions as more appropriate in outgroups and with lower status others than the Americans did. These results are consistent with Scherer's (1988) work on antecedents of anger, which found that the Japanese subjects reported anger antecedents involving strangers more frequently than the Americans.

The Empowering Effect of Anger Displays in Individualistic Societies

In individualistic societies such as the United States, people are reinforced to assert their own rights and independence. Anger, properly channeled and expressed, can empower individuals and lead to positive interpersonal outcomes (Averill, 1982). Anger also has the function of pointing out wrong doings when things are not done according to cultural rules.

Historically, in the United States, the importance of anger management is evidenced in the existence of an extensive literature on anger control (Stearns & Stearns, 1986) and, more recently, the training of assertive behaviors and related social skills in behavior therapy. Assertive behaviors are "actions that secure and maintain what one is entitled to in an interpersonal situation without impinging on the rights of others" (Spiegler & Guevremont, 1993, p. 265). Extreme caution is exercised in teaching response differences among assertive, aggressive, and unassertive behaviors because each response exerts a different impact on interpersonal relations.

However, these topographic response differences may be interpreted differently in interethnic situations. The literature on social skills training for African Americans reveals that White Americans may perceive the same pattern of social behaviors as assertive for Whites, but aggressive for African Americans (Caldwell-Colbert & Jenkins, 1982). That is, "blacks are perceived as aggressive by whites when they express their feelings, raise questions, or are assertive" in interracial situations (Caldwell-Colbert & Jenkins, 1982, p. 182). Furthermore, empirical studies (e.g., Matsumoto, 1993) indicate significant ethnic differences in perceived intensity of emotional expressions in the face.

In summary, the consensus in the literature is that culture plays a major role in regulating anger: "People everywhere get angry, but they get angry in the service of their culture's rules. Sometimes those rules are explicit . . . ; more often they are implicit, disguised in the countless daily actions" (Tavris, 1982, p. 47).

WHEN ANGER MANAGEMENT FAILS: CLINICAL IMPLICATIONS

Acts of norm violations, perceived injustice, and socially offensive behaviors occur every day. The inability to cope with such situations can have serious implications for individuals and society. Cultures attempt to cope with individuals who exhibit extreme outbursts of temper and aggressive behavior by developing transient roles under certain social conditions. Averill (1982) illustrated this with several examples. There are unique names such as *running amok* in Malaysia, *wild-pig syndrome* (or *wild-man syndrome*) in New Guinea, and *to nu* among the Kaingang Indians of Brazil. In New Guinea, the wild-pig syndrome is described as a culture-bound, time-limited psychotic behavior pattern involving a variety of overtly aggressive acts, including looting and shooting arrows at a bystander. After a few days of playing the role of a wild pig, the afflicted young man disappears into the woods and returns as a normal man. The Gururumba believe that the aggressive acts are caused by the "bite of a ghost of recently deceased individual" (Averill, 1982, p. 56). The aggressive behaviors are believed to show the inability of the young man to cope with frustrations imposed by society. After the episode of the wild pig, he must accept social obligations in a society that emphasizes conformity. The wild-pig syndrome shows that the young man is not capable of controlling his own behavior. Thus, culture gives a socially sanctioned label and permits specific role behaviors of a wild man.

It is obviously important to study the different ways in which individuals and their cultures cope with anger-management failure. As concluded in an extensive review of the literature on cross-cultural behavior therapy (Tanaka-Matsumi & Higginbotham, in press), clinicians must develop knowledge of cultural norms, display rules, and specific and common antecedents to assess the function of their clients' anger. This will lead to effective and efficient treatments for individuals and families who seek help for anger disorders.

Chapter 6

Anger and Criminality

Sergei V. Tsytsarev

St. Petersburg State University, Russia, and Hofstra University, Hempstead, New York

Gustavo R. Grodnitzky

Federal Correctional Institution, Danbury, Connecticut

To understand the relationship between anger and aggression, it is important to understand the concept of *crime*. Crime is behavior—specifically that subset of behavior that violates criminal laws. According to Pallone and Hennessy (1992), crime is any behavior (an act or omission) officially prohibited by public law. Thus, it concerns those transgressions committed against the public order; crime is not focused on moral or private events. Of course, official prohibitions of specific behaviors tend to vary over time (e.g., sale of alcohol, age of accepted use of alcohol, voluntary abortion, etc.). Thus, the specific behavior of one person is actually not a criminal act until it has been adjudicated as one. Acts are criminal when they are specified in written laws (thus, they differ across societies). However, although federal, state, and local jurisdictions often vary in their definitions of *minor crimes*, they seldom disagree in their definitions of *serious*, *violent*, and *aggressive crimes*.

In terms of classification, a *violent crime* is an unlawful behavior, such as homicide, rape, robbery, and assault, that may result in injury to a person. A *property crime* is an unlawful act that is committed with the intention of gaining property (e.g., car theft, burglary, etc.), but that does not involve the use of verbal threat or physical force against an individual. To say that a person is a *criminal* (i.e., to use it as a noun) suggests a state of being, or (as a trait) that there are criminal personality characteristics that reside inside the person. This is a rather nonbehavioral view (see Salzinger, chap. 4, this volume for an objection to the trait perspective). In contrast, as an adjective, *criminal* indicates a property that a particular behavior acquires in relation to a body of law. This perspective analysis is simply definitional, and suggests that criminal behavior can become non-criminal immediately if the law changes.

Crime often involves anger and aggression. However, Pallone and Hennessy (1992) also noted that "a psychology of [anger and] aggression is not a psychology of criminal behavior" (p. 40). Psychology and the other behavioral sciences may study acts that are aggressive and/or antisocial, as well as private internal events such as brooding and sullenness as signs of anger. Indeed, such low-level and sometimes private events experienced only by the person may be presumed to be antecedents of behavior that is formally criminal. However, anger only sometimes leads to (or is associated with) aggression, and not all aggression is criminal. Thus, the fields of criminology and psychology overlap, but also have fully distinct elements.

Congruent with the analysis presented earlier, Erikson (1966) noted that, "Deviance is not a property inherent in any particular kind of behavior; it is a property conferred upon that behavior by the people who come into contact with it" (p. 6). In contrast, Hennessy and Pallone observed that some behavior is considered to be "wrong in itself" (p. 47). This might include acts such as child abuse, elder abuse, murder, and so on, which take life or unjustifiably deprive others of their property. These behaviors seem to offend what ethicists call *pristine moral principle* (i.e., acts that are not colored by the norms of specific societies or the laws in place at a particular time in a society). Indeed, acts that ethicists define as *wrong* may not even violate the law of a society.

In summary, it is likely that some anger and aggression is bejudged as wrong in some societies, or some parts of some societies, or at some time in the life of a society, while being judged elsewhere or at another time as acceptable. Certainly laws relating to monogamy versus polygamy fit this description. In contrast, other behaviors are assumedly *wrong* (as defined by ethicists) because they violate some pristine principle, such as peacetime murder.

With this as background, it is nevertheless important to govern society—to develop laws to punish and segregate transgressors, and to serve as a warning to those about to transgress. Yet because of the high level of anger and aggression, this model (as currently structured) is questionable. The medical community has identified violence in the United States as a significant public health issue (Koop & Lundberg, 1992). Injuries, both fatal and nonfatal, resulting from interpersonal violence are rampant, and the Centers for Disease Control (CDC) has made violence prevention one of its top priorities (Rosenberg, O'Carroll, & Powell, 1992).

According to the Federal Bureau of Investigation and the U.S. Department of Justice's (1991) *Uniform Crime Reports*, one violent crime occurs every 17 seconds in the United States. An average of 733 shootings take place each day, and there is one murder approximately every 22 minutes. Novello, Shosky, and Froehlke (1992) indicated that homicide is the second leading cause of death among 15- to 24-year-olds, and the leading cause of death among 15- to 34-year-old African American males. The United States has the highest homicide rate of any Western industrialized nation.

According to the 1991 *Uniform Crime Reports*, aggressive acts typically occur between people who know each other, and frequently occur during some kind of disagreement. More than 50% of murder victims know their assailants— only 14% of victims are murdered by strangers. Moreover, 34% of all murders committed in 1990 were preceded by some kind of disagreement or argument. This indicates that murder usually occurs in a social context, and is not random. Anger is also more often experienced between acquaintances (Averill, 1983). When coupled with contextual information, which suggests that violence is often preceded by arguments between people who know each other, the possibility of a relationship between anger and aggressive behavior emerges. Yet as noted by Kassinove and Sukhodolsky (chap. 1, this volume), the relationship between these two variables is unclear. Some hostile or emotional anger seems to lead to aggression, but some aggression is clearly a product of cool and thoughtful action.

In the context of this chapter, it is important to note that, according to Pallone and Hennessy (1992), the American Law Institute developed a list of mitigating factors, ". . . the presence of which may not exculpate an alleged offender, but influences the severity of the sanction imposed upon conviction" (p. 52). Thus, the way murder is seen varies with circumstances. Many of these mitigating factors are psychological in nature, and they go on to mention such variables as the influence of mood-altering drugs, alcohol, the prior relationship between the victim and the offender, whether the victim may have invited or colluded in his or her own victimization, and so on. It is especially important to note that in the criminal justice systems of most industrialized countries, including the United States, passionate angry affect is seen as a mitigating factor in criminal aggression.

PREVALENCE AND PREDICTION

The prevalence of violent acts is clearly documented. However, relatively little is known about the prevalence of anger, or about the relationship between anger and aggression. In addition, because of the need to focus on aggression, no studies that systematically study anger in criminal groups exist. However, in a series of surveys by Averill (1982, 1983), American college students and community residents were asked to describe their most recent anger episodes. Another group described the experience of being the target of another person's anger. The most frequent response to anger was nonaggressive. Only 10% of the angry responses recorded were described as leading to physical aggression. More than 50% of the anger episodes involved a loved one or someone well known, and only 13% involved strangers. In 85% of the cases, subjects indicated that the cause of anger was reported to be a perceived injustice by another person that was preventable and voluntary. Finally, although most subjects regarded the actual experience of anger as negative, the short-term consequences of most anger episodes were generally evaluated as positive and useful, even by the targets of another person's anger. These data are generally consistent with the data on violent crime. Anger and aggression occur most often in an interpersonal context, among people who know each other well. Regrettably, although the outcome of anger may often be positive, the outcome of criminal aggression is not.

Another area of interest to practitioners and theoreticians alike concerns the lack of predictability of aggressive behavior. Although Averill's (1983) data show self-defined anger to be a daily experience, violent behavior (e.g., homicide, rape, etc.) is quite infrequent even among angry, violence-prone individuals (Tsytsarev & Callahan, 1995). For example, convicted murderers and even serial murderers are nonviolent in most of their interactions with people. In fact, according to Hillbrand, Foster, and Hirt (1988), less than 2% of violence-prone individuals commit violent crimes. Most are able to find alternate, socially acceptable, institutionalized ways to express anger at work, at home, and in a variety of other environments. Such realities are not usually considered in the empirical research on aggressive behavior and violence. Thus, it behooves clinicians to look for those final triggers that lead to criminal violence.

Deffenbacher (1993) described a variety of characteristics of persons with generalized anger (which he uses to develop the ideal intervention programs he describes in chap. 9, this volume). His model has relevance for criminal aggression, and includes two levels of event appraisals: primary and secondary. *Primary appraisal* (Lazarus, 1991) is an evaluation or interpretation that a violation has transpired in one's personal domain; that is, there has been some trespass on personal rules or expectations and/or an interruption of a goal-directed behavior. Further, during primary appraisal, anger is thought likely to arise if the act is judged to be: (a) intentional (i.e., the angry person attributes a purpose to the event that happened), (b) preventable (i.e., the angry person believes the event was controllable, but was not avoided), (c) unjustified (i.e., the event has violated the angry person's sense of what is fair and just, therefore it is perceived as unwarranted and undeserved), and (d) blameworthy (i.e., in the angry person's sense of perceived righteousness, the source was wrong and should or must be punished).

Secondary appraisal (Deffenbacher, 1993; Lazarus, 1991) involves a person's perception of his or her own ability to cope with the negatively perceived situation. The person may perceive his or her own ability to cope as inadequate, and thus experience anger. However, the person may also perceive his or her own ability as inadequate, but experience anger because of one of the primary appraisals previously described.

Deffenbacher (1993) and others (e.g., DiGiuseppe, chap. 8, this volume) suggested that angry individuals tend to possess several cognitive information-processing patterns that distort and lead to excesses in normal levels of anger. Among these are the following: (a) poor estimation of probabilities (i.e., angry people overestimate the probability of negative outcomes, events, and/or personal resources and underestimate the possibility of positive ones), (b) misattribution of cause (i.e., angry people quickly and automatically perceive events as negative, even when information suggests alternative possibilities. They believe others have engaged in intentional, personal, and malicious attacks, and there is a quality of mind reading and a belief in the certainty about the future. Angry people believe that they know what others are thinking, how others will behave, and the consequences of the situation for all involved), (c) overgeneralization (i.e., angry people use broad constructs when evaluating time [e.g., *always, never*] and others [e.g., *stupid, crazy, worthless*]. This exaggerates their sense of injustice and unfairness), (d) dichotomous thinking (i.e., also referred to as *black-and-white thinking*, this refers to a style of perception where constructs lie on juxtaposed poles [e.g., people are either winners or losers, things are either right or wrong, people either like me or hate me]. When the positive extreme cannot be confirmed, or when the situation is ambiguous, the negative polarity is automatically assumed), (e) inflammatory or provocative labeling (i.e., this involves the perception of persons involved in the event as highly negative [e.g., ass, shithead, etc.]. Anger escalates as a function of the highly emotionally charged language, instead of the realistic problems the individual is facing), (f) demandingness and/or dictatorial thinking (i.e., perceived injustice escalates when moral expectations or guidelines are unfulfilled, and is often followed by beliefs that others should not or must not act as they did) and, (g) catastrophic evaluations (i.e., angry individuals tend to perceive unmet demands or dictates in an exaggeratedly negative manner and define them as *horrible, unbelievable, awful*, etc.).

For generally angry, and probably aggressive, persons, these cognitive processes tend to make them intellectually rigid and inflexible, and prevent the possibility of entertaining alternative interpretations of a given event or situation. When hopes, personal desires, goals, and aspirations become moral imperatives and are then unfulfilled, anger can be expected to ensue. If unresolved and if combined with other elements that lead to aggression, such as alcohol or drug usage or fatigue, criminal aggression can result.

Anger antecedents and consequences have been investigated in a series of studies by Deffenbacher and colleagues (Deffenbacher, Demm, & Brandon, 1986; Deffenbacher & Sabadell, 1992; Story & Deffenbacher, 1986). College students of high and low anger levels were asked to rate their most angering, ongoing situations, as well as their day-to-day responses of anger. High-anger individuals reported more frequent and intense daily anger reactions. Using qualitative analyses, Deffenbacher (1991) reported two interesting findings. First, although high-anger people reported more frequent and intense anger on a daily basis, the antecedent situations they were responding to did not differ from those faced by low-anger subjects. Low- and high-anger subjects encountered similar situations, but high-anger subjects responded with greater anger. Second, anger occurred primarily in an interpersonal context. As noted previously (see chap. 1, this volume), this is congruent with Averill's (1983) findings. Deffenbacher reported that, of the most severe ongoing situations, 53% involved nonfamily interpersonal relationships (e.g., roommates, friends), 15% involved family, 10% arose from one's own behavior, 6% involved work and school, respectively, and

9% involved miscellaneous events (e.g., driving into inanimate objects). Analysis of day-to-day sources of anger revealed somewhat similar results, with 40% of anger-provoking situations coming from interpersonal situations, 5% from family interactions, 22% from one's own behavior, 7% from school, 3% from work, and 22% from miscellaneous situations.

In Deffenbacher and Thwaites (1991), anger consequences/outcomes of angry responses were evaluated. In this study, although insufficient anger responses were given to rate consequences into categories of severity, seven types of consequences were identified: (a) physical damage to self, (b) physical damage to others, (c) physical damage to objects, (d) damage to interpersonal relationships, (e) vocational/school problems, (f) legal/quasilegal difficulties, and (g) damage to self-esteem. In this study, a questionnaire was used to gather more detailed information about the two worst anger incidents for both the high- and low-anger groups. Findings revealed that high-anger subjects reported more negative consequences than low-anger subjects on all dimensions, except for legal and work/school. There were no gender differences.

Specific comparisons for high- versus low-anger subjects in the worst anger-related event were 45% versus 17% for physical damage to self, 20% versus 4% for physical damage to others, 26% versus 8% for physical damage to objects, 80% versus 60% for damage to relationships, and 35% versus 25% for work/school consequences (Deffenbacher, 1991). In the second worst anger-related event, again, there were no gender differences; however, high-anger individuals experienced more severe damage to physical objects, personal relationships, and self-esteem. Thus, high-anger subjects experienced significantly more frequent and negative long-term consequences for their angry responses (Deffenbacher, 1991).

In summary, current findings in anger studies find that angry men and women have cognitive processes that seem to predispose or lead to angry responses. They respond more frequently and intensely with angry emotions, and they tend to be provoked most often by interpersonal interactions that are perceived negatively. Behaviorally, angry persons are more likely to respond in an uncontrolled manner. Furthermore, angry persons do suffer long-term effects from their anger, experiencing more frequent and more negative personal, physical, and social consequences.

DEFINING BASIC CONCEPTS

A motivational approach to understanding criminal behavior is presented in this section. However, it is important to clearly define the phenomenon of interest. *Crime* has already been defined as behavior that violates criminal law. Law is discussed, voted on, and, in that sense, written into reality. Clinical constructs are harder to define and do not come into existence by the democratic method. Scholars rarely vote on hypotheses and theories. Thus, when Averill (1982), Tavris (1989), and Spielberger and his colleagues (Spielberger, 1988; Spielberger,

Jacobs, Russell, & Crane, 1983; Spielberger et al., 1985) reviewed various attempts to define anger, aggression, and hostility, they concluded that providing definitions remains a difficult task, and that researchers have not yet agreed on uniform definitions. Historically, *anger* has been confused with *hostility* and *aggression*, and the terms have been used interchangeably. In chapter 1 (this volume), Kassinove and Sukhodolsky defined *anger* as:

> a negative, phenomenological (or internal) feeling state associated with specific cognitive and perceptual distortions and deficiencies (e.g., misappraisals, errors, and attributions of blame, injustice, preventability, and/or intentionality), subjective labeling, physiological changes, and socially constructed and reinforced organized behavior scripts. Anger varies in frequency. Some people report feeling angry almost all of the time, whereas others rarely feel angry. Anger varies in intensity, from mild (typically labeled as *agitation* or *annoyance*) to strong (typically labeled as *fury* or *rage*). Anger varies in duration, from transient to long term (i.e., holding a grudge). However, people express their anger experiences differently, thus many different behaviors (e.g., sulking, yelling, glaring, avoiding eye contact, leaving, making snide comments, etc.) are associated with the internal experience. It is the totality of specific cognitive and phenomenological experiences that differentiate anger from other feelings such as anxiety, sadness, and so on. (p. 7)

Their definition emphasizes the phenomenological nature of anger, and it underscores the importance of subjective self-report in the assessment of anger. We agree with their position. Yet observer inference from behavioral reactions, facial expressions, and/or measures of physiological arousal is important. These measures alone disregard the centrality of subjects' self-report when evaluating an emotion such as anger. For example, several authors attempted to define *anger* without the phenomenological component. *Anger* has been defined in almost entirely cognitive terms (Ellis, 1977; Lazarus, 1991), in terms deemphasizing the influence of cognition (Novaco, 1975), or in terms emphasizing the relationship between anger and aggression (Rubin, 1986). But as pointed out in chapter 5 (this volume) by Tanaka-Matsumi, cultures differ widely in their display rules and scripts for the expression of anger. Thus, clinicians who rely on facial expressions, physiological arousal, cognitive patterns, or even verbal behavior alone are likely to make mistakes in anger assessment. Indeed, anger is the totality of specific cognitive and phenomenological experiences.

Aggression (Baron, 1977; Berkowitz, 1993; DiGiuseppe, Tafrate, & Eckhardt, 1994; Spielberger, 1988) is overt motor behavior enacted with the intent to do harm or injury to a person or object. There is, first and foremost, behavioral and observable aspects of the construct. Second, there is a motivational component (i.e., intent) that allows us to differentiate aggression, which is accidental (i.e., knocking someone to the ground while attempting to enter the subway), from aggression, which is deliberate (knocking someone to the ground during a robbery or assault). Crime concerns aggression, typically intentional aggression, and anger may or may not be part of its root.

For most authors (e.g., DiGiuseppe et al., 1994), *hostility* is a personality trait evidenced by cross-situational patterns of anger and hostile attitudes (Spielberger, 1988), possibly in combination with (criminal) aggression. Although this term is currently in vogue and has been used interchangeably with *anger* and *aggression*, this definition of *hostility* emphasizes a long-standing personality style, not a one-time behavioral response evoked by a specific stimulus perceived as threatening, undesirable, or noxious.

ANGER, AGGRESSION, AND CRIMINAL BEHAVIOR

We now focus on three of many aspects of the problem of anger and crime. First, we present the motivational perspective to violence to understand how habitual experiencing and expressing of anger under particular circumstances and in certain subcultures can become a form of addictive behavior—so-called "process addiction" (Schaef & Fassel, 1988; Tsytsarev, 1989). Second, we present the symptoms and dynamics of *pathological affect* and *physiological affect*. These terms refer to two states of strong anger that underlie certain types of crime known to the general public as *crimes of passion*. Third, we discuss the expression of anger within a subculture of criminals being detained for violent crimes. This is important from the perspective of preventing the development of new violent behavior patterns.

THE MOTIVATIONAL PERSPECTIVE

As has been stated by many researchers (e.g., Averill, 1982; Berkowitz, 1993; Guldan, 1986; Rogachevsky, 1984; Tsytsarev & Callahan, 1995), aggressive behavior is a complex, multiaxial phenomenon. To understand its nature, one must explore the meaning of aggressive behavior both for the individual behaving violently, and for his or her social environment. The psychological meaning of violent behavior depends on both its overt and covert functions (i.e., on the drive states underlying the criminal behavior, which to some extent are satisfied by, and may be reinforced by, violent behavior). In this regard, an approach previously developed in Russia for the motivational analysis of sexual behavior (Kon, 1988), the behavior of psychopathic individuals (Guldan, 1986), and for addictive behavior (Nemchin & Tsytsarev, 1989) appears applicable to the analysis of violent behavior as well. In the United States, a similar approach has been developed by Cox and Klinger (1987, 1990).

The central concept in this model is *craving*. In our earlier research (Boky & Tsytsarev 1987; Nemchin & Tsytsarev 1989), we found that cravings develop as the motivational process unfolds: from the individual's need to the goal object capable of satisfying it, to need satisfaction, and finally to motivational tension reduction. (Note: *need* in this model does not refer to biological processes, and may be considered as the equivalent of drive in other models because the needs referred to are often social in nature. Other theorists would thus call them *drives*, a term used to encompass both needs and wants.) To be defined as a *craving*, motivation must meet the following three requirements: (a) a significantly higher level of motivational tension (e.g., affective arousal, frustration, anguish, etc.) than what the individual typically experiences, such that there is considerable strain and discomfort; (b) a great attractiveness of the goal object, which is thought to be capable of satisfying the need; and (c) two groups of obstacles impeding access to the goal object—objective barriers arising in the environment, and subjective barriers resulting from personality traits or problems.

If the object corresponds to the basic need (i.e., it is natural and adequate to fulfill the need), and the individual is capable of coping with both objective and subjective obstacles and finally reaches the object of his or her need, then a normal craving is formed and fulfilled. Normal cravings result in real need satisfaction and motivational tension reduction, and thus play an important role in personality growth because the individual involved is compelled to change either the social environment (coping with objective obstacles) or his or her own personality (coping with subjective obstacles). Thus, if there is a need for love and an attractive person could fulfill it, but is unavailable (perhaps the person is married—an objective obstacle), or the person has low self-esteem (subjective obstacle), there is a normal craving that may or may not be fulfilled.

If the object is not adequate to the basic need (i.e., the normal object is supplanted by another that is unable to provide real need satisfaction—alcohol or drugs are substituted for the person being sought), a certain discharge of motivational tension associated with the strained need occurs. However, the individual achieves no real satisfaction and thus becomes frustrated, and the basic frustrated need is repeatedly recycled into a state of tension. In time, the individual is unable to follow a normal course of need satisfaction, and gradually becomes dependent on the substitute object. The motivation underlying such behavior can be defined as an abnormal or pathological craving.

Using this model, the ultimate goal of the psychological study of violent criminal behavior is the investigation of mechanisms involved in its development. Therefore, one must evaluate the subjective and objective meanings of violent behavior, and how they derive from the needs being satisfied with violent conduct. From this perspective, Tsytsarev and Callahan (1995) considered violent behavior to be: (a) a means of tension reduction—anger and violence are elicited by inner impulses that demand to be discharged by any means, and violent behavior is one possibility; (b) a means for temporary self-esteem growth—violence may provide a strong feeling of self-confidence, and even omnipotence and grandiosity; (c) a means of emotional state transformation and sensation seeking, obtaining unusual affective experience and escaping from emotional emptiness and boredom; (d) a means of compensation or substitution—a profound frustration of any basic need (e.g., love, affiliation, power, social achievement, security, etc.) results in excessive motivational tension and anger that can be directed toward others or, rarely, at the subject him- or herself; and (e) a means of communication—violence is an integral part of certain specific subcultures (e.g., criminals, drug and alcohol abusers, etc.), wherein violent behavior shows group affiliation and is a means to establish a hierarchy of interpersonal relations. Moreover, violent/aggressive behavior substantially simplifies the complex emotional relationships within these groups. It is commonly employed as a means of manipulation of others, and is aimed at achieving otherwise unattainable goals.

When analyzing different types of violent behavior, it is important to bear in mind that, initially, some kind of motivation (i.e., a frustrated need), playing the role of a psychological predisposition to become violent or express other abnormal behavior, facilitates violent manifestations. But later, reaching no satisfaction, the need becomes progressively stronger and results in more intense aggressive or destructive motivation. Moreover, the individual who becomes accustomed to using violence to satisfy needs, thereby reducing the associated tension and frustration, is likely to subsequently employ the same mode of gratification for other frustrated needs. Thus, violent behavior may become a "process addiction," as characterized by Schaef and Fassel (1988). Compulsive craving, with denial as a prevalent defense mechanism, and confusion, self-centeredness, dishonesty, perfectionism, "frozen feelings," and ethical deterioration may predominate (Schaef & Fassel, 1988). Other significant features may be present as well, including crisis orientation, depression, stress, abnormal thinking processes, forgetfulness, dependency, negativism, defensiveness, projection, tunnel vision, and fear (Schaef, 1987).

Thus, it is important to learn about the types of objects that are sufficient for normal need gratification (fulfillment) but are, in fact, unavailable for subjects displaying violent behavior. There are three common avenues available in different cultures to provide society members with goal objects to satisfy needs and normal cravings. The first is well known and widely used in free societies, wherein individuals are granted access to choices and opportunities that allow them to fulfill their lives by searching for and finding appropriate goal objects. The second is commonly observed in so-called "addicted" societies (Shaef, 1987), where various opportunities are replaced by some form of "harmless" substitute, such as gambling, excessive work, and so on, which pseudosatisfy individuals' needs. The third is directly related to anger and aggressive behavior—when society is unable to offer socially acceptable ways to satisfy needs, but, rather, allows conflicts and problems to be resolved from positions of power.

Therefore, positive reinforcers (rewards) for expressions of anger and violent behavior that occur in the culture (or subculture) must be investigated, and several types of cultures can be differentiated. Some, termed *repressing violence cultures*, reinforce nonviolent behavior while punishing and suppressing violent behavior. An alternate type can be termed *permissive violent cultures*, where violent ways of resolving conflicts and achieving goals through expressions of anger are highly valued and respected. Criminal, violence-prone subcultures positively reinforce expressions of anger and violence (Berkowitz, 1993). Within predominant relationships in that type of culture, anger, rage, and aggressiveness can be seen as personality traits (i.e., consistent across time and situations). The behavior of such criminals is highly predictable.

There are intermediate variations between these two extremes, and in each a certain amount of anger and violence is allowed and positively reinforced under certain circumstances (e.g., military combat; police work; sports such as hockey, karate, or football; some workplace activities, etc.). Such permitted violence is a ready source for the overwhelming violence in a society where the aforementioned conditions arise (i.e., violent behavior serves as a means of pseudosatisfaction of the frustrated basic needs; Tsytsarev & Callahan, 1995).

An illustration of how anger experiences and expressions can become involved in a vicious circle of addictive behavior is shown in cases of serial killers. It was found, through testifying in Russian courts, that, for some serial killers, experiences of anger, followed by aggressive behavior, play a special role in their need satisfaction. Each murder committed by them is done while being truly "possessed" with anger, rage, and outrage. Murderers usually misattribute the cause of their anger to their victims, and accuse the victims of being immoral (e.g., serial murderers who kill prostitutes), overly seductive and spoiled (e.g., those who kill underage girls), dangerous for society, and/or simply "totally bad" in a sense that they create. In fact, the outburst of anger followed by sexual, physical, and/or verbal aggression provides them with tension reduction experienced as relief, satisfaction, and happiness, which last for a significant period of time and prevent further aggressive behavior. However, as their needs get strained and the feelings of dissatisfaction and frustration increase, they become unable to control impulses leading them to the next episode of murder, sexual assault, and so on.

Two examples of this behavior pattern are widely known today. The first is the case of Ted Bundy, the former assistant to the chairperson of the Washington State Republican Party, who (from 1974 to 1978) stalked, attacked, killed, and then sexually assaulted as many as 36 victims in Washington, Oregon, Utah, Colorado, and Florida. The second is V. Tchikatillo, a Russian high school teacher, who killed, mutilated, and sexually assaulted more than 50 victims in the 1970s and 1980s in various cities of southern Russia. They both maintained a facade of charm so that acquaintances described them as fascinating, charismatic, and compassionate. Some authors believe this is a characteristic of the psychopathic or sociopathic personality (Wrightsman, 1991). Regardless of the labels that are used, the behavior of those perpetrators evidently represents the addictive nature of some forms of violent behavior.

The issue of motivation is especially important because both its semantics (subjective meaning) and juridical qualification depend on how and in what terms various motivational factors are identified, measured, and interpreted. Within the constraints of this chapter, we are unable to discuss the many different motivational approaches to criminal behavior. Therefore, we limit our discussion to the identification of emotional factors in the motivation of aggressive criminal conduct, and specifically to the role of anger, rage, and hostility.

THE CONCEPT OF AFFECT OF ANGER

In traditional European criminal codes, such as in Germany, France, and Russia, the concept of *affect of anger* was introduced about 100 years ago to refer to specific types of crime—called *crimes of passion* in America. In these crimes, there is a state of emotional overexcitement caused by certain behaviors of the potential victim (often perceived to be illegitimate), followed by the brutal aggressive acts. In this conception, affect of anger is both (a) a pathological state that resembles pathological intoxication in its clinical picture, and (b) a psychophysiological state that develops through the same stages as does pathological affect, but does not cause extreme forms of disorders of consciousness (such as dramatic cognitive distortion, loss of consciousness, falling asleep immediately after the aggressive act, etc.). If a crime is committed in a state of pathological affect, the perpetrator, in most cases, is found insane, and the physiological affect is considered as a mitigating factor that substantially diminishes criminal responsibility, and therefore the level of punishment.

Definition of some of these terms helps clarify the model. *Affect* is an impetuous and stormy emotional process, displayed in an extremely intense explosion of anger (or/and other emotions) that might be followed by an outburst of uncontrollable actions (e.g., aggressive or self-destructive behavior). The word *physiological*, as traditionally used in Russian, French, and German forensic psychology and psychiatry, is used to emphasize that this emotional state does not have to be considered pathological (in the framework of insanity and related concepts), but rather represents an extraordinary reaction of an individual expected by neither him- nor herself nor other people to external stimuli. It is a response to circumstances such as interpersonal conflict or arguments that are perceived to markedly lower the individual's self-esteem, insults or humiliates him or her, and/or are a real or perceived threat for the person's life or the life of his or her significant other. An example of physiological affect is presented in the case of Anna.

> Anna, a 42-year-old elementary school teacher and mother of 2-month-old Ivan, her first and only child, was standing at an intersection with her baby carriage. Suddenly a truck passing through the intersection hit the carriage and killed the baby. The truck immediately stopped. Anna opened the driver's door, jumped inside, and strangled the driver to death. At that moment, she was truly possessed with anger, and, according to her later testimony, she didn't see or hear anything around her. Her attention was concentrated on the person who had killed her son. Although the driver had stopped breathing, she continued to hold his neck for another 15 minutes until police arrived. Then she felt extremely tired and fatigued, and could barely walk. She looked like a person who had lost her way,

and for a while she did not recognize the streets or other familiar places, or people she knew before. A full hour later, she exclaimed, "He killed my son!"; she then began to cry and her emotional responses became appropriate.

Anna responded to a specific and traumatic stimulus, and her reaction was a surprise even to her. Her response was acute. All cases of physiological affect are characterized by three stages (i.e., by sequential changes in the emotional state). Depending on various factors, the duration of each stage may vary, but the sequence is always the same. The first stage is characterized by the occurrence and/or accumulation of emotional excitement and tension in response to an external stimulus perceived as an awful, horrible, catastrophe (e.g., a threat to life, humiliation or insult, or other factors significantly decreasing self-esteem and provoking a feeling of helplessness). Regardless of whether the stimulus is objectively threatening, the person perceives it as so. In one class of Stage 1 reactions, there is an immediate response to the anger provoking stimuli. In the second class of Stage 1 reactions, the response occurs as a function of prolonged conflict between the perpetrator and his potential victim. Over time, the person is exposed to the excessive humiliation, is consistently insulted, and so on, and this leads him to an accumulation of the emotional tension. These two models are shown in Figure 6.1. In these cases, a specific trigger playing the role of what is called the *final drop* in Russian or the *last straw* in English is needed to elicit the outburst of anger and aggression. The appraisal of the trigger depends on various

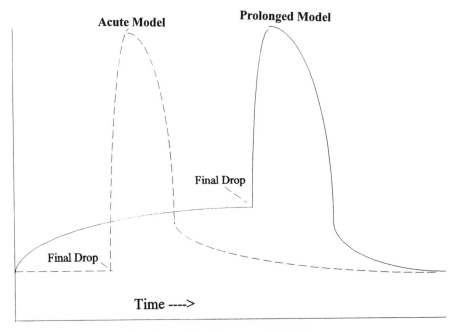

Figure 6.1 Acute and prolonged development of affect of anger.

individual characteristics and experiences of the perpetrator, so it can never be taken for granted by mental health professionals and lawyers, but rather examined in terms of its subjective meaning for the individual at the time of affective response.

> Vladimir, a 19-year-old soldier, was serving his first year in the Soviet Army. He was systematically humiliated by the senior soldiers, who beat him and made him work for them, cleaning toilets, doing their laundry, and so on. He experienced enormous anxiety and fears, yet he could not resist because he was threatened by a group of aggressive older soldiers. One day two of the older soldiers invited him to go to the woods. In the woods, one of them said, "It's time to initiate Vladimir," and they explained they would like to have sex with him. Vladimir grabbed the first object he saw—a heavy stone—and beat one of them more than 10 times. He screamed, cried, used obscenities, and did not stop beating the older soldier until he became totally exhausted. The second soldier ran away. Thirty minutes later, Vladimir returned to the regiment and reported what had happened.

As shown in this example, the second stage is characterized by an extremely powerful emotional outburst that occurs unexpectedly for the perpetrator. The accumulated affective tension turns into an explosion of anger and rage, and is usually accompanied, or preceded, by intense feelings of humiliation and despair. Observers testify that the person shows symptoms of extremely intense emotional arousal, displaying dramatic changes of facial expressions, gestures, postures, tone of voice, and so on. Anger and rage control all aspects of behavior.

As the emotional process dramatically and drastically develops from the first stage to the second, it is accompanied by the massive cognitive distortions previously described. The person's consciousness typically becomes concentrated entirely on the target, and the threshold of perception changes so that the individual can see and hear only what is related to anger. He loses the ability to consciously control his own behavior, as well as the ability to predict possible consequences of his behavior.

The perpetrator often shows extreme forms of behavior never shown before, which do not reflect his stable personality characteristics. The aggressive behavior often contradicts the perpetrator's moral and ethical beliefs about what is right and wrong, and the behavior is impulsive in the sense that nothing besides the feelings of anger or rage underlie it. In many cases, the aggression is directed toward a person seen as a threat or a source of damage to the perpetrator's self-confidence. The aggression becomes compulsive, automatic, and totally out of conscious control. The perpetrator may stab the victim numerous times, and may continue to do so even when the victim is obviously dead. Sometimes multiple victims are involved in this type of aggression. Although rare, bystanders or people indirectly involved in the conflict may become victims of the person possessed with this level of anger. The perpetrator may use any available murder weapon: his own hands, knives, guns, heavy objects, and so on. It is clear that homicides committed under that kind of circumstance are not premeditated. Aggression at this stage of affect is mainly physical. For most perpetrators, however, aggression is alien to their typical behavior. The unjustifiable aggressive and often cruel behavior of such perpetrators does not make sense for the witnesses or, sometimes, even experienced law enforcement officers.

The third stage is characterized by exhaustion, fatigue, apathy, and depression. However, the overall level of awareness and conscious control over behavior progressively increase, and the emotional tension, anger, rage, and excitement decrease. In many cases, the perpetrator may experience intense repentance, may try to help the victim, may call the police and ambulance, and may cry and show feelings of guilt and depression. The feelings experienced by the perpetrator in this final stage of physiological affect may be categorized into two groups. In the first, anger is followed by reduced tension, decreased frustration, and satisfaction. The person feels better and may believe that his mission now is completed, even though some perpetrators admit that other ways of handling their problems could have been chosen. This type of behavior after the criminal act can be called *self-justifying behavior*. In the second group, the climax of anger and aggression is followed by intense shame, guilt, and remorse. These perpetrators might call the police and an ambulance, report themselves, and quite often (65%–75%) have suicidal ideation and intentions (Guldan, 1989). In individuals who do not have anger and aggressiveness as personality traits, anger-out reactions displayed during the third stage can be immediately redirected inward. In that case, anger-in feelings could be a cause of self-destructive, suicidal behavior, and police are on alert for suicidal gestures in such persons.

The difference between physiological affect and pathological affect is in the magnitude of cognitive distortion and/or disorders of consciousness. In the case of pathological affect, the intensity of emotional arousal reaches a psychotic degree and is generally associated with amnesia for the crime. The individual may be totally unable to remember the sequence of events of the crime, and sometimes may show true blackouts, wherein periods of time and particular events become totally forgotten. The exhaustion that follows is very intense. The perpetrator may even fall asleep next to the dying victim; when he wakes up, he may not remember anything related to the criminal offense committed in the state of pathological anger (Mayer-Gross, Slater, & Roth, 1974). The next case illustrates pathological anger.

> Julia was the 45-year-old wife of an alcoholic and abusive husband who constantly humiliated and physically abused her and her children from a previous marriage. One day, Julia's husband came home drunk and angry, and an argument took place between him and Julia in their bedroom. In the midst of their heated interchange, he said that he is going to kill "a bastard," her 11-year-old son, unless he stops smoking. Julia became enraged, took a knife and stabbed him more than 20 times, and then fell asleep next to his body in their bed. When she awoke the next morning, she was totally unable to recall what happened the night before. She was scared and agitated, called police, and reported that she

found her husband dead in their bed. She believed someone else had entered the house at night and killed him.

Anger and pathological affect is an important, but certainly not the single motivational factor in aggressive criminal behavior. Some forms of aggressive criminal behavior have little or nothing to do with anger, such as some crimes of organized criminal groups. This is the reason that emotional factors are taken into account by the courts; it is their responsibility to decide whether those emotional factors should be seen as mitigating factors.

DISPLAY RULES FOR ANGER AND AGGRESSION IN CRIMINAL SUBCULTURES

Display rules are defined as those social or cultural scripts that govern behavior in a particular environment. As delineated by Tanaka-Matsumi (see chap. 5, this volume), these rules change from one environment to the next. In the United States, when two people meet for the first time, they typically shake hands. This can be considered a display rule for initial interpersonal contact. In some Latin cultures (e.g., Spanish, Italian), upon meeting for the first time people will likely exchange two kisses. This is the initial interpersonal contact display rule for these cultures.

In the United States, there are different display rules for anger and aggression, depending on the environment. Different modes of expression are permitted on the football field, in bed with a lover, during a karate class, and in a university classroom. Although there are some exceptions, society generally does not condone unwanted physical aggression, but may endorse anger. There are, however, subgroups wherein displays of anger are rejected, and aggression is not only endorsed but rewarded. In the world of gangs, focused anger and aggression are both permitted and required. This is a world where unfocused anger is not to be displayed (because it shows a loss of control); aggression is the preferred pattern of behavior. Violence is a means of achieving a goal. Non-goal-directed, unfocused anger (such as yelling, screaming, demonstrations of frustration, etc.) is not respected, and is seen as a sign of weakness. The individual who executes an aggressive act may have no animosity toward the victim, but behaves aggressively to achieve the goal. This is instrumental aggression, and it is without anger.

Thus, anger and aggression are not always related. However, in organized crime, if an order is given to kill someone and the shooter has never performed this behavior, anger may be used to energize the shooter. Those in law enforcement repeatedly hear the statements, "The first murder is never easy," and "I remember getting really angry the first time, but now it's just like killing a bug." Anger-energizing statements are used to instigate new violent acts, and perpetrators describe a process of "psyching up" for the job. Self-generated anger is an energizer. A first-time shooter, in organized crime, uses anger statements to increase physical arousal, get adrenaline flowing, decrease inhibition, and propel the aggressive behavior that follows. This process involves using anger-energizing statements and images, which may be completely false, to create the perception of personally and voluntary directed threat, harm, or perceived injustice. Just as football players may think of "killing" the opponents, criminals imagine that the target has "raped my wife, killed my mother, molested my sister, assaulted my grandmother, or threatened my son/daughter." These cognitions lead to observable physical arousal, such as increased muscle tension, increased heart rate, sweating, and rapid shallow breathing. It is this extreme level of angry arousal that appears to propel the individual to carry out the new aggressive behaviors.

For the well-experienced shooter, the experience is different. When the behavior is well established, the shooter reports the ability to kill between bites of a sandwich, as is often displayed in Hollywood movies, without displaying signs of arousal or discomfort. Killing can become routine. When killing occurs without anger, efficiency increases, which, in turn, decreases the probability of being caught.

Is aggression preceded by anger? Sometimes. The answer is often yes if the performance of the aggressive behavior is new. Criminals use anger in the service of aggression. This model of anger as an energizer or disinhibitor for new violent aggression allows anger to be a point of intervention for practitioners who work with new and/or young felons, people on probation, and so on. If we can assist in the management of anger experiences, we may prevent or diminish the number of people developing new aggressive behavior patterns. Men who batter their wives may never hit their wives if they can learn to manage their anger. Likewise, parents who learn anger control may not abuse their children. However, once a pattern of physical violence is set, anger may no longer be a point of intervention because it may not be present in the cycle; as with the violent criminal, the only point of intervention will be the consequence for aggression and violence after they have been exhibited.

ISSUES

Forensic experts are often questioned about the reliability of the assessment of an emotional state at the time of the offense. The evaluation of whether the person was in a state of pathological angry affect at the time of offense is one of the most critical issues, both in theory and in the practice of court-ordered evaluations. This issue is complex, and joint efforts of forensic social science experts and lawyers have to be made to develop a conceptual bridge between the legal concept of *temporary insanity* and psychological conceptions such as being in states of pathological angry affect, which in turn lead to dissociative reactions. In that regard, we support Eckhardt and Deffenbacher's (chap. 2, this volume) suggestion to establish *anger disorder* as an independent diagnostic category. Perhaps an additional subcategory would be *pathological angry affect with dissociation and aggressive criminal behavior.*

The greatest difficulty in assessing emotional states at the time of offense is related to the necessity of conducting a retrospective study of the behavior, emotions, and cognitive functioning of the perpetrator. Although there is no simple answer to this problem, Goldstein (1992) and Melton, Patrila, Poythress, and Slobogin (1987) noted that the reliability of information obtained from the perpetrator, the victim (if he or she is alive), and eyewitnesses is basically as high (or as low) as reliability of information obtained by the administration of standardized psychological tests.

The forensic psychological evaluation of emotional states (pathological angry affect) at the time of the offense includes an analysis of the following (Tsytsarev, 1987): (a) situational factors facilitating affective reactions; (b) personality traits such as attitudes, values, beliefs, motives, self-esteem, and cognitive ability/intelligence; (c) prior behaviors in extreme conditions; (d) psychophysiological states of the perpetrator immediately before the offense; (e) mental states of the perpetrator during and after the offense; and (f) how the behavior of the offender was seen by himself immediately after the offense, some days after it, and at the time of the interview. Interviews, self-reports, and psychological tests can assess some of these quite reliably. Others, at least for now, remain as judgments to be made by knowledgeable and experienced professionals.

CONCLUSION

Criminal behavior often involves both anger and aggression. For this reason, an understanding of the nature and causes of anger, and its relationship to aggression, will help in our goal of reducing criminality. Of importance, it would be wise to recognize that, within the criminal world, the anger that is dealt with is often very strong, and at a level labeled as *pathological affect*. It differs in intensity and quality from that found in other populations. It can be associated with abnormally strong cravings that motivate the person to act in antisocial ways. Crimes of passion, based on strong angry affect and unusual cravings, often lead to complex aggressive and antisocial behaviors, such as rape and serial murder. Therefore, we believe it is important for mental health workers who work with criminal populations to have diagnostic categories that reflect such crimes. The recognition that anger can be very intense, and can lead to antisocial behavior of which we may be unaware, is the first step toward resolution of the problem. This will be helped with the development of a reliable diagnostic classification system.

Chapter 7

Evaluation of Treatment Strategies for Adult Anger Disorders

Raymond Chip Tafrate

Institute for Rational-Emotive Therapy, New York

and

Hofstra University, Hempstead, New York

Given the potential seriousness of anger-related problems, it is surprising that anger has received such little attention in the psychological literature. In comparison with other emotions, such as anxiety and depression, little is known about the incidence and frequency of anger problems. Practitioners are just beginning to develop schema and methods to assess and diagnose clients who present with anger-related difficulties (see Eckhardt & Deffenbacher, chap. 2, this volume).

Information on anger treatment is also limited because advances in treatment typically follow a clear conceptualization of a particular problem. This has not happened with anger-related disorders. Nonetheless, those in the therapeutic trenches must routinely assist clients with their anger, and clinicians who turn to the scientific literature for assistance find little research from which to guide treatment.

The purpose of this chapter is to provide a comprehensive quantitative review of the psychotherapy outcome literature on anger. This chapter provides much needed clarity about which programs work, which do not, and which strategies have not yet been examined by researchers. The chapter begins with a description of the methods used in creating the quantitative review or meta-analysis. A vignette of a client with an anger problem is then presented, along with several questions that may arise for clinicians treating such a case. The rest of the chapter is organized around different therapeutic approaches that may be useful when working with anger-disordered clients. Each treatment approach is reviewed in two ways. First, the application of the treatment to help the client with his anger problem is briefly discussed; then, where available, an examination of the controlled outcome research for that approach is reviewed. Finally, the limitations of the present state of anger research are discussed, as well as implications for clinical practice. The following treatments are reviewed:

1   Cognitive therapies: self-instructional training, Beck's cognitive therapy, rational-emotive behavior therapy;
2   Relaxation-based therapies: relaxation, systematic desensitization, anger-management training;
3   Skills training therapies: social skills training, assertiveness training, problem-solving therapy;
4   Exposure-based treatments;
5   Cathartic treatments; and
6   Multicomponent treatments.

META-ANALYSIS

The technique of meta-analysis (Hedges & Olkin, 1985) was used to evaluate each strategy's effectiveness for the treatment of anger. For those who are unfamiliar with this technique, the following brief review clarifies what was done. Results from each study were converted into a common and comparable unit, known as the effect size. An *effect size* is simply an estimate of how effective a particular treatment is for subjects who received the treatment, in comparison with subjects who were not treated. The advantage of meta-analysis is that results from different psychotherapy outcome studies can be combined to yield an overall estimate of a treatment's effectiveness. Obviously, conclusions based on the integration of results from a series of studies are likely to be stronger than those from individual studies (Hedges & Olkin, 1986).

However, there are some problems associated with meta-analysis. The most noteworthy and relevant for this chapter is the "file drawer problem" (Rosenthal, 1979). Studies that show statistically significant results are more likely to be submitted for publication by researchers, and are more likely to be accepted by editorial review boards. Those that show nonsignificant results tend to get allocated to the file drawer. Therefore, the possibility exists that any group of published studies in a chapter such as this one may overestimate the effects of a given treatment. An in-depth discussion of the advantages and disadvantages of meta-analysis can be found in Rosenthal (1984).

METHOD

A computer search of psychological abstracts was performed for the period 1974–1994. Anger was cross-referenced with key words and synonyms for each treatment examined in this chapter. In addition, the references of articles located by computer were manually searched. The criteria for including articles in this chapter were: (a) anger was the focus of treatment and was mentioned in the title of the article, (b) the study tested the effectiveness of some treatment for anger against a control condition, (c) subjects had to receive at least two treatment sessions, and (d) subjects had to be adults. Unpublished doctoral dissertations were not included. Given the lack of attention that has been paid to anger, it is perhaps not surprising that only 17 studies (see appendix, this volume) met the four criteria. Effect size calculations were performed with D-STAT (Johnson, 1989). Where given, the difference between the means of the experimental and control group was divided by the combined standard deviation of the two conditions (Hedges & Olkin, 1985). Where no means and standard deviations were given, effect sizes were estimated from t and F statistics, or r values.

As discussed in earlier chapters of this volume, researchers have not yet agreed on a definition of *anger*. This lack of definitional clarity continues to be a significant factor thwarting anger research (Averill, 1982; Chesney, 1985; Tavris, 1989); any review that confuses anger, hostility, and aggression, or is otherwise unclear, would only further muddle the anger arena. For this reason, the characteristics of the definition of *anger* proposed by Kassinove and Sukhodolsky (chap. 1, this volume) and Eckhardt and Deffenbacher (chap. 2, this volume) were adopted. Thus, *anger* is defined as the totality of a transient, internal negative experience with associated physiological reactions (activation of the sympathetic nervous system, release of adrenal hormones, increased muscle tension), cognitive processes (inflammatory labeling, demandingness, low frustration tolerance, various cognitive distortions, attributions of injustice, intentionality, blameworthiness), and subjective labeling (identifying and labeling the reactions on a continuum ranging from annoyance and irritation to fury and rage).

Effect sizes were only calculated for outcome measures that adhered to this definition of anger. The following classes of dependent variables were accepted: (a) self-report measures such as standardized anger assessment instruments, reported anger ratings following in vivo or imaginal laboratory experiences, and subjective ratings of the intensity and frequency of anger in real-life situations; (b) physiological measures such as heart rate, blood pressure, and skin conductance; and (c) articulated thoughts rated by objective observers. Because anger has frequently been confused with aggression, and because there is little agreement about which behaviors are clear markers of anger, measures of aggression and related behaviors were excluded, as were other constructs such as *self-esteem, assertiveness*, and *anxiety*.

Most studies contained multiple outcome measures and compared several treatment approaches against a control condition. To avoid weighing studies according to their number of dependent measures, the following procedure was followed. Individual effect sizes were calculated for each acceptable dependent measure in each treatment group. Effect sizes were then averaged across outcome measures to yield one effect size estimate for each treatment approach within each study. This means that studies that compared one treatment against a control condition ultimately yielded one effect size. Studies that compared three treatments against a control condition produced three effect sizes, one for each approach. Effect sizes for similar treatment approaches were then averaged across studies to get an overall estimate of each treatment's effectiveness. In following this procedure, the 17 studies included in this chapter produced 30 effect sizes.

Cohen (1977) offered some rough guidelines to evaluate the meaningfulness of an effect size. For psychotherapy outcome studies, an effect size of .2 is considered small, an effect size of .5 is considered medium, and an effect size of .8 is considered large. Although these are statistical guidelines, it is important to keep in mind that even small reductions on anger measures may be meaningful to clients, as well as to the people around them.

> Ken is 29 years old. He has been married for 3 years, and recently had a son. He reports that he has had a bad temper ever since he can remember. Although his wife has been urging him to get help since they have been together, it was the birth of his son that motivated him to seek treatment. Ken states, "I want to get my life together and I don't want to be angry around my kid."
>
> Ken's problems with anger are most prominent at work. He has lost three jobs in the past 5 years due to his angry outbursts. Ken has been at his current job for 3 months, and reports difficulties dealing with his supervisor. He complains about unfair treatment, and claims that his work is singled out as being below par far more frequently than that of his co-workers. He attributes this to the fact that he doesn't play politics: "I don't hold back, when I'm upset about something I let people know it." Ken also has anger problems at home. He reports frequent feelings of anger toward his wife, and describes their relationship as being stormy right from the beginning. According to Ken, he has never hit his wife, but admits to pushing her during several arguments. He also has problems with his anger while driving. He finds himself yelling at other drivers at least once a week, and he occasionally gets out of his car to confront people. This has resulted in a fistfight on at least one occasion.
>
> Ken says that when he gets angry he can feel the tension building up in his body. He feels it primarily in his neck and arms, and his face feels hot. Sometimes he notices that his heart races and his hands tremble. When asked about his thoughts, Ken states, "Sometimes I get so angry that my thoughts race and I can't think straight." In addition, Ken reports that he frequently ruminates about the targets of his anger, "I just can't get it out of my head." Ken also indicates that he gets most upset in situations where he thinks he has been deliberately treated unfairly. Behaviorally, Ken has responded to the difficulties at work by being argumentative with his supervisors, and sometimes insulting and yelling at co-workers. At home, he says that he occasionally throws things, and that he has put his fist through the wall on several occasions.
>
> Besides some sadness about his difficulties at work, Ken does not present with symptoms of depression. In addition, although he is definitely concerned about his anger and with keeping his job, these feelings and thoughts are neither intense nor intrusive. Thus, he does not meet the diagnostic criteria for an anxiety disorder.

ANGER TREATMENTS

In addition to raising important issues about diagnosis, the case of Ken also raises a number of questions about treatment. How can he be helped with his anger problem? What strategy is best used? What would be the target of the intervention: ruminative thoughts, cognitive distortions, specific behaviors, physical arousal, and so on? Which treatments are likely to be effective? Which are not?

Although very much in its infancy, the current scientific literature on anger does hold some preliminary answers, and this literature is reviewed herein. Each treatment strategy is briefly discussed, using the case of Ken as a model of a client with an anger disorder. The current empirical status of each approach is then examined. Because a variety of treatments are reviewed, it is impossible to provide an in-depth discussion of each approach, given space limitations. The brief descriptions provided for each of the treatments are intended only as a guide for those clinicians who are unfamiliar with them. References are given for more detailed information.

Prior to implementing a particular strategy, it is important to establish a quality therapeutic relationship, and for agreement to be reached between the client and therapist as to the goals and tasks of therapy. A more comprehensive discussion on the method of establishing a working therapeutic relationship with angry clients and the problems associated with this relationship can be found in DiGiuseppe, Tafrate, and Eckhardt (1994) and DiGiuseppe (chap. 8, this volume).

COGNITIVE THERAPIES

Cognitive therapies are based on the hypothesis that a person's thoughts, interpretations, and self-statements about external events exert a strong influence on emotional and behavioral functioning. The goal in cognitive treatments is to help clients identify and challenge their irrational and distorted thinking patterns, and to assist them in constructing more adaptive belief systems (Beck, 1976; Ellis, 1973). At present, there are three dominant models of cognitive therapy: self-instructional training (Meichenbaum & Goodman, 1971), Beck's cognitive therapy (Beck, 1963), and rational-emotive behavior therapy (Ellis, 1962).

Self-Instructional Training

The premise of self-instructional training (SIT) is that people's verbal self-statements or instructions influence their behavior. New self-instructions can be developed; these can interrupt old thinking and behavior patterns, and also direct new responses to problematic situations (Rehm & Rokke, 1988). For the reader who is unfamiliar with SIT, a brief description follows.

In applying SIT to Ken, the therapist would first identify situations where Ken becomes angry. For example, one problem for Ken emerges when interacting with his supervisor at work. The specific self-talk that Ken engages in when he is angry, and the relationship between Ken's self-talk and his anger, would be discussed and evaluated. Ken might reveal that, prior to getting angry at his boss, he says to himself, "It's unfair, and I don't have to take this crap from him! I'll tell him a thing or two! He needs to be put in his place!" Once identified, this statement would be replaced with a self-instruction likely to reduce anger and help Ken stay in control. New self-instructions preferably would be developed in a collaborative fashion with Ken. In this example, a new self-instruction might be, "I can handle criticism from my boss, blowing up only makes the situation worse. It's better to let it go, than to tell him off. Be calm." Ken would practice rehearsing this new statement out loud and silently, both in and out of the sessions.

This procedure of identifying and changing anger-related self-statements, and practicing the new self-instructions, would be used for the other anger-provoking situations that Ken reported. Self-instructional strategies have been used for a number of clinical problems, to treat both children and adults. Additional information can be found in Meichenbaum and Cameron (1973) and Rehm and Rokke (1988).

Cognitive Therapy

During the 1950s, psychiatrist Aaron Beck began to examine the content of thoughts in psychiatric patients. Beck (1976) proposed that, during upsetting events, individuals react with a stream of unplanned, automatic thoughts or cognitions. Some of these thoughts are appropriate to the situations at hand, whereas others are likely to be distorted and illogical. According to Beck (1971), emotional disorders stem from such cognitive distortions and unrealistic appraisals of events.

In applying this form of cognitive therapy to Ken, the therapist would begin by having Ken monitor his automatic thoughts that occur when dealing with his supervisor. Some of Ken's automatic thoughts in this situation might be, "He's out to get me. He is my enemy. He is always picking on me and never picks on anyone else." The therapist would then help Ken examine and test the accuracy of these thoughts. For example, after careful observation, we might find out that the supervisor is also critical of several other employees. As for the supervisor "always" being critical, it might be discovered that, in reality, Ken is criticized only about once a week, and that this frequency is not dissimilar to the negative feedback given to other employees.

The next step would be to help Ken replace these thoughts with more realistic appraisals of the situation, such as, "It's not just me, he is critical of others as well. He generally leaves me alone and only occasionally is critical of my work" and "He is neither my friend nor my enemy. As a supervisor his job is to review and evaluate my performance." In this form of therapy, Ken would be taught to evaluate his own thinking and to identify and replace cognitive distortions in a variety of situations. A broader discussion of those cognitive distortions thought to lead to emotional disturbance and a full description of cognitive therapy can be found in Beck (1976) and Burns (1989).

Rational-Emotive Behavior Therapy

Rational-emotive behavior therapy (REBT) was developed by Albert Ellis in the 1950s. According to Ellis' (1962) A-B-C model, emotional disturbance (Point C) is the result of illogical and irrational thinking (Point B) about external events (Point A), and not the events themselves.

In applying REBT to Ken, the therapist would help Ken identify the irrational beliefs and ideas that are hypothesized to lead to and maintain his anger. Beliefs are characterized as irrational if they are demanding and rigid, inaccurate, and unhelpful in assisting people to achieve their goals (Walen, DiGiuseppe, & Wessler, 1980). Some of Ken's irrational beliefs about being criticized by his boss might be: "He should not tell me how to do my job," "It's awful to be treated so unfairly," and "I can't stand this."

In REBT, the therapist would not challenge Ken's perception that he is being treated unfairly. Instead, Ken's conclusions about the unfair treatment would be scrutinized and debated through a process called *disputation*. The therapist might ask Ken, "Must you always receive fair treatment? Do you have the power to make him act fairly? Let's assume that you are being treated in an unfair manner; why is that awful and horrible?" A detailed discussion on disputation can be found in Walen, DiGiuseppe, and Dryden (1992).

Once these beliefs have been challenged and disputed, Ken would be assisted in developing alternative beliefs that are hypothesized to lead to healthier emotional functioning and more adaptive behavior. Such rational beliefs might include: "It would be nice if my boss treated me fairly, but he doesn't have to," "Although I want to be treated fairly, I can't control the way others act," and "I can stand being criticized and treated unfairly, it's not awful only uncomfortable." The desired result with Ken would be a philosophical shift in his thinking—to a mode that would be less demanding and more accepting of his situation. Since Ellis developed this model in the 1950s, a large literature base on it has developed. For the reader who wishes to learn more, an in-depth discussion of REBT and rational-emotive theory is presented in Ellis and Harper (1975) and in Walen et al. (1992).

Empirical Status

Studies that have examined cognitive treatments for anger are presented in Table 7.1. Overall, this class of treatments produced an average effect size of .93, which is considered a rather large treatment effect. The cognitive strategy with

Table 7.1 Effectiveness of the Cognitive Therapies

Category and study	Subjects per comparison	Number and type of sessions	Effect size
Self-instructional training			
Deffenbacher, Story, Brandon Hogg, & Hazaleus (1988)	30 male and female undergraduates	8 group sessions	1.00
Hazaleus & Deffenbacher (1986)	39 male and female undergraduates	6 group sessions	.70
Moon & Eisler (1983)	20 male and female undergraduates	5 group sessions	1.46
Novaco (1975)	17 students and community members (male & female)	5 individual sessions	.84
Beck's cognitive therapy			
Whiteman, Fanshel, & Grundy (1987)	21 child-abusing parents	6 individual sessions	.64
Rational-emotive behavior therapy			
No studies	Effectiveness currently unknown		

Note. Average effect sizes according to category: self-instructional training, 1.00; Beck's cognitive therapy, .64; rational-emotive behavior therapy, unknown. Overall average effect size for cognitive therapies, .93.

the greatest empirical support is SIT. Based on the results of four controlled studies, SIT appears to be an effective treatment for anger, with an average effect size of 1.00. The one study that used Beck's cognitive therapy achieved an effect size of .64.

Regrettably, there are currently no controlled outcome studies that directly examined the effectiveness of REBT for clients with anger problems. However, two studies that did not meet the inclusion criteria (Conoley, Conoley, McConnel, & Kimzey, 1983; Woods, 1987) suggest that REBT may be a promising treatment for anger. In addition, several books for both professionals (Dryden, 1990) and the public (Ellis, 1977) address the application of REBT to anger disorders. However, until controlled outcome studies are undertaken, it is difficult to draw a conclusion about the effectiveness of REBT for the treatment of anger.

RELAXATION-BASED THERAPIES

Many clinicians and researchers have noticed that the experience and expression of anger are often accompanied by high levels of physiological arousal (Ax, 1953; Berkowitz, 1990; Novaco, 1975), and therefore the definition of *anger* includes physiological markers that can be used as dependent variables in research studies. Hence, it is not surprising that relaxation has been applied to the treatment of anger problems. Historically, of course, relaxation and desensitization procedures have been primarily used for anxiety disorders. When relaxation treatment is given in isolation, the focus is on teaching clients to reduce physiological arousal levels, as noted by muscle tension, breathing rates, and so on.

When relaxation is used in a desensitization program, the goal is to countercondition or extinguish the "power" of or reactivity to anger-provoking stimuli by pairing those stimuli with relaxation.

Relaxation

Many techniques are available to help clients reduce physiological arousal. These include: progressive muscle relaxation, guided imagery, autogenic training, biofeedback, and various forms of meditation. Perhaps the most widely used procedure is a modified (shortened) version of Jacobson's (1938) original method of systematically tensing and relaxing a series of muscle groups. Although his original procedure was very elaborate, in modern versions relaxation can be produced within 15–30 minutes, either by a therapist or by having the client listen to an audiotape. Relaxation can also be practiced at home to further strengthen its effects. A full description of relaxation procedures can be found in Masters, Burish, Hollon, and Rimm (1987).

In helping Ken, the therapist would teach him one or more relaxation techniques. Ken would then practice the technique both in and out of session until he is proficient. Proficiency is shown by self-report and by therapist observation of breathing rates, spontaneous sighs, and so on. The desired result would be a voluntary, increased ability to dampen sympathetic nervous system arousal in anger-provoking situations. This would hopefully translate into more self-control. Relaxation skills are commonly used in conjunction with other procedures, and Ken would likely be given a variety of homework assignments to strengthen his skills. A detailed discussion of what has become known as *the relaxation response* has been provided by Benson (1975).

Systematic Desensitization

Systematic desensitization is a well-known treatment developed by South African-trained psychiatrist Wolpe (1958). The history, theory, and application of this intervention have been presented in detail in a number of places (e.g., Masters et al., 1987; Wolpe, 1982). We review the basic points for the reader who is unfamiliar with this approach.

In using systematic desensitization, the therapist would have Ken describe in detail those situations where he typically experiences anger. A realistic scene would then be developed from each anger-arousing situation. The scenes would then be organized into a hierarchy, from least anger provoking to most anger provoking. Those events that would be low on Ken's hierarchy might include waiting on line at the bank or not being understood by his wife. Situations associated with moderate levels of anger might be having his wife disagree with him or being stuck in a traffic jam. At the top of Ken's hierarchy might be being cut off by another driver or having his work criticized by his supervisor in front of other employees.

While the hierarchy was being developed, Ken would be taught a relaxation technique such as progressive muscle relaxation. Once Ken could easily put himself in a state of relaxation, he would be asked to vividly imagine the lowest anger-provoking scene on the hierarchy. Ken would imagine the scene until he experienced an anger response similar to what might occur in real life. Once this occurred, he would be instructed to shift back to relaxation. The anger-provoking scene would be repeatedly presented and paired with relaxation until Ken reported that it no longer produced anger. Over the course of therapy, Ken would be guided in a similar fashion through each item on the hierarchy until anger was no longer elicited.

Anger-Management Training

Another form of therapy that emphasizes relaxation skills is anxiety-management training, or anger-management training (AMT; Richardson & Suinn, 1973). This strategy has been used in a number of research studies specifically targeting anger.

In applying AMT to Ken, the therapist would help Ken develop several anger scenes based on real events. The first scene would be associated with a moderate level of anger, and the second with a high level of anger. For Ken, the first scene might be about a disagreement with his wife, and the second scene about being criticized by his supervisor. In addition to the creation of the anger scenes, Ken would be trained in relaxation skills. Once he is proficient in relaxation, the first anger scene would be presented in imagery. The purpose of the anger scene is to help Ken practice relaxation skills in a relevant context. He would repeatedly practice using relaxation in response to the moderate level scene, both in session and at home. Once he successfully uses relaxation during the moderate scene, the higher level scene would then be practiced. A detailed discussion of AMT application to both anxiety and anger problems can be found in Suinn (1990).

Empirical Status

Studies that have examined relaxation-based treatments for anger are presented in Table 7.2. Overall, the effectiveness of this class of treatments is quite high, with an average effect size of 1.16. Of the nine studies that incorporated some form of relaxation in the treatment, two examined the effectiveness of progressive muscle relaxation, four used systematic desensitization, and three tested the effects of AMT.   Relaxation by itself appeared to be the least effective treatment with an average effect size of .48. Anger-management training yielded a larger treatment effect, with an average effect size of 1.01. Systematic desensitization appeared to be quite effective, producing an effect size of 1.63. It should be noted that several studies that examined systematic desensitization produced unusually

Table 7.2 Effectiveness of Relaxation-Based Therapies

Category and study	Subjects per comparison	Number and type of sessions	Effect size
Relaxation			
Davison, Williams, Nezami, Bice, & DeQuattro (1991)	58 borderline hypertensive males	7 group sessions	.49
Whiteman, Fanshel, & Grundy, (1987)	25 child-abusing parents	6 individual sessions	.46
Systematic desensitization			
Evans, Hearn, & Saklofske (1973)	20 female nursing students	15 individual sessions	2.02
Hearn & Evans (1972)	34 female nursing students	15 individual sessions	3.47
Novaco (1975)	16 students and community members (male & female)	5 individual sessions	.36
Rimm, DeGroot, Boord, Hieman, & Dillow (1971)	30 undergraduate males	3 individual sessions	.65
Anger-management training			
Deffenbacher, Demm, & Brandon (1986)	29 male and female undergraduates	6 group sessions	1.12
Deffenbacher & Stark (1992)	39 male and female undergraduates	8 group sessions	1.34
Hazaleus & Deffenbacher (1986)	40 male and female undergraduates	6 group sessions	.57

Note. Average effect sizes according to category: Relaxation, .48; systematic desensitization, 1.63; anger-management training, 1.01. Overall average effect size for relaxation-based therapies, 1.16.

large effect sizes. These studies were conducted by the same authors and used similar outcome measures and subject samples.

Regrettably, research on the effectiveness of systematic desensitization for anger problems seemed to end in the 1970s. This is unfortunate because more studies are needed to replicate what appears to be a strong treatment effect. This is similar to the reduction of studies on systematic desensitization for anxiety disorders. Psychotherapy clearly has moved to a focus on cognitively oriented treatments, or to cognitive–behavioral procedures. Systematic desensitization, although highly effective, is quite boring for the therapist, and this may partially explain the loss of focus on this important treatment.

SKILLS TRAINING THERAPIES

The underlying premise of skills training approaches is that many psychological problems, including anger disorders, stem from interpersonal skill deficits. These deficits may inhibit people from dealing effectively with difficult situations and prevent them from achieving their personal goals. This, in turn, may contribute to emotional upset. According to D'Zurilla and Goldfried (1971), "ineffectiveness in dealing with problematic situations, along with its personal and social consequences, is often a necessary and significant condition for an emotional or behavioral disorder requiring psychological treatment . . ." (p. 109). The goal of treatment is to help clients learn new behavioral responses that are likely to increase their chances of achieving the desired outcomes. A number of skills training approaches have been developed. The most noteworthy include: assertiveness training, social skills training, and problem solving.

Assertiveness Training and Social Skills Training

Assertion training involves teaching clients to appropriately express their feelings. Social skills training involves teaching socially accepted and proper motor and verbal skills for interpersonal situations. These approaches are similar because assertion training can be viewed as one subset of the larger domain of social skills. Although there are many variations in the skills training therapies, both assertion and social skills training involve the application of the same procedures, including modeling, coaching, rehearsal, and feedback, to achieve their end goals.

In applying this approach to Ken, anger-related behaviors could be identified through a variety of procedures, such as self-monitoring, interview, or behavioral role-plays. The therapist would note those social responses that are not likely to be effective for Ken. For example, when Ken is criticized by his supervisor, Ken usually raises his voice and immediately begins to argue with his boss. If Ken agrees to work on a new approach, the therapist would develop and then model improved responses to the supervisor's criticism. The therapist might demonstrate how to first listen to the supervisor's complaint and then respond to it in a calm tone of voice. This new response would hopefully increase Ken's chances of keeping his job and, perhaps, result in less supervision.

Next, Ken would rehearse the new response. This could be done through behavioral role-plays, where the therapist would play the part of the difficult supervisor and Ken would repeatedly practice the new way of responding. Finally, Ken would be given specific feedback about his performance. As with the other approaches discussed in this chapter, much has been written about these techniques. A detailed discussion of assertiveness and social skills training can be found in Masters et al. (1987).

Problem Solving

Another skills training approach that has been applied to anger is problem solving. Like social skills training, there are a number of problem-solving approaches (D'Zurilla & Goldfried, 1971; Spivack, Platt, & Shure, 1976). The five steps in the D'Zurilla and Goldfried model are now described as they might be used with Ken.

Problem solving would begin by having Ken collect data about situations where he typically becomes angry, and examining the consequences of his angry feelings and behaviors. Ken would likely report that raising his voice and arguing with his boss usually result in him being singled out more frequently and being threatened with suspension. Once Ken agrees that the consequences of his current actions are undesirable, he would then be asked to generate as many alternative responses as he can think of to deal with the critical supervisor, no matter how good or bad they might be. For example, Ken could walk away from his boss, hit him, listen to him, ignore him, continue to argue, try talking to him at a later time, not respond immediately, and so on. Working collaboratively with the therapist, Ken would assess the probable consequences of each alternative. The best one would then be selected and put into action. In sessions that follow, the effectiveness of the new response would be evaluated. This procedure could be repeated for other situations related to Ken's anger.

The problem-solving approach differs from social skills and assertiveness training, in that there is more emphasis on the client developing the new strategies, rather than having the therapist solve the problem. However, problem solving is a skills-based approach because it teaches the client how to identify, evaluate, and implement alternative responses to problematic situations. For a more detailed discussion on problem-solving therapies, see D'Zurilla (1988).

Empirical Status

Studies that have examined the effectiveness of skills training therapies are presented in Table 7.3. Overall, skills training approaches appear to be effective in helping clients manage their anger problems. The average effect size for this class of treatment was .82.

Four controlled outcome studies for assertiveness and social skills training and three outcome studies for problem solving were identified. Both strategies yielded large treatment effects. However, social skills and assertiveness training produced slightly better results, with an average effect size of .86. Problem solving yielded an average effect size of .76.

EXPOSURE THERAPIES

Exposure treatments such as implosive therapy and flooding have been used extensively in the treatment of anxiety disorders. The central hypothesis is that if clients expose themselves to high levels of relevant anxiety-inducing stimuli, while being prevented from engaging in anxious (avoidance) responses, the anxiety-eliciting properties of the events will be extinguished (Masters et al., 1987).

There are several reasons why exposure-based treatments, both in vivo and imaginal, may hold promise for the treatment of anger. First, anxiety and anger are physiologically and functionally similar. Both are associated with high levels of autonomic nervous system arousal, such as increased heart rate, blood pressure, and respiration, and both seem to energize an individual for action against a potential threat. Treatment packages for anxiety, which include an exposure component, have been shown to be quite effective (Barlow, Craske, Cerny, & Klosko, 1989). Because there are similarities between the two emotions, exposure techniques may also be applicable to help clients with anger problems.

Another reason that exposure treatments may be effective for anger can be found in the earlier review of the relaxation-based treatments. There is a marked difference in effectiveness among the relaxation-based treatments in Table 7.2. Strategies that emphasize only relaxation appear to be less effective than strategies that also incorporate an imaginal exposure component, such as AMT or systematic desensitization. This suggests that the addition of exposure may, in general, result in more effective treatment.

With regard to our hypothetical client, Ken, there are two main ways to implement exposure techniques. The first would be through the use of in vivo procedures. Ken would identify situations and statements that are most likely to trigger his anger. For example, he might reveal that he gets angry when his boss says, "Ken if you don't pay more attention I'll have to have someone else do this project," or when his wife says, "You're really selfish and never help out around the house." These negative statements would be repeatedly presented to Ken in session by the therapist. Ken would be instructed not to respond, but "just to hear" the statements. The intensity level of the exposure would be altered by the therapist by changing the tone of his or her voice, moving closer to or farther away from Ken, and using threatening posture and hand gestures. Ken would practice

Table 7.3 Effectiveness of the Skills Training Therapies

Category and study	Subjects per comparison	Number and type of sessions	Effect size
Social skills and assertiveness training			
Deffenbacher, Story, Stark, Hogg, & Brandon (1987)	35 male and female undergraduates	8 group sessions	.83
Deffenbacher, Thwaites, Wallace, & Oetting (1994)	95 male and female undergraduates	8 group sessions	.61
Moon & Eisler (1983)	20 male undergraduates	5 group sessions	.98
Rimm, Hill, Brown, & Stuart (1974)	13 male undergraduates	6 group sessions	1.02
Problem-solving therapy			
Deffenbacher, Thwaites, Wallace, & Oetting (1994)	93 male and female undergraduates	8 group sessions	.77
Moon & Eisler (1983)	20 male undergraduates	5 group sessions	.73
Whiteman, Fanshel, & Grundy (1987)	24 child-abusing parents	6 individual sessions	.77

Note. Average effect sizes according to category: social skills and assertiveness training, .86; problem-solving therapy, .76. Overall average effect size for skills training therapies, .82.

hearing each statement at increasing intensity levels until he reports reduced feelings of anger and good control. In addition to desensitizing Ken to certain triggers, in vivo exposure could be used as a context to enhance the learning of new skills, such as relaxation, new self-instructions, or specific behavioral responses.

In vivo techniques such as this have recently been implemented in a treatment outcome study on anger reduction (Tafrate, 1995). In this study, the use of repeated exposures to aversive verbal stimuli for decreasing anger, as well as the effectiveness of different types of self-statements, were evaluated. Subjects were 45 adult males, recruited from the community, who were experiencing problems with anger control. Each man received 12 individual exposure sessions. Almost all of the clients who participated in this study reacted well to the exposure technique, as long as there was an established therapeutic alliance, sufficient motivation for change, and a clear rationale for the procedure. Data from the project look promising.

The second way to implement exposure procedures with Ken would be with the use of imagery. Anger scenes would be developed and repeatedly presented to Ken in session, and they would also be rehearsed at home. Each scene would be reviewed until it no longer elicited anger. This approach differs somewhat from systematic desensitization and AMT mentioned earlier, in that relaxation skills would not be practiced. More information on the application of exposure techniques to other disorders can be found in Stampfl and Levis (1967) and Shipley (1979).

Empirical Status

Although exposure-based treatments may hold promise for the treatment of anger problems, no controlled studies using exposure techniques for anger have appeared in the scientific literature.

CATHARTIC TREATMENTS

The underlying idea in catharsis is that negative energy or affect can build up over time and accumulate within an individual. This pent-up anger is thought to be a major source of problems for people, resulting in aggressive behaviors, as well as a variety of emotional and physical disorders (Bach & Goldberg, 1974; Janov, 1970). According to proponents of this approach, built-up anger must be drained off or released by some form of expression. Thus, the participation in harmless aggressive acts can hypothetically prevent anger and aggressive energy from building to dangerous levels (Lorenz, 1966).

In applying this model to Ken, the therapist would encourage Ken to routinely "get his anger out" or "to blow off steam." This would be done through a variety of techniques. For example, in trying to ventilate anger about his critical supervisor, Ken might be asked to beat his bed every night with a tennis racket while repeating loudly, "I hate you! You're such an asshole!" Other activities might include hitting a punching bag, watching violent movies, screaming, participating in sports, smashing objects, and even venting anger directly at his boss. The desired result of such activities would be to drain off and decrease the amount of pent-up anger that Ken experiences from work.

Empirical Status

The idea of catharsis has been around for a while, thus many psychological experiments have examined the effects of participation in cathartic activities. In a review of over a dozen studies conducted in the 1960s, Berkowitz (1970) concluded that both the observation and participation in aggressive behaviors leads to more, not less, anger and aggression. In the 1980s, Warren and Kurlychek (1981) reviewed approximately 15 studies, in which experimental subjects engaged in verbal, written, or physical aggressive behaviors. They also concluded that the rehearsal of verbal and physical aggression leads to increases, rather than decreases, in hostile attitudes and behaviors. In a review of eight recent studies that examined anger expression, Lewis and Bucher (1992) concluded that catharsis leads to an escalation of anger. In addition, they noted that cathartic activities influence the client to see him- or herself as a helpless victim, and thus distract both the client and therapist from developing more functional ways of dealing with conflict. They stated, "It appears that catharsis of anger has no appropriate place in psychotherapy and should be confined to its origin—the theatre!" (p. 391).

Although there is a (somewhat) voluminous literature on catharsis, it is surprising that no controlled outcome studies using cathartic procedures to reduce anger in clinical subjects have been conducted. However, the results of three decades of psychological experiments indicate that encouraging clients to blow off steam is not likely to be an effective strategy for reducing anger. It may even have the opposite effect. Nevertheless, it should be kept in mind that the effectiveness or ineffectiveness of cathartic procedures has not been put to the test in actual treatment outcome studies.

MULTICOMPONENT TREATMENTS

Multicomponent treatments are those strategies that combine several techniques, such as relaxation, self-instructional training, and behavioral rehearsal. The premise here is that the combination of several techniques will yield superior effects over any single approach. Combined approaches have dominated the treatment literature on anger ever since Novaco's (1975) pioneering study. He found that the combination of cognitive and relaxation interventions was superior to either treatment alone. Novaco's multicomponent treatment package for anger is called *stress inoculation*.

Stress Inoculation

The stress inoculation procedure involves three basic steps: cognitive preparation, skill acquisition and rehearsal, and application/practice (Novaco, 1977). In the first step, situations, self-statements, and signs of bodily tension that precede anger are identified. The situations where Ken has difficulties controlling his anger are with his supervisor at work, with his wife at home, and while driving. In these situations, Ken reports feeling tension in his neck and arms, and often is aware of his face getting hot. The self-talk that Ken usually engages in when he is angry at his supervisor for criticizing him is, "It's unfair and I don't have to take this crap from him!" With his wife, Ken sometimes says, "She should not disagree with me"; while driving, Ken says, "I would never be that inconsiderate. I'll show this creep!"

The second step involves teaching, modeling, and rehearsing of coping self-statements and relaxation procedures. The substitution of new self-statements would follow the same procedure described earlier for self-instructional training. In addition, Ken would be taught progressive muscle relaxation or another relaxation technique, and would practice until he was proficient.

In the final step, Ken would be exposed to anger-provoking situations either through imagery or role-plays. In doing this, Ken would practice rehearsing the new self-statements, as well as trying to keep his body relaxed. In addition to practicing these skills in session, Ken would also be encouraged to implement them in real life. For a detailed description of how to apply stress inoculation, the reader is referred directly to Novaco (1977).

Empirical Status

Multicomponent treatments appear to be effective in helping clients with anger problems. Nine studies that have examined multicomponent approaches are presented in Table 7.4. The average effect size of these studies was 1.00, and the majority demonstrated large treatment effects. However, it is too early to tell exactly which combination of techniques is likely to be most helpful. Although stress inoculation is probably the most widely used treatment for anger, other combinations of techniques may also be effective, although they have not yet been examined by researchers.

SUMMARY

The average effect size for all of the treatment conditions examined in the psychotherapy outcome literature is .99 (Table 7.5). This is actually quite high, and indicates that there are several effective therapeutic approaches currently available for clinicians working with adult clients suffering from anger disorders.

There are several broad classes of therapies that have some degree of empirical support. Cognitive therapies, relaxation-based treatments, skills training approaches, and multicomponent treatment packages have all demonstrated large treatment effects. However, exposure-based therapies and cathartic techniques have not yet been examined in controlled outcome research.

Among the cognitive therapies, self-instructional training has the greatest level of empirical support. In contrast, only one study examined the use of Beck's cognitive therapy, and no studies that met the inclusion criteria tested the effects of REBT. There were some differences in the effectiveness of relaxation-based approaches. Progressive muscle relaxation by itself appeared to be moderately effective, whereas AMT and systematic desensitization produced large effect sizes. Although systematic desensitization produced the largest effect size, it is too early to conclude that it is the most effective treatment for anger. Two of the studies that produced the greatest effects were conducted by the same authors, and used similar outcome measures and subject samples. Replication of these results is needed. Both of the skills training therapies produced large effect sizes. However, the more active-directive assertion and social skills model seemed to yield slightly better results than did the problem-solving approach. In the research literature, multicomponent treatments have received a good deal of attention, and have been shown to be quite effective for anger problems. Several researchers (Novaco, 1975; Whiteman et al., 1987) have concluded that certain combination approaches are more effective than single techniques. This conclusion was not supported in

Table 7.4 Effectiveness of Multicomponent Treatments

Study	Subjects per comparison	Number and type of sessions	Effect size
Deffenbacher, McNamara, Stark, & Sabadell (1990a)	32 male and female undergraduates	8 group sessions	.55
Deffenbacher, McNamara, Stark, & Sabadell (1990b)	29 male and female undergraduates	8 group sessions	.46
Deffenbacher & Stark (1992)	36 male and female undergraduates	8 group sessions	1.07
Deffenbacher, Story, Brandon, Hogg, & Hazaleus (1988)	30 male and female undergraduates	8 group sessions	1.07
Deffenbacher, Story, Stark, Hogg, & Brandon (1987)	32 male and female undergraduates	8 group sessions	1.06
Deffenbacher, Thwaites, Wallace, & Oetting (1994)	94 male and female undergraduates	8 group sessions	.76
Novaco (1975)	17 students and community members (male & female)	5 individual sessions	1.03
Stermac (1987)	40 male prison inmates	6 group sessions	1.82
Whiteman, Fanshel, & Grundy (1987)	24 child-abusing parents	6 individual sessions	1.14

Note. Average effect size for multicomponent treatments, 1.00.

Table 7.5   Average Effect Size for Each Therapy Type

Therapy type	Number of studies	Effect size
Cognitive therapies	5	.93
Self-instructional training	4	1.00
Beck's cognitive therapy	1	.64
Rational-emotive behavior therapy	0	unknown
Relaxation-based therapies	9	*1.16*
Relaxation	2	.48
Systematic desensitization	4	1.63
Anger-management training	3	1.01
Skills training therapies	7	*.82*
Social skills and assertiveness training	4	.86
Problem solving	3	.76
Multicomponent treatments	9	*1.00*
Exposure-based treatments	0	*unknown*
Cathartic treatments	0	*unknown**

Note. The average effect size for all anger treatments (.99) was calculated based on 30 effect sizes obtained from 17 studies. A separate effect size was calculated for each type of treatment examined within each study.
*Evidence from analog studies suggests caution because catharsis may increase anger and aggression.

this chapter. Self-instructional training, AMT, and systematic desensitization appear to be as effective as multicomponent interventions.

It is important to note that techniques based on catharsis may not be helpful for clients with anger disorders. Although no controlled outcome studies on catharsis were identified, several reviews of the experimental analog research have appeared (Berkowitz, 1970; Lewis & Butcher, 1992; Warren & Kurlychek, 1981). These reviewers unanimously concluded that participation in cathartic activities leads to increases, rather than decreases, in anger.

LIMITATIONS OF THE RESEARCH

Although the available research studies can help guide the treatment of anger, substantial limitations exist in the literature. The most obvious is the small number of treatment outcome studies on anger. Only 17 studies were identified in which anger was the target of treatment. As noted by Kassinove and Sukhodolsky (chap. 1, this volume), when compared with depression and anxiety, there is significantly less research on anger to guide clinical practice.

Another important issue is the nature of the subjects. In over 60% of the studies, the subjects were undergraduate students who volunteered for treatment (Tables 7.1–7.4). For example, the studies conducted by Deffenbacher and his colleagues used volunteer introductory psychology students who indicated a personal problem with anger and scored in the upper 25th percentile on the Trait Anger Scale (Spielberger, 1988). As discussed in earlier chapters, clients with anger problems may be coerced into therapy by courts, family members, or employee assistance programs. Undergraduate volunteers may represent a substantially different population than other adults, children, and adolescents with anger problems.

As indicated in Tables 7.1–7.4, most of the treatment studies used a group format as opposed to individual treatment sessions. In addition, treatment length was rather short. The average number of sessions was only 7.5. The possibility exists that protocols involving individual sessions and longer treatment lengths may lead to increased effectiveness.

Another limitation in the anger literature is that approximately half of the studies were conducted by the same researcher, Deffenbacher of Colorado State University, who contributed chapter 9 of this volume. These studies were well designed, used a variety of outcome measures, and have tested important treatment questions. Much of what is known about the treatment of anger comes from these studies. However, little replication exists from other researchers using similar or different methodologies. This leaves open the possibility that unknown factors are actually accounting for the treatment effects.

CONCLUSIONS

This chapter described several therapeutic approaches that may be effective for helping clients, such as Ken, better manage their anger. Based on a quantitative review of two decades of published anger research, several treatments emerge with some degree of empirical support. Strategies that target self-statements, physiological arousal, and behavioral skills all appear to be effective. In addition, although a combination of these strategies is also likely to be helpful, it does not appear that a combination is superior to any single intervention applied alone.

Treatments that have received little or no attention from researchers are Beck's cognitive therapy, Ellis' rational-emotive behavior therapy, and exposure-based approaches. Although no controlled outcome studies on cathartic treatments have appeared, reviews of experimental analog research indicate that this approach may not be helpful, and may actually be harmful. There are currently only a handful of treatment outcome studies on anger. However, the quality of research in this area appears to be improving, and the number of studies is increasing. It is hoped that this chapter helps set the stage for increased research and development of more effective anger treatments.

APPENDIX

Davison, G.C., Williams, M.E., Nezami, E., Bice, T.L., & DeQuattro, V.L. (1991). Relaxation, reduction in angry articulated thoughts, and improvement in borderline hypertension and heart rate. *Journal of Behavioral Medicine, 14*(5), 453–468.

Deffenbacher, J.L., Demm, P.M., & Brandon, A.D. (1986). High general anger: Correlates and treatment. *Behavior Research and Therapy, 24*, 481–489.

Deffenbacher, J.L., McNamara, K., Stark, R.S., & Sabadell, P.M. (1990a). A comparison of cognitive-behavioral and process-oriented group counseling for general anger reduction. *Journal of Counseling and Development, 69*, 167–172.

Deffenbacher, J.L., McNamara, K., Stark, R.S., & Sabadell, P.M. (1990b). A combination of cognitive, relaxation, and behavioral coping skills in the reduction of general anger. *Journal of College Student Development, 31,* 351–358.

Deffenbacher, J.L., & Stark, R.S. (1992). Relaxation and cognitive-relaxation treatments of general anger. *Journal of Counseling Psychology, 39*(2), 158–167.

Deffenbacher, J.L., Story, D.A., Brandon, A.D., Hogg, J.A., & Hazaleus, S.L. (1988). Cognitive and cognitive-relaxation treatments of anger. *Cognitive Therapy and Research, 12*(2), 167–184.

Deffenbacher, J.L., Story, D.A., Stark, R.S., Hogg, J.A., & Brandon, A.D. (1987). Cognitive-relaxation and social skills interventions in the treatment of general anger. *Journal of Counseling Psychology, 34*(2), 171–176.

Deffenbacher, J.L., Thwaites, G. A., Wallace, T.L., & Oetting, E.R. (1994). Social skills and cognitive-relaxation approaches to general anger reduction. *Journal of Counseling Psychology, 41*(3), 386–396.

Evans, D.R., Hearn, M.T., & Saklofske, D. (1973). Anger, arousal, and systematic desensitization. *Psychological Reports, 32,* 625–626.

Hazaleus, S.L., & Deffenbacher, J.L. (1986). Relaxation and cognitive treatments of anger. *Journal of Consulting and Clinical Psychology, 54*(2), 222–226.

Hearn, M.T., & Evans, D.R. (1972). Anger and reciprocal inhibition therapy. *Psychological Reports, 30,* 943–948.

Moon, J.R., & Eisler, R.M. (1983). Anger control: An experimental comparison of three behavioral treatments. *Behavior Therapy, 14*(4), 493–505.

Novaco, R.W. (1975). *Anger control.* Lexington, MA: D.C. Heath.

Rimm, D.C., Hill, G.A., Brown, N.N., & Stuart, J.E. (1974). Group assertive training in treatment of expression of inappropriate anger. *Psychological Reports, 34,* 791–798.

Rimm, D.C., DeGroot, J.C., Boord, P., Heiman, J., & Dillow, P.V. (1971). Systematic desensitization of an anger response. *Behavior Research and Therapy, 9,* 273–280.

Stermac, L.E. (1987). Anger control treatment for forensic patients. *Journal of Interpersonal Violence, 1*(4), 446–457.

Whiteman, M., Fanshel, D., & Grundy, J. (1987). Cognitive-behavioral intervention aimed at anger of parents at risk of child abuse. *Social Work, 32*(6), 469–474.

Chapter 8

Developing the Therapeutic Alliance with Angry Clients

Raymond DiGiuseppe
St. John's University
and
Institute for Rational Emotive Therapy

In reviewing the literature on psychotherapeutic methods for treating anger, I was struck by how little information exists. Compared with depression and anxiety, there is considerably less research and theory to guide clinical treatment of anger-related disorders (Tafrate, chap. 7, this volume). Perhaps this state of affairs exists because most of the original psychotherapy theorists, such as Freud (1920), Adler (1931), Rogers (1951), Ellis (1962), Beck (1976), and so on, developed their theories from the clients they saw, who were primarily self-referred neurotics presenting with anxiety- and depression-related disorders. However, mental health services expanded greatly in this century, and psychotherapists have been asked by courts and society at large to serve more diverse populations. Thus, there are now numerous treatment programs designed to serve spouse abusers, juvenile offenders, jail inmates, drunk drivers, and substance abusers. These populations typically did not receive mental health services when most of the originators of psychotherapies formulated their theories and practices.

Psychotherapists who provide treatment in family violence programs, jails, and juvenile offender facilities frequently complain that angry clients are resistant to treatment. Perhaps these clients are resistant to psychotherapy because they simply do not wish for treatment. In fact, the major premise of this chapter is that angry clients are frequently unmotivated to change because they are typically coerced into treatment. Thus, our initial and still basic theories of psychotherapy may be inadequate as they stand to address anger-related disorders because they were designed for self-referred populations who recognized their own problems. Although a separate chapter in this book focuses on empirical studies on anger psychotherapy outcomes (see Tafrate, chap. 7) and others deal with suggestions for treating anger-related disorders in adults (see Deffenbacher, chap. 9) and children and adolescents (see Feindler, chap. 10), the present chapter focuses on the basic problem of motivating angry clients for treatment.

THE PROBLEM OF THE THERAPEUTIC ALLIANCE

Initially, clients often respond with shock and disbelief to the suggestion that they change their behavior. For example,

> A man referred to me because of spouse abuse responded with surprise to the suggestion that he target his anger for change. He readily admitted that he had never considered *not* feeling angry because he did not know what emotion he might experience instead.
>
> In a family therapy session, I failed to convince a father to give up his anger and to stop yelling at his children. The father confronted me for trying to change his anger, and argued that anger was necessary for a parent. Without anger, he said, he would make no attempts to discipline his children. Anger was a cue that the children's behavior required attention. He thought not experiencing anger meant that he would be ignoring his parental responsibility.
>
> During a marriage counseling case, a wife refused to discuss changing her level of anger toward her husband. Giving up her anger, she said, would mean that she accepted or condoned his inappropriate behavior.
>
> An adolescent boy referred by the court for frequent fighting resisted all attempts to help him control his anger toward his peers. He believed that failure to express anger would result in others failing to respect him.
>
> The president of a small corporation sought consultation because of continued conflict with his staff. His "incompetent staff had failed to reach their sales quota." He defended his anger with reports of its success at controlling sales personnel and secretaries. Surrendering anger, he confided, would be abandoning his only management tool.
>
> A business executive expressed concern that eliminating her anger when she interacted with her family after work would prevent her from expressing the anger she built up at work during the day. She said that failure to have an outlet for her anger would result in more explosive outbursts.
>
> One husband I treated resisted attempts to target his anger for change because he concluded that my attempts to change his anger meant that I did not believe that his wife mistreated him. He persisted in attempts to convince me that her behavior was inappropriate and needed changing.
>
> A 14-year-old boy diagnosed as having an attention deficit disorder was rebellious toward his special education teacher. He refused all attempts to control his anger in class because he believed the teacher was wrong to call the students *dummies* and to read the newspaper rather than teach.

Spouses, courts, teachers and other school officials, employee assistance programs, and other agencies or individuals often instigate the referral for treatment for angry individuals. Thus, angry clients are typically either coerced into treatment or seek help because they want assistance in changing the target of their anger, not in changing their own anger. Those angry people who are self-referred often do not seek treatment. Rather, they seek supervision and want to learn how to change the target of their anger. Typically, they want the target (spouse, employees, students, etc.) to comply with their own demands, and they have low frustration tolerance for the individuality of these targets. As a result, there is often difficulty forming a therapeutic alliance with angry clients (DiGiuseppe, 1991; Ellis, 1977).

In psychotherapy supervision, one often finds therapists working to change their clients' anger while the clients are working to change the person at whom they are angry. The clients fail to agree to change their anger because they do not even recognize that it is problematic to them. They typically believe that they are justified and that it is appropriate to feel anger, or they may not believe that any other emotional reaction would be appropriate to the event. Therapists and clients clash because they disagree on the goal and target of intervention. Therapists desire to change the angry emotionality, whereas patients desire revenge, condemnation, or change in the transgressor. It is not surprising, therefore, that conversations with other therapists who treat angry children, adolescents, and adults led to the conclusion that the failure to develop a therapeutic alliance with angry patients is a common problem.

Although considerable research exists on the therapeutic alliance in psychotherapy, none of this research appears to focus on angry clients (see Horvath & Luborsky, 1993; Horvath & Symonds, 1991). Research and theory need to explore the nature of the therapeutic alliance with angry clients, and propose if and why clients with anger disorders have a greater problem forming a therapeutic alliance than do clients with other emotional problems. It is also important for research and theory to explore the nature of the therapeutic alliance with angry clients, and propose why the problem of formulating a therapeutic alliance might exist for this emotional disorder more than for others.

The concept of *therapeutic alliance* involves more than the therapeutic relationship. Bordin (1979) proposed that a successful therapeutic alliance includes three elements: (a) agreement between the therapist and client on the goals of therapy, (b) agreement on the tasks of therapy, and (c) the bond—a warm, accepting, trusting relationship. This last aspect of the alliance—the bond—is what most psychotherapy theories refer to as the *therapeutic relationship*. However, a successful alliance is more than the therapeutic bond. Angry clients appear less likely to reach agreement on the goals of therapy than clients with other emotional problems. DiGiuseppe (1991) and Ellis (1977) both suggested some attitudes commonly found among angry persons that may be instrumental in preventing the development of the therapeutic alliance. Specifically, these beliefs may prevent clients from reaching an agreement with therapists that the goal is to change their own anger. These attitudes include the following.

Strong Anger Is Justified and Appropriate   Angry clients may not experience their emotions as deviant because they cling to emotional scripts that sanction their anger. This may occur because clients may not have been socialized to react with alternative emotions. That is, their culture, family, or peer group may not have modeled alternative emotional reactions, or they may have actually sanctioned high levels of anger. In such situations, these persons may fail to evaluate their angry reactions as deviant.

Emotional Responsibility and Other Blame   Angry people often fail to take responsibility for their emotions; they assign responsibility for their emotions to external events. It is common to hear angry clients report, "He (She or It) made me angry." As long as the cause of anger is perceived to lie outside of themselves, angry persons are unlikely to act to change the emotion. Because someone else is thought to be responsible for the anger, by behaving badly, this other person is perceived to need to change. Even if the angry clients perceive their emotion as deviant (i.e., excessive and personally harmful), they may not take steps to manage the emotion if it is thought to be externally controlled.

Other Condemnation   Anger usually occurs along with the belief that the target of one's anger is a totally worthless human being. The angry person does not differentiate the person from the person's acts. In turn, because the transgressor responsible for the person's anger is a worthless, condemnable individual, he or she deserves the angry person's wrath and must pay for the transgression. The worthless individual is perceived to be a deserving target of the anger outburst, or at least of contempt. This belief works against changing the anger.

Self-Righteousness   Angry patients almost always report believing that they have been wronged or treated unfairly. The transgressors are portrayed as morally wrong, whereas the patients see themselves as the aggrieved parties. Angry clients are rarely willing to examine their own role in an interpersonal conflict, and rigidly adhere to the correctness of their behavior and the folly or immorality of their enemies. Self-righteousness leads angry people to believe that justice and God are on their side.

Cathartic Expression   Most angry clients believe that people must release their anger. American culture (i.e., teachers, TV and radio commentators, psychodynamic psychotherapists, etc.) seems to promote a hydraulic model of anger, which includes the notion that anger must be dissipated or it will build up to a high level and the person will explode. Clients believe that holding their anger "inside" will eventually lead to greater anger outbursts and psychosomatic illness, and that anger expression is healthy and necessary. Again, such a belief mitigates against attempts to change the anger.

Short-Term Reinforcement   Angry patients are often temporarily reinforced for their temper tantrums by significant others' compliance with the former's demands. Of course, these rewards are offset by the negative consequences
of using coercive processes in interpersonal relationships. Although significant
others often comply (at least initially), they may remain resentful, bitter, and dis-
tant. However, the angry patients seem unaware of the negative effect the anger
has on their interpersonal relationships. This belief is similar to Beck's (1976)
cognitive error of selective abstraction. Angry patients selectively abstract into
awareness the positive reactions to their anger outbursts, but ignore the information on the negative side of the hedonic calculus. Attending to the short-term
reinforcement of one's behavior and ignoring the long-term negative consequences of the same behavior is a common human foible, and is a common social
trap seen by therapists who work with angry clients and patients.

Reactance and Perceived Lack of Empathy by Others   Therapists'
attempts to change their patients' anger are often perceived by the patients as
indicating that the therapists do not believe that the transgressor is responsible for
the problem, that the therapists do not agree that the patients were aggrieved, or
that the therapists do not believe the transgressor was wrong (Walen,
DiGiuseppe, & Dryden, 1992). Patients may experience therapists' attempts to
change their anger as invalidating their experience of being wronged and dis-
pelling their moral outrage against the offender, or as disagreement by their therapists with their moral standard.

MODELS OF CHANGE

New models are needed to suggest how clinicians can motivate clients to change
and avoid the previously discussed resistances. Prochaska and DiClemente (1988)
investigated the process of change both inside and outside of psychotherapy. They
identified five stages of attitudes people have about change. In (a) the precontemplative stage, people are not even thinking about changing. In (b) the contemplative stage, people are evaluating the pros and cons of changing, but have not yet
made the decision to change. During (c) the readiness stage, people have decided
to change and are preparing to take some action. During (d) the action stage, people actually implement some change strategies. Finally, (e) the maintenance stage
encompasses people's attempts to continue and strengthen changes that have
already been made (Prochaska, DiClemente, & Norcross, 1992).

Most consumers of psychotherapy arrive for treatment in the contemplative,
readiness, or action stages. They are thinking that they might change and wish to
explore that possibility, or they have already decided to change. In contrast, using
Prochaska and DiClemente's scheme, most angry clients seem to arrive in the
precontemplative stage for changing *their* anger, but in the action stage for
changing *others*. They want to change others who, they believe, make them
angry. I predict that research using Prochaska and DiClemente's stages of change

measure would provide evidence for the hypothesis that most angry clients have not reached the decision to change their anger when they arrive for therapy. Prochaska and DiClemente suggested that clients in the precontemplative stage of change may not respond to active directive therapeutic procedures. Instead, therapists should utilize strategies that focus on self-awareness.

To help angry clients focus on changing their destructive anger, it may first be necessary to acknowledge and validate their frustration and disappointment at the hands of "the enemy." Even then, however, changing the anger may not become a goal for patients until they gain self-awareness and reach two insights. First, they must understand that their present emotion (i.e., anger) is dysfunctional in the long run, even though it may temporarily lead to satisfaction; second, they must be able to conceptualize an alternative emotional reaction that is socially and personally acceptable to them. These two insights are prerequisites to formulating a therapeutic alliance for any problem. Such insights are usually reached quite readily by anxious or depressed, self-referred clients before they arrive for therapy. These may even be the motivators that instigate clients to seek treatment. Regrettably, angry clients do not have such insights.

One of the primary tasks in formulating a therapeutic alliance with angry clients and patients is to move them from the precontemplative stage of change to the action stage of change. This accomplishes an agreement on the goals of therapy. To agree on the goal of changing people's anger, it must be agreed that the anger is dysfunctional and that there is an alternative emotional reaction to replace the anger. Before discussing methods to achieve these goals, it would be helpful to review the script theories of emotions, which serve as a model for changing how clients think about their anger.

CULTURE, LANGUAGE, AND ANGER

Ekman (1974) listed anger as one of the six basic prototypical human emotions, along with sadness, happiness, fear, surprise, and disgust, that all humans experience regardless of culture. Although there has been substantial debate on the universality of basic emotions, Soloman (1984) and Izard (1977) stated that if any emotion is universal to the human condition, it is anger. However, Wierzbicka (1992) identified several cultures that have no word for anger. She demonstrated that words initially translated as *anger* actually represented emotions that have no translation in English; thus they concluded that there is no reason to think that the English word *anger* represents a "pan-human prototype."

If anger is not an innate emotion, perhaps it (and other emotions) is more influenced by culture than previously thought. A substantial literature exists on the sociology of emotions that psychologists rarely reference (see Kemper, 1991, for a review). It is proposed here that script theories of emotions (Abelson, 1981; de Sousa, 1980; Fehr & Russell, 1984; Hochschild, 1983; Sabini & Silver, 1982; Tomkins, 1979) are helpful in understanding anger. According to this position, emotional experiences and expressions result from a socially derived scheme concerning a group of subevents. Accordingly, emotional scripts consist of schemes that include the eliciting stimuli, the evaluations and beliefs about those events, culturally sanctioned emotional experiences, and the social expression and behavioral displays associated with the emotions. Hochschild (1983) presented the most elaborate theory. She posited that people choose, often unconsciously, from the culturally appropriate and available options according to perceptions of five categories of experience: motivation, agency, value, and the relationship between the self and the agent. Emotions are experienced that match proscribed combinations of perceptions. For example, in a given culture, anger could be the emotional experience tied to these five perceptions: (a) I want to be treated with respect, (b) I do not have X's respect, (c) It is terrible not to have X's respect, (d) X is wrong for not respecting me, and (e) X is a less worthwhile person than I am.

Kemper (1991) pointed out that such theories can be useful to psychologists because the mechanisms by which the culture has its effect, the five categories of perceptions (or cognitions), are hypothesized to match the emotional experience. The five categories of perceptions that Hochschild posited are similar to constructs in cognitive-behavioral therapy, such as automatic thoughts (Beck, 1976), attributions (Seligman, 1975), and irrational beliefs (Ellis, 1962).

Sociocultural theories also provide clues to help identify when people are motivated to change their emotions. Hochschild (1979) proposed a concept called *emotional deviance*, which represents persons' perceptions that the emotion experienced differs from one of the socially prescribed, appropriate emotions. Thoits (1985) then proposed that people are motivated to change their behavior, physiological reactions, and emotionality when they experience emotional deviance. Therefore, people's recognition that their emotional reactions are inappropriate or socially unacceptable becomes a primary motivation for emotional change.

Several between- and within-culture hypotheses relevant to the diagnosis and treatment of anger follow from this perspective on emotion. First, immigrants to a new culture actually live in two cultures, and thus may fail to recognize that some of their emotions are regarded as deviant in the new culture. As a result, they may not wish to change a reaction that brings disdain from others in the mainstream culture. Second, immigrants may not have acculturated the scripts that guide the emotional reactions proscribed by the mainstream culture in which they now live, and they may be perplexed and frustrated by their inability to perceive others' emotional reactions. Such individuals may experience confusion because they do not know what to feel. Third, they may be surprised when they respond emotionally with a script from their culture of origin, and this emotional experience is perceived as deviant by the new adopted culture. As a result, they may believe that their emotional reactions are invalidated by members of the mainstream culture.

Another implication of script theory concerns individuals learning the proper scripts of their own culture. Individuals may have learned culturally unacceptable scripts during their developmental period, or failed to learn accepted ones because of deviant socialization in their family, clan, or subgroup. This is shown in cases of children raised in inner-city slums, where anger/aggression and gang membership are normative.

Because emotional scripts evolve in a culture across time, cultures may contain numerous or few scripts of each emotion prototype. That is, there can be few or many variations of anger, guilt, sadness, and so on. Sadly, cultures and subcultures can fail to contain a script or schema for an adaptive form of anger. The *emotional script* concept appears helpful in understanding maladaptive anger reactions and in treating anger disorders. Based on this perspective, it is hypothesized that American culture possesses too few scripts concerning the prototype of anger. As a result, people often respond with an anger script that is inappropriate because of its frequency, intensity, or duration, and because of the maladaptive interpersonal and intrapersonal effects it produces.

Kemper (1978, 1991; Kemper & Collins, 1990) suggested that emotions need to be understood in the context of the social structure in which individuals reside, and Kemper and Collins believed that the factors of power and status are important influences on emotional scripts. Scripts that include the suppression of anger in relationships with superiors, or those in power, may be particularly problematic because suppressed anger is related to physical illness. For example, Hochschild (1979) studied flight attendants, a group that must suppress any annoyance, anger, or irritation to passengers' aversive and obnoxious behaviors to ensure future business. Flight attendants report feeling emotionally "numb" and experience considerable emotional problems. Hochschild generalized from these results to suggest that any individual in an occupational or social role that includes strong rules to suppress anger will experience difficulties similar to flight attendants. Some immigrants, members of minority groups, and women often have rules that encourage the suppression of emotional expression when they interact with those perceived as having higher status, and as a result experience detrimental, suppressed anger. Such persons lack an adaptive script to react to negative reactions from those perceived as having higher status.

CULTURE, FAMILIES, AND EMOTIONAL SCRIPTS

Cultural considerations can be quite important in helping clients reach an agreement with therapists on the goal to change their anger. The development of nondisturbed, functionally alternative emotional scripts such as annoyance or "nondisturbed anger" may depend on the availability of such scripts in the clients' (and therapists') culture and family. Over the years, I have had considerable world-wide experience training therapists in rational-emotive behavior therapy. Based on observations during these training sessions, it has become clear that therapists from different cultures have varying degrees of difficulty understanding Ellis' (1977) notion that there are both disturbed and nondisturbed types of anger. People from English-speaking countries have some difficulty understanding the difference between disturbed anger and nondisturbed annoyance. It is not that the English language does not have alternative words for anger-related emotions. Rather, it appears that the term *anger* is used quite indiscriminantly in English to describe a variety of internal experiences. One can use the word *anger* to reflect a range of similar but unique emotions, from the mildest level of infrequent irritation to persistent homicidal rage (e.g., "I was so god-damned annoyed with what I saw that I beat the shit out of her!"). Therapists from Spanish-speaking countries seem to grasp Ellis' distinction easily. They report that their language has words similar to English to express disturbed variations of anger, such as *rabio* and *furioso*. These words are used much more precisely in Spanish to describe inappropriate or exaggerated anger experiences. In my experience, Israeli therapists have the greatest difficulty attempting to apply Ellis' distinction in their language. They claim that there is one commonly used word for what Americans call anger, which is translated literally as, *I am nervous at you*. Not surprisingly, they report difficulty helping clients accept the goal of changing their anger and have few culturally accepted alternative scripts available to replace clinically dysfunctional anger. These examples are similar to the distinction in Russian reported by Kassinove and Sukhodolsky (chap. 1, this volume) between *gnev* and *zlost. Gnev* is generally seen as mature and appropriate anger that requires no psychotherapeutic intervention. *Zlost* is an immature and inappropriate experience that requires intervention if it is frequently experienced. In Russian, these are moderately intense emotions that are different both from annoyance and rage (see chap. 5, this volume, for further discussion of cross-cultural perspectives on anger).

Thus, vocabulary words in clients' language that make distinctions between emotions may not actually influence the availability of the scripts to clients. Instead, the frequency with which such distinctions are made in the language (i.e., that the words actually reflect distinct scripts, and that the person has learned these distinctions through socialization) affects the availability of alternative emotional scripts to the person. The greater number of words that are used in common conversation to describe alternative scripts to similar events, the more these alternative scripts will be accessed in the culture. It follows that cultures, subcultures, or linguistic groups whose languages do not have many commonly used words to represent alternative emotional reactions to the same situation will have fewer emotional scripts. The fewer alternative emotional scripts that can be accessed by common words, the more difficulty people in that group will have with that emotion. Simply stated, the lack of a variety of acceptable, socially sanctioned emotional scripts leads to inflexibility of emotional reactions to troublesome situations. This hypothesis can be tested by cross-cultural research that attends to the emotional scripts and the vocabulary used to express them in various cultures.

Cultural scripts for anger are likely to differ by gender. Many researchers propose gender-specific patterns of anger expression and inhibition (e.g., Tavris,

1989, 1992). Biological arguments suggested that because infrahuman males tend to be more aggressive, so, too, are human males (Lorenz, 1966). Another view suggests that men and women are equally capable of anger expression, but America's male-dominated society inhibits female anger expression. However, Averill's (1983) data showed that men and women experience and express anger at a similar frequency, with similar intensity, and for similar reasons. Nevertheless, one gender difference did emerge: When angry, women reported crying significantly more often than did men.

Cultures and their languages may vary greatly in the distinctions they make between affective states. Therapists need to be aware of how the emotional scripts for anger (or any other emotional state) are valued in a patient's culture or subculture, and what alternative scripts are available within that culture. If the patient's cultural, subcultural, or family group has no alternative script for a functional emotional response, the therapist should attempt to build a scheme for him or her. Of course, clinicians need to be sensitive to what the client's subculture considers "acceptable alternative scripts."

Clinical experience suggests that families (and subcultures) have idiosyncratic scripts that differ from those of their larger culture. In addition, it has been found that families with anger problems have few emotional scripts, and that family members fail to make distinctions between the various reactions they *could* have to events. Perhaps because only one script has been modeled, clients behave rigidly with the same emotional reaction. This lack of flexibility results in dysfunctional family interactions. Failure to have an emotional script for a type of adaptive, nondisturbed anger will likely lead to a failure to want to change one's anger. This will translate into a failure to agree to change one's anger as a goal of therapy.

DISTINGUISHING TYPES OF ANGER

Ellis' rational-emotive theory (Ellis, 1989; Ellis & DiGiuseppe, 1994; Walen, DiGiuseppe, & Dryden, 1992) posits that people may fail to target any emotion for change because of the lack of semantic precision in words for affective expression. Anger is a particular problem in this regard. Colloquial American use of the word *anger* includes a wide range of affective states with numerous behavioral and physiological responses. Americans appropriately use the word *anger* to express a range of emotions, from mild levels of irritation to very strong murderous rage. One could conclude from this that Americans have few emotional scripts from which to choose. However, the English language makes the distinction between the distressed emotion of *depression* and the experience of *sadness*. Also, *anxiety* (a response to imagined threat) is often differentiated from *fear*, which is a reaction to real threat. Although other standard English words may fall in the same arena as anger (e.g., *animosity, annoyance, ire, irritation, indignation, wrath*, and *vexation*), they are not as commonly used. Thus, I propose that the lack of common usage of a nondisturbed affect word in the anger arena prevents people from distinguishing between disturbed and nondisturbed emotional scripts.

Most patients and therapists consider anger as varying along one quantitative continuum. In contrast, rational-emotive theory maintains that emotions differ not only on a quantitative continuum. It posits that adaptive and maladaptive variants of each emotion exist and differ qualitatively as well. Izard's (1989) analysis indicates that each emotion has four characteristics: (a) phenomenological experience, (b) social expression, (c) behavioral predisposition, and (d) physiological arousal. Of these, only physiological arousal is a quantitative dimension.

To accept one's anger as a target for mental health intervention requires one to recognize at least two different anger-related emotional scripts. The first, called *adaptive nondisturbed anger* (or what Ellis, 1977, referred to as *annoyance*), would have several components. Cognitively, it would acknowledge that the person was aggrieved and that the transgressor's action was perceived to be wrong. It would include an experiential negative affect along a continuum from mild to moderate. It could lead to clear assertive communications by the aggrieved party communicating his or her feelings and desires. It could lead to other adaptive behaviors that would avoid victimization in the future. If no adaptive behavior was readily available in the person's repertoire, this emotion might initiate problem-solving activities to consider and evaluate new responses. Also, this state would not lead to the unnecessary disruption of the person's functioning. Such an emotion may have moderate, although not excessive, affective arousal.

The second anger script, called *dysfunctional or clinical anger*, would lead to a much more unpleasant phenomenological experience. It would include a more intense hostile and attacking form of social expression, which might cause additional long-term problems. It may interfere with problem solving, and could restrict consideration of more adaptive behavior that would avoid victimization in the future. Finally, it would lead to disturbed affect and rumination, which greatly interfere with the individual's functioning. A third common script is similar to the second in all ways except expression. Here the person avoids any mention of the problem or confrontation with the transgressor.

Averill (1982, 1983) supported the view that people can distinguish between disturbed clinical anger and nonclinical, functional annoyance types of anger. His data suggest that people view anger as a more intense emotional experience than annoyance. They also view anger as a more serious or inappropriate emotional reaction. The rational-emotive theory of emotions is similar to the script theories of emotions mentioned earlier. Discussion of the *script* concept with angry clients usually results in several themes. First, they typically defend their anger script, and report that it is necessary to attack their transgressors lest they be overwhelmed by them. Second, they often insist that it is important to express anger to avoid the negative health consequences that accompany anger suppression.

In essence, it seems that American culture has limited scripts for anger. Common American cultural scripts usually incorporate an instinctual link between anger and aggression, and they (wrongly) stress the importance of cathartic release of anger. It is proposed that anger and its treatment can be better understood if researchers and clinical practitioners investigate: the common scripts that people hold concerning anger, how these scripts relate to adaptive behavior, and how scripts relate to labeling anger as a problem. A common perspective between therapists and clients on understanding scripts should help the therapeutic alliance.

BUILDING THE ALLIANCE

To reach an agreement on the goal of changing patients' anger, the following steps/strategies are suggested.

Acknowledge the Transgression to the Client

The first obstacle that therapists usually encounter is their clients' belief that anger is justified because they were wronged by the target of the anger. Frequently, clients' anger is out of proportion to the actual transgression that occurred. Often they have been participants in a "menage a deux," where they and their anger target have both acted poorly. It is easy for therapists to skip over the transgression and challenge other issues. However, most angry clients believe they have been purposely and voluntarily treated unfairly, and they desire (or demand) to be heard. Therapists' attempts to change or reduce anger are often perceived by patients as a sign that the therapists do not agree that the patients were aggrieved, do not believe the transgressor was wrong, or believe that the transgressor was not responsible for the problem (Walen, DiGiuseppe, & Dryden, 1992). Patients often experience therapeutic attempts to change their anger as invalidating their moral outrage against the offender, or they feel as though the therapists disagree with their moral standard. Many clients respond to attempts to change their anger by accusing therapists of taking the side of the significant other at whom their anger is directed.

To help clients focus on the goal of changing their anger, it may be necessary to first acknowledge and validate their frustration and disappointment at the hands of their enemy. Therapists' acknowledgment that a negative event or transgression has occurred to the clients helps them move on to evaluate the adaptiveness of their anger. The importance of the acknowledgment of patient frustration is shown in two case studies, described in the following.

> A couple sought help for their arguments about the husband's 21-year-old daughter from a previous marriage who lived with them. The daughter had dated a drug user who stole from the couple's house to support his habit. The father felt hurt, but forgave the daughter. The wife felt angry at the daughter for allowing the family home to be violated, and was angry at the father for forgiving the

daughter. The therapist's first intervention was to evaluate and challenge the wife's dysfunctional anger. However, this resulted in more anger. The wife believed that attempts to change her anger meant that the therapist and the husband believed that the daughter had done no wrong, and that the wife had not been harmed. The therapist then switched, and acknowledged the wife's hurt and validated her sense of vulnerability and betrayal by the daughter before implementing other anger-reduction strategies. Agreeing that one goal of therapy would be to discuss how to prevent the daughter from putting the family at risk helped the alliance and allowed the wife to examine whether her anger toward her husband actually accomplished her goal. Although her anger toward her husband appeared unjustified because he did not encourage the thievery, the wife believed that her emotions and issues were not addressed.

A family was referred by child protective services because of physical and verbal abuse by the father toward his wife and two children. Whenever his anger was addressed, the husband responded by justifying his anger. He claimed that his wife was an ineffectual parent and did not discipline the children. Focusing on his anger increased his anger and blame toward her. The therapist then switched, and allowed the father to report his litany of sins of the mother, many of which were valid from a purely behavioral perspective. An agreement was made that his issues of parenting would be addressed. However, it was pointed out that his anger resulted in his family avoiding any discussion with him. Again, this man's anger was out of control and disproportionate to the wife's transgressions. Acknowledging his concerns, pointing out that he was unsuccessful at addressing them, and agreeing to address them in conjoint sessions allowed the therapist to discuss whether the husband's anger was effective in attaining his goals. Thus, an alliance was established.

Assess Client Goals

The therapist needs to clearly assess whether angry clients have as their goal a change in their anger. This is a simple matter of overt verbal agreement between patient and therapist. Failure to closely attend to the issue of agreement on therapeutic goals will surely lead to an alliance rupture.

Agree on a Goal to Explore   If the client does not wish to change the anger and the therapist believes that anger is a problem, the therapist may seek an agreement with the client that they spend some time reviewing the functionality and adaptiveness of the client's anger. At the very least, this will put the matter of the anger on the table; it also will provide an opportunity for the therapist to educate the patient about the maladaptive anger pattern.

Explore the Consequences of Anger   Therapists can lead clients, by Socratic dialogue, through an analysis of the consequences of anger. Exploring the consequences of clients' anger usually involves challenging some of the beliefs mentioned earlier, which help maintain anger.

Emotional Responsibility   Angry clients are quick to blame the transgressor who elicited their angry reaction. Teaching clients that *they* are responsible for their anger is much easier after the therapist has acknowledged that the transgressor has done some wrong. When challenging emotional responsibility, it is important to ask, Does your anger get you what you want? Many clients are so stuck on the issues of moral blame of the transgressor that they fail to focus on the practical aspects of their reaction. If the transgressor does not and will not change, which is often true, then how will the client cope with the situation and how does the anger help in problem solving? The useful clinical strategy here is to repeatedly acknowledge the transgressor's behavior, acknowledge the client's emotion, and then ask how he or she is solving the problem and how the anger will help reach the goal.

> A middle-level manager was referred by a friend because of persistent anger at his company and supervisors after he was passed over for promotion. The man reported that he deserved the promotion more than the person who received it, but was passed over because his immediate supervisor personally liked the successful candidate. During the ensuing 2 years, the client had openly berated his superiors, the upper management, and the company. Most of his peers avoided contact with him because of his continual angry tirades. For the first four sessions, the client attempted to convince the therapist of how he was mistreated and how guilty were all of those involved or who failed to appreciate his work. The therapist responded, "All right, so you were treated unfairly, and you are unappreciated. How are you coming to live with these facts? How has your anger and your ranting and raving helped you to cope with the situation?" Further conversation resulted in the client admitting that his behavior had alienated his peers, reduced the quality of his work, prevented him from considering a job change, and prevented him from doing good work to impress other managers in the organization. Although he had "gotten even" by reducing his productivity, he hurt himself because others in his industry perceived him as an angry person whom they neither wished to promote nor employ. Continued focus on the consequences helped to develop these insights and an alliance to change his anger.

It Is Healthy to Express Anger   Although cathartic expression of anger is frowned on by most scientists who have studied it, it is difficult to dislodge the notion that it is healthy and desirable (chaps. 1 and 7 explore the notion of cathartic expression of anger more fully). This is a particularly difficult belief to challenge Socratically. Clients may not have sufficient information about the long-term effects of anger expression to allow their experiences to lead them to the correct conclusions. Instead, I have found it better to use more didactic teaching to challenge this belief. Clients who believe in cathartic expression are correct in their belief that holding in one's anger results in illness. However, this definitely does not mean that the opposite—the outward expression of anger—results in psychological or physical health. Research has demonstrated that the outward expression of anger also leads to physical illness (Chesney, 1985; Diamond, 1982; Diamond, Schneiderman, Schwartz, Smith, Vorp, & Posin, 1984; Spielberger, 1992). Thus, one can become physically ill regardless of whether one holds one's anger in or expresses it outwardly.

Similarly, psychological adjustment is not accomplished by inwardly harboring anger. The internal rumination that angry people experience can consume their lives. However, the outward expression of anger does not lead to psychological health, but rather to more anger. This is often difficult for angry clients to see because they often feel better (immediately and temporarily) after they unload their anger on someone. They may feel better after an anger outburst because they stop ruminating, and because their muscles may actually relax after the long period of preparing to "tell that person off." Thus, there is a moment of relaxation similar to what one might feel in deep muscle relaxation when tense muscles are released. Unfortunately, this emotional improvement is short lived. Cathartic expression results in an increase in the probability that the person will respond to a similar situation with anger (Tavris, 1989). Thus, the belief that catharsis is a corrective experience that reduces the buildup of anger is false. Instead, catharsis leads to temporary relief and increases the chances that one will become angry in the future. I usually remind clients of the old joke, "How do you get to Carnegie Hall?" Answer: "Practice, practice, practice." So, "How do you become a really angry person?" Answer: "Practice, practice, practice."

Angry clients appear stuck in a conundrum. Do they hold their anger in or let it out? Neither, most of us would argue; they would best find a way to control/eliminate/dissipate the anger and work toward experiencing another emotion. Spielberger (1992) used the metaphor of a *pressure cooker*: To deal with the buildup of steam, one can wait until the cooker explodes or one can periodically reduce the pressure by siphoning off some of the steam. However, a better solution would be to just lower the flame and reduce the heat.

Anger Is an Effective Way to Control Others   As noted, clients are likely to focus on the immediate consequences of their anger, rather than the long-term social consequences. Thus, clients might focus on the outcome of an anger ventilation, such as succeeding in getting someone to comply with their rules, but ignore the fact that they seriously damaged the relationship. Frequently, clients lack empathy about how their anger affects others. Thus, it is helpful for them to recount how they feel when others are angry at them, and to use this to imagine how significant others feel when the clients get angry. It is important to make the distinction between short- and long-term consequences. Clients can usually convince the therapist that the short-term consequences are in their favor. Because immediate reinforcement is more effective than delayed reinforcement, it is not surprising that clients have difficulty focusing on long-term effects. It is important to ask about the outcome of previous anger outbursts on social relationships, and about social relationships, wherein the client does not express anger. Clients usually answer by saying that they do not express anger to those in a higher social position for fear of consequences, or to people who would not or have not tolerated the anger expression. This information can be used to make the case that people do not like anger.

Empathetic role taking is a successful strategy to help angry clients become aware of the social relationship consequences of their anger. I ask clients how they have reacted to those who have expressed anger at them. Most clients relate well to this exercise, and report disliking and distancing themselves from angry persons in their lives.

> The corporate president mentioned previously reported numerous bosses who expressed anger at him while he was moving up the corporate ladder. He reported that he always responded with an attempt at revenge through passive–aggressive behavior. He did only what they asked and nothing more. When asked how he would feel if sales personnel and secretaries would do the same to him, he got the point and agreed to change his anger.

The importance of empathy and contemplation are also seen in the following case.

> The angry father discussed earlier was asked who treated him with anger in his life. He reminisced about how his father yelled and hit him. He thought that his father was successful at demanding obedience. But he then went on to describe how he hated his father and avoided contact with him since becoming an adult. The hard question was whether he sought the same relationship with his children when they became adults. After contemplating the fact that generations can easily repeat the cycle, he was eager to learn better ways to discipline his children than yelling in anger.

Explore Alternative Scripts Once clients agree that it is in their best interest to reduce or eliminate their anger, they still can be thwarted because they may not know what to replace it with. They may have a limited number of alternative scripts to apply to the situation that they consider socially appropriate to the individual's status in the group. Helping clients generate alternative scripts is similar to generating alternative solutions in the problem-solving model of adjustment (Spivack, Platt, & Shure, 1976). This can often be achieved by having clients recall the successful, but nonangry reactions of others whom they respect. It also helps to generate a model for an alternative script. Clients from dysfunctional families may have few such models. Thus, therapists may have to suggest models from the general culture or from the literature, folklore, or films of the clients' culture. After a model is chosen for an alternative script, it is important to review the consequences of the model's behavior following the script. Next, clients are asked to imagine that they react in the same manner as in the script and imagine that the consequences happen to them. In this way, clients can provide information about how they believe the script may not be socially or personally acceptable to them. This process is repeated until the clients accept an alternative emotional script.

A male adolescent, Sal, was referred by his father because he was continually angry and fought with peers at least once a day. Sal was quite proud of his anger. He believed it was functional, despite several losses of friendships and being expelled from four parochial high schools. It was easy to convince him that the anger was dysfunctional, given that his father almost always learned of the fights from school authorities and punished him severely. However, Sal could not conceptualize any socially acceptable alternative reaction. Fortunately, Sal was enamored with the "Godfather" movies. The therapist pointed out how Sal's behavior was similar to the behavior of Sonny Corleone. Like the character in the film, Sal got intensely angry, expressed his anger in a histrionic manner, and impulsively attacked his instigators. The therapist asked, "What happened to Sonny?" The client reported how Sonny's enemies knew how he acted. They provoked his anger, ambushed, and killed him! "Well, you're just like Sonny! How long before the same thing happens to you?" the therapist responded. After examining how the client's and film character's behavior was similar, the therapist suggested that other models were available. Sal imagined himself reacting like the other son, Michael Corleone, who eventually became the new "Don." This character rarely reacted impulsively, but thought through his reactions and never let others know of his emotions. This client identified with the character and was now able to conceptualize an alternative reaction. Therapy was highly successful after this intervention.

Of course, the value of using a gangster as a model for an adolescent boy may be questioned. After all, Michael Corleone was a violent man who eventually killed all of his enemies. However, it is important that the model is respected by the client. We focused on prosocial aspects of the model's behavior—remaining calm and not letting others know what you are thinking until you decide how best to respond—and we downplayed the negative aspects of the model's behavior. Sal could always decide to avoid retaliation once he calmly thought through the situation.

After a model is chosen for an alternative script, it is important to review the consequences of the model's behavior following the script. Clients are asked to imagine that they react according to the script and to consider what consequences will likely follow. In this way, clients provide information concerning whether they view the script as socially or personally acceptable to them. In the case discussed previously, we asked the boy how the character Michael would respond to a situation the boy was angry about. Then we asked if he could react the same way, and if he thought the character's reaction was appropriate. Once the client agreed that he could accept the new model, we established an alternative script. With some clients, the behavior of three or four persons will have to be reviewed before an acceptable model is found.

Jamil was an inner-city African American adolescent referred by the school psychologist because of his frequent conflicts with authority figures. School authorities were considering placing him in an out-of-district school for disruptive children. Jamil reported that his anger was justified because he believed that the

White staff members at his school were racist. He gave quite convincing report-ing situations where the teachers used racial slurs and derogatory remarks about Jamil and other African American students. Jamil's angry outbursts usually resulted in the teachers and administrators perceiving him as violent and out of control. The therapist told Jamil that his anger and violent reactions gave the racist teachers an excuse to place him in a special school. His anger was, in fact, making it easy for them to ensure that Jamil did not get a quality education. Jamil agreed that his reactions were self-destructive. However, he reported that anger was the only reaction available to him. Any other reaction would fail to acknowledge the injustice committed by the transgressors.

The therapist asked Jamil if he knew of a person or character who responded to prejudice in a more productive, successive manner—that is, with-out losing control and acting impulsively in a manner that played into the hands of his tormentor. Jamil discussed several people and eventually reported a scene from the movie "Malcom X." In this scene, one of Malcom's friends is seriously injured by the police for no reason. Malcom leads an orderly military march of the Black Muslims to the police station. All of the Muslims stand at attention outside the police station while Malcom confronts the police desk sergeant. Jamil said that Malcom's behavior was intense, but controlled. He did not act or speak in any manner that would give the police an excuse to retaliate violently. Jamil called this reaction "controlled anger." The person experiencing it is react-ing to a real injustice. It is a strong, but not destructive emotion. The person can think clearly about the best course of action. Jamil decided he would use this scene from the film as a model. He rehearsed how Malcom X might respond to his teachers' racist comments. He practiced responding directly in a controlled voice, pointing out the insult that had been made without yelling or resorting to verbal abuse.

Once Jamil agreed that his anger was disruptive and discovered a socially acceptable script, we focused on how he could begin to respond with the new script. A therapeutic alliance to change his anger had been made.

THE MOTIVATIONAL SYLLOGISM

Once the therapist and client have successfully accomplished these steps, the therapist can continue with treatment of the client's anger with any strategy that is agreed on mutually. These strategies and steps constitute what I term the *moti-vational syllogism*. The first premise is: My present anger is dysfunctional. The second premise is: There is an alternative script that is more functional. The third premise is: I can control which reaction I have to the activating event. The con-clusion is: I need to examine ways in which I can change my emotional reaction. It is helpful to quickly review the motivational syllogism at the initiation of a dis-cussion about a new anger-arousing event, or at the beginning of each session. In this way, the client is reminded of the previous points that have been agreed on earlier in therapy, and the reason to change the anger; the review also strengthens the therapeutic alliance and allows for further interventions. Well-researched and effective interventions are most likely to be successful when the *client* believes it is desirable to begin a program aimed at anger elimination.

CONCLUSION

Because angry clients are often forced into treatment, they typically enter with a low level of motivation to work toward change. Working with anger-disordered persons, therefore, requires that special attention be paid at the initial stage of therapy to building a positive therapeutic alliance. If this is done, the outcomes of our interventions are far more likely to be successful. The first step is to acknowledge to clients that a transgression has actually occurred, and that the clients are angry. This can then be successfully followed by helping the clients to understand the causes, short- and long-term consequences, and disadvantages of strong and so-called "cathartic expressions" of anger. Once they recognize that their prior verbal and behavioral anger scripts have been limited, and that there are more constructive ways to resolve interpersonal difficulties, they often become more receptive to developing new goals, practicing them, and incorporating them into their daily repertoire of behavior.

Chapter 9

Ideal Treatment Package for Adults with Anger Disorders

Jerry L. Deffenbacher

Colorado State University

In chapter 2, anger was conceptualized as an internal cognitive-affective-physio-logical experience in response to (a) external and/or internal prompts, (b) primary and secondary appraisals, and (c) momentary and enduring person characteristics. In turn, anger may manifest itself in various functional and dysfunctional ways.

Interventions might target different points in this sequence of arousal and expression to alter the probability, intensity, or frequency of anger. For example, external triggers of anger might be changed or avoided, thereby aborting the rest of the sequence. Cognitive interventions might change primary and secondary appraisals, such that provocative stimuli are no longer perceived or responded to in the same way. Likewise, cognitive and attitude change strategies might change the individual's enduring ways of coding the world, leading to more benign, less hostile interpretations. Of course, anger might be addressed directly. For example, the individual might learn relaxation skills to reduce angry feelings and physiological arousal or cognitive restructuring strategies to change angry self-talk and imagery. Additionally, the mode of expression might be targeted with problem solving, assertion, social and communication skills, time out, and the like. Escalation of anger and dysfunctional expression would be reduced as the individual modified the form of expression.

In the ideal treatment of adult anger problems, the therapist and client form a strong therapeutic alliance and engage in a careful, collaborative assessment, in which anger is identified as a significant personal problem; treatment strategies are then developed and tailored to those elements thought to be primary for that

Preparation of this chapter was funded, in part, by a grant (#P50DA0707) from the National Institute of Drug Abuse to the Tri-Ethnic Center for Study of Prevention Research.

client. That is, client and therapist work together to define *anger* as a primary concern, and then focus intervention on altering critical elements of the anger problem complex. In summary, the ideal treatment of adult anger problems is a highly individualized assessment and intervention process for anger issues that are owned as a problem by the client.

Ideal treatment can become disrupted in at least two general ways. First, the client and therapist may not develop a shared definition of the problem and/or the relationship necessary for therapy. Quite simply, many angry individuals do not define anger or anger expression as their primary problem (i.e., they do not own anger as a problem). Therefore, anger reduction is either irrelevant to or rejected by them. Such people may be brought into therapy by some other person (e.g., spouse or employer) or by some other social system (e.g., court or school) who identifies them as having an anger problem. However, from the individuals' perspective, they do not have an anger problem, but may come to get others off their back. However, until such clients acknowledge anger as a personal problem, conditions for the ideal treatment of anger are not present. Interventions for such persons should focus on readiness for anger reduction and attempt to move them from pretherapy and contemplative stages (Prochaska & DiClemente, 1988). Second, the therapist may not have a sufficient repertoire of anger-reduction strategies (i.e., he or she does not possess enough of the necessary interventions to tailor them to the presenting concerns and to reduce anger effectively).

This chapter addresses these two issues. The initial portion identifies common issues or themes that interfere with the client owning anger as a problem. Clinical suggestions to move the client toward defining and owning anger as a personal problem are then offered. The remainder of the chapter outlines specific interventions with which to target different elements of anger elicitation and expression.

DIFFERENTIAL DIAGNOSIS AND REFERRAL

Not all anger, even if owned by the client as a problem, should necessarily become a focus of anger-reduction intervention. Anger may only be a part of another problem or syndrome. For example, anger and irritability are common to depression, paranoia, and psychotic reactions. Anger may also be reflective of hormonal imbalances or neurological conditions. Such possibilities should be considered, carefully assessed, and ruled out before anger becomes the primary focus of therapy. When anger is part of another presenting problem, the alternative disorder should be the focus of treatment and potential referral.

Anger may also be a reaction to abusive, coercive, or intimidating individuals or social systems (e.g., spouse abuse or sexual harassment at work). Such possibilities, too, deserve careful assessment and attention. If anger is a reaction to a highly negative environment, therapeutic effort may shift appropriately to crisis intervention or to empowering the individual to make significant environmental changes (e.g., leaving the toxic environment) and/or behavioral limit setting and assertiveness. Anger too may be the concomitant of an individual's violent or destructive behavior (e.g., child or spouse abuse). Intervention should shift to the immediate control of the violent behavior first to protect the welfare of the individual or others. Anger management may be relevant as part of therapy, but is not likely to be the full answer. However, the clinician should be aware that such individuals may seek anger-reduction therapy to reduce the vocational, social, or legal consequences for current or past violent, destructive behavior, and may not be really invested in changing anger per se. In summary, it is important for the clinician to resist making anger the automatic target of intervention. Differential diagnosis, alternative conceptualizations and treatment plans, referral, and/or crisis intervention may be more relevant for some cases.

THE ANGRY CLIENT WHO IS NOT READY FOR THERAPY: ENHANCING READINESS

As noted previously, not all angry individuals enter therapy for the treatment of anger. This section identifies common themes that interfere with the identification and owning of anger as a personal problem and suggests strategies for enhancing readiness.

Lack of Awareness

Many angry individuals are relatively out of touch with their feelings and the ways in which they are expressed. This is not to suggest that they are highly defensive, which they may in fact be, but that they have little self-awareness of and insight into their feelings and their expression. They simply do not know how different their experience and expression patterns are from the norm.

Self-monitoring is a basic strategy to help such individuals. The format should be flexible and tailored to the individual, but, over time, should include tracking of affect, physiological reactions, self-talk, imagery, memories and associations, behavioral reactions, and the contexts in which these occur. Self-monitoring is explored within sessions, with the therapists aiding the client in understanding patterns and relationships among self-monitored experiences. Psychometric tests may also be useful. For example, the Trait Anger Scale (Spielberger, 1988), Anger Inventory (Novaco, 1976), Anger Expression Inventory (Spielberger, 1988), or the more comprehensive State–Trait Anger Expression Inventory (Spielberger, 1988) might be given. These instruments can be used normatively to help the individual gain a sense of their anger relative to peers. Tests can also be used idiographically as well. For example, the individual's pattern of anger expression—anger-in, anger-out, and anger-control—could be noted, with the client being asked what determines when one is used over another, increasing awareness of the situational and emotional parameters that influence anger expression. In going over the Anger Inventory, the clinician might ask why the client responds strongly to some events and not to others. The contrast of reactions may help clarify cognitive and situational parameters that influence the meaning of an event and the reaction to it. Feedback from others about how the person comes across may also provide a more defined personal picture of the individual. Mirrors and video-recording equipment may also be enlightening. For example, the client and therapist might role play an angry interaction in front of a video recorder. Replaying the tape provides direct feedback on both verbal and nonverbal aspects of behavior, and stopping the tape at different places allows for inquiry into more subjective aspects of thoughts, feelings, images, and the like. An alternative strategy is for the client to recall in detail previous anger experiences. As the client visualizes the event, the therapist can solicit information about experiential elements and behavioral expression. Regardless of the strategies chosen, the goal with the unaware client is to increase the level of awareness of the experience, expression, and contexts of anger.

Lack of Awareness of, or Empathy for, the Impact of Anger

Some individuals are aware of their anger, but not of its influences on others. For example, they may not know that others are put off, frightened, or intimidated, or that they feel hurt, rejected, disliked, or criticized when they are subjected to the individuals' anger. Such clients need to increase their awareness of and empathy for the impact of their anger so that they can identify it as an area on which they wish to work.

Many interventions described in the prior section—on enhancing general awareness—may be adapted to clients who do not understand the impact of their anger. However, the therapeutic focus shifts to having them identify with the feelings of and consequences to others. For example, clients might self-monitor, but track how others felt or reacted when they were angry, or they might interview others and ask them about emotional and other consequences when they were angry. Such clients might also be asked to vividly recall childhood or adolescent experiences where they were exposed to emotions and behaviors similar to those that they demonstrate.

The focus is on having clients identify the negative feelings and reactions they had so that they can anticipate that others would feel similarly when exposed to their anger. They might also be assigned to periodically take the role of another, asking themselves what another is thinking, feeling, or experiencing. A gestalt two-chair technique might be adapted such that an individual expresses angrily how he or she feels and then changes chairs and expresses how another person who is exposed to this anger thinks and feels. This might increase the person's appreciation for both the emoting and the receiving end of the interaction. Because some consequences of anger are delayed, these might be identified, and the client can be asked to visualize them, thereby bringing the more distal negative consequences into the present. For example, within actual treatment sessions, one angry individual visualized his coronary arteries slowly occluding, another imagined his children shaking in fear and terror, and a woman thought of her husband leaving and her children voluntarily joining him because of her angry tirades. In using this technique, it is useful to have clients visualize anger as part of a "movie" in their head, with color, music, and drama. Overall, the goal of any of these interventions is to increase the client's awareness of and feeling for the consequences of his or her anger to others, so that anger becomes personally meaningful and a target for change.

Anger Is Identity or Role Congruent

Anger, and sometimes aggressive behavior, can be fully congruent with an individual's self-concept (i.e., the person sees him- or herself as an angry person and likes it that way). For others, however, anger is more consonant with a role they periodically fill, such as parent, spouse, child, adolescent, or supervisor. Such individuals are often deficient in alternative ways to conceptualize the role and, perhaps, in behaviors with which to implement the role effectively.

As long as anger is central to general identity or part of an important role, anger will feel natural and right. Therefore, anger reduction is alien to or a threat to the individual's identity or role. He or she is not motivated to change, and typically resists direct intervention because to do so would be ego or role alien, an attack on something valued. Therefore, intervention should work on reframing anger as identity or role dissonant, and as something that is working to the client's detriment, rather than something positive, so that the client is motivated to change.

There are four ways to intervene to enhance readiness for this type of client. First is an exploration of the consequences of current identity or role conceptualizations. A series of open-ended questions can be illuminating (e.g., Is your anger getting you all of what you want? Are there less angry ways to deal with this and still feel ok? Is this the way you really want to see yourself?). Answering such questions often leads to the identification of unforeseen negative consequences, many of which are role or identity incongruent. In turn, these may motivate change. A variant of these interventions is to analyze long-term outcomes—specifically, how the person would like to have others describe or view him or her in the future. Because most people want to be liked, or at least respected, they might visualize feedback from others at some future date (say at retirement) and be asked how others would describe them generally and in terms of their anger. If reactions were negative, this might provide the motivation for change.

A second kind of intervention focuses on creating dissonance directly within the individual's identity or role constructs. That is, a client may hold other valued role or identity dimensions that are inconsistent with being highly angry. For example, he or she may see him- or herself as kind, loving, giving, tolerant, helpful, strong, smart, and the like. Interventions that reframe anger and aggression within these constructs create dissonance for the individual. Calmer, problem-oriented, negotiative approaches, for example, are reinterpreted as being smarter, stronger, or more tolerant. If the person is going to continue to view him- or herself in these other ways, then anger needs to be changed. Generally, it is suggested that the clinician stay within the client's frame of reference. For example, an angry tirade of a 21-year-old might be juxtaposed with valued concepts of being tough and cool, rather than responsible and mature. It might be suggested that a 5-year-old can cuss someone out, but that to be strong and cool requires being able to keep one's emotions under control and being able to negotiate effectively.

A third set of interventions considers the possibility that there is a lack of alternative role or identity concepts available to the individual. If this is suspected, the therapist can work to increase the range and depth of alternative role models. For example, the individual might interview and observe others and how they approach life situations (e.g., an angry 30-year-old might interview peers to find out how other grown adults handle parents in less angry, abrasive ways). Alternatively, the person might take a class on or read about certain roles (e.g., being a parent or supervisor). He or she might develop detailed pictures and scripts of him- or herself with and without anger, and then visualize these images, assessing how he or she feels about him- or herself in each. Observations of, and discussions of, some TV characters who have better conflict-resolution strategies than the client may be helpful as well.

In addressing role or identity congruent anger, the clinician may encounter and be ready to deal with other self- or role concepts that interfere with taking on a new role or identity. For example, if a client labels him- or herself as *dumb*, *a wuss*, or *rolling over*, he or she is unlikely to try out new concepts. When this is encountered, it is suggested that these concepts be reframed in terms of current, positive concepts as suggested earlier.

Arousal and Expression Are Reinforced

Anger and dysfunctional forms of expression may be maintained because of reinforcement. The form of reinforcement, however, is often quite varied. For example, an angry outburst may be negatively reinforced because it lowers an aversive state of arousal. Moreover, such emotion and behavior are often socially supported (Tavris, 1982) by cultural premises about anger (e.g., "You gotta let off steam," and "Keeping anger bottled up is bad for you"). Anger and its expression can also be positively reinforced. For example, tantrums and intimidating behavior may lead to desired outcomes or wear others down until they give in. A variant on this theme is where others provoke one's anger because it leads to reinforcement for them, as in the case of children who provoke parents knowing that when they cool down they become guilty and give in. The child's provocation is positively reinforced and the parents' anger is strengthened by negative reinforcement in terms of the initial emotional release and subsequently in terms of guilt reduction. Sometimes reinforcement is one step removed. For example, a couple may argue and then become more emotionally intimate, reinforcing the angry interaction as the lead into greater closeness and emotional expressiveness.

Anger and aggression may be normative in deviant subgroups or in cultures where anger and its negative expression are reinforced and condoned by that group. An extreme example is gangs, where anger and violence are strongly sanctioned by the gang. However, many more subtle and frequent examples exist. For example, an 18-year-old may receive considerable peer support for angrily confronting an authority figure at work, and anger may be a part of sanctioned adult peer behavior (e.g., "bitch sessions" about children, spouses, and employers). As long as anger and its expression are reinforced, they are likely to be maintained.

Readiness interventions for these cases should focus on changing the reinforcement structures, making anger less reinforced (see chap. 7, this volume, for further descriptions of anger-reduction techniques). For example, interviews may analyze anger-related consequences to the individual. It is important to help the individual distinguish among all of the outcomes, particularly the difference between short- and long-term fulfillment. Anger may, in fact, improve immediate chances of the individual getting his or her way. However, in the long run, the same expression may lead others to avoid or counterattack the individual. Either way, the person is less likely to meet the goal of long-term relationships or friendships. Another strategy is to directly change the consequences for anger and dysfunctional expression (e.g., time out for and ignoring of tantrums, or use of response cost procedures contingent on dysfunctional levels and expressions of anger). Also, as discussed earlier, distal negative consequences may be visualized to balance the short- and long-term reinforcement structures. Whatever the method, the goal is to alter reinforcement patterns to make anger less attractive and anger management more attractive.

Anger Is Not Immediately Apparent

Anger may be suppressed, denied, intellectualized, or otherwise not immediately obvious. Sometimes as individuals self-monitor they become aware of greater amounts of anger, but for many, anger simply is not part of the presenting problems because it is mixed with and buried in other issues, only becoming apparent as the case moves forward. For example, a client may present with anxiety, depression, interpersonal distance, and mild substance abuse, with anger only surfacing later as the person deals with childhood sexual or physical abuse. Other clients may have learned to deny anger and express it in indirect, often passive-aggressive ways. They are not likely to own anger as a problem, at least not at the beginning of therapy.

The goal for intervention is twofold: getting clients to experience and own the emotion of anger, and assisting them in changing dysfunctional elements. Paradoxically, in the early stages, it is often important to legitimize and normalize anger as an appropriate emotion, one worthy of expression, because many clients are anger phobic. That is, because anger is a taboo emotion in American society, it is important to legitimize the emotion and make it acceptable before it can be explored and have its dysfunctional elements treated.

Anger Is Not My Problem—It's Theirs

Perhaps the most common reason that anger is not owned is because individuals do not see it as belonging to them. Anger is believed to be *caused* by someone or something outside of the person, and therefore they have no responsibility for it. That is, clients' belief structures define situations in irrational (Dryden, 1990; Ellis, 1977) or absolute (Beck, 1976) ways, and then they attribute blame and deflect responsibility for their anger to other people or events. Thus, clients use phrases such as, "*He* made me angry" or "*It* pissed me off." They almost never say, "*I* got myself angry when my spouse came home later than I expected." Rather, the spouse is blamed as the agent or cause of anger. In essence, there is a demand that things *should* be a certain way; when things are not so, the world should change. Therefore, anger and its expression are justified and the source of anger is externalized, hence the locus of anger control and any source of change. As long as people conceptualize anger in this manner, anger is not a personal problem and there is little motivation to change.

If readiness-enhancement strategies are to be effective for these individuals, they need to bring about basic cognitive and attitudinal change. The clinician may begin exploring issues by means of open-ended, Socratic questions. For example, questions such as, Where is your evidence for that? and Why does it have to be that way? may open alternatives other than people's habitual externalizations. Repeated exploration often lays bare egocentric, circular logic (i.e., it should be this way just because I say so). Questions such as, What's another way of looking at that? and Do you know anyone who would look at it differently? may also raise alternative perspectives and interpretations. Clients might also interview others or read about other points of view.

Sayings, bumper stickers, analogies, and metaphors may also be helpful in making philosophical and attributional changes. For example, clients might be introduced to the notion that "Bad things happen to good people," with the direct suggestion that bad things happen to good people like the clients—or, as the bumper sticker says, "Shit happens." The notion of inevitable pain and injustice is put forth directly, especially for clients with low frustration tolerance (Dryden, 1990; Ellis, 1977). A series of Socratic questions then might be employed to challenge assumptions that negativity should not happen to the clients. Some questions may be relatively benign such as, And why shouldn't this happen to you? or perhaps more challenging such as, And who appointed you God? The latter question is excellent, but often frustrates and puzzles clients. It can be pointed out that gods get to dictate, but that humans only get to want; because individuals were dictating how the world should be, they must be gods. If they appointed themselves to the status of a god, then they can unappoint themselves and stay with their wants and preferences. Another useful analogy is the difference between the elegant and practical solution. In the elegant solution, life never again provokes individuals to anger—an ideal, but unrealistic solution. In the practical solution, individuals accept that life has negative events and focus on how to deal with them. That is, life has negativeness, unfairness, and injustice, and individuals cannot start over, but practically can choose how to go on from there.

Another strategy is the paradox of freedom. Individuals might be asked a question such as, Do you always do exactly what others ask of you? The answer is usually emphatically negative. This is followed with a question regarding why not. The response is usually on the order that they have the freedom and the right to make their own choices. They are then asked if other people have the same rights and freedoms, to which they usually reply affirmatively. Then the paradox is pointed out—namely, that the clients are abridging others' freedoms by insisting that they have to do things the clients' way. That is, if freedom is to be protected, others (e.g., husbands, wives, children, teachers, parents, etc.) have to have the right to be wrong and the right to ask and do dumb things. The clients have the right to set limits and hold others accountable, but not the right to impose their will on others and coercively remove their freedoms—freedoms that clients value dearly and jealously guard for themselves. Regardless of the specific interventions employed, the goal is to move clients toward accepting, at least tentatively, that life naturally has painful events. This is not to be denied. However, coping with, making, and enacting painful decisions is more fruitful than angrily trying to force fit the world in a way it will not bend.

In dealing with these issues, clinicians should be prepared to deal with two therapeutic traps. First, angry clients are adept at stating their position and getting others to argue them out of that position. Therapeutically, this leads to many frustrating interactions and impasses, where the therapist cannot persuade the client. The therapist would be wise to avoid this trap by continually keeping the focus on the client and having him or her show the therapist how things follow, not the other way around. Second, because the therapist challenges the client's automatic "shoulds," the client may suggest, directly or indirectly, that the therapist does not believe anything is important or of value, and by implication that he or she can reject the therapist's input. The therapist should address this directly and indicate clearly that this is not the case. Specifically, the therapist supports the client's right to want, prefer, and hold dear anything he or she wishes, and to expend time, money, energy, and other resources in the pursuit of those values. This often leads to a number of successes and a sense of fulfillment, as well as some frustrations and disappointments. However, what is not being supported is the client's right to impose on, demand, or coerce others into meeting his or her definition of what is valued. Thus, values are supported, but angry dictates are not.

INTERVENTIONS FOR ANGER REDUCTION

Even when the therapist is working with a motivated client who owns anger as a personal issue, ideal treatment involves a careful tailoring of strategies to the nature of the client's anger. This section outlines and provides examples of several interventions, and relates them to the portions of the anger arousal and expression sequence to which they have the greatest application.

Self-Monitoring and Enhanced Awareness

Many individuals can slow their reactions and make them less automatic and impulsive if they are aware of the conditions to which they are vulnerable and the ways in which they typically respond. Therefore, interventions to enhance awareness extend self-monitoring activities from assessment (as discussed earlier) and target the entire prompt-appraisal-anger-expression sequence. Increased awareness alone is unlikely to make major, lasting change, but it is important for at least two reasons. First, especially early in therapy, increased awareness provides the client with a rudimentary sense of control. Second, greater sensitivity to the internal and external cues of anger arousal provides the basis for prompting other skills developed in therapy.

Stimulus Control and Response Disruption

These interventions describe a number of strategies that intervene between the prompts of anger and anger itself, or that disrupt anger once it is aroused. Avoidance is one such strategy; the individual avoids provocative situations or conditions that increase the probability of anger reactions, particularly those momentary person characteristics such as fatigue, illness, and so on. Examples include: (a) an angry driver who located a different route home to avoid the provocation of drivers cutting across several lanes of traffic to make certain exits, (b) parents who agreed not to confront their adolescent when his friends were present because nasty scenes always ensued, and (c) a couple that agreed not to discuss finances and other family difficulties after 9:00 p.m. because fatigue increased anger and arguments.

Sometimes provocation cannot be anticipated or avoided. However, the individual can remove him- or herself from the angering situation once provoked. Anger is reduced when the individual is no longer exposed to the provocative cues. For example, the individual might leave the situation without explanation, or, alternatively, he or she could explain why he or she is leaving (e.g., "I'm getting really pissed now. If I continue this discussion, I'm going to say something that I'll regret. I'm going for a walk, and when I get back, we can talk about it"). Social systems, such as schools or families, where anger is repetitive may negotiate and legitimize the taking of time outs. For example, a family might agree that anyone in the family could take a time out at any time, without explanation, simply by asking for it. Such time outs or removal from provocation can be very effective. However, the therapist should make sure that the client can give him- or herself permission to take a time out, does not hold attitudes that would interfere with taking a time out (e.g., labeling him- or herself as *weak* or *giving in*), and has sufficient practice taking time outs to have high skill and efficacy expectations.

Anger may also be suppressed or disrupted through the contingent presentation of aversive stimuli. For example, a businessman who tended to make angry, aggressive comments in staff meetings learned to place a pen or pencil between his thumb and index finger and squeeze it to the point of pain when he felt angry and had the urge to make derisive comments. A woman who ruminated angrily about her ex-husband placed a rubber band around her left wrist and snapped it firmly when she started to brood about him. Of course, not all aversive stimuli have to be physical. For example, a conservative businessman who, when angry, made cutting, sarcastic remarks to his employees agreed to place a campaign button of a liberal candidate on his shirt for 30 minutes if he started to make such comments. Finally, a client mentioned earlier visualized either his coronary arteries occluding or fear and intimidation in his children whenever he had the urge to engage in angry yelling.

At other times, clients can engage in behavior that disrupts anger because it is incompatible with it. Such behavior provides time for the individual to collect him- or herself and consider alternative ways of reacting, and may remove the person from angry prompts. For example, an individual might employ thought stopping to disrupt angry ruminations or engage in anger-interruptive behavior, such as going for a walk, taking a shower, or planning grocery lists. A final example of this type of intervention is that of either seeking a delay in responding or finding an alternative form of response. For example, a client might indicate that he or she needs time to think the issues over, to check out additional information, or to pull thoughts together before responding to someone who angered him or her. During the delay, the individual has the opportunity to calm down and plan for constructive action. The angered individual may also request the opportunity for an alternative form of response, such as an individual who communicated by written summaries rather than impulsive angry comments in meetings, or by letter rather than by phone when angry. In these examples, the alternative response tends to be slower and provides for more thought and control, often with an opportunity for editing or changing the response.

Although stimulus-control and response-disruption strategies are rarely sufficient, they can give clients some easily implemented strategies for anger management. This can be especially helpful early in therapy, when a quick boost in self-efficacy is welcome. Many of these strategies can be elicited by asking clients what they typically do to manage their anger successfully, and then extending and tailoring these strategies to problematic situations.

Palliatives

These involve clients engaging in mental, emotional, or behavioral activities that reduce arousal and/or increase the tolerance for and endurance of difficult, anger-engendering situations. As with many other strategies, they are rarely sufficient in and of themselves. However, they increase the capacity to endure angering situations and often, at least modestly, cognitively reframe the situation and prepare individuals for coping action.

Many palliatives can be provided through self-instruction or written reminders. Client examples include: "And this too will pass"; "Vietnam was hell, and I survived. I certainly can handle one grumpy boss"; "She's just doing her job. It's in a teenager's job description that they are supposed to try to drive their parents crazy. My mom put up with me, and I can put up with her"; "Who will know or care about this in a week, anyway?"; "Hang in there. There will be a better day. It always sunshines after it rains"; "This is nothing compared to my open heart surgery. Just relax and cope with it"; "This is disturbing, but not dangerous"; "This is just like the barn. Shovel it out and get on with it, rather than spending lots of time complaining about the smell"; "They have a right to be wrong. Boy, are they ever exercising their rights, but it is their right to be that way."

Other palliatives are enacted as mental images, often with metaphorical meaning. For example, one young adult, responding explosively to comments and put-downs from peers, imagined he was a turtle and their barbs simply bounced off his shell. Moreover, he viewed the turtle as a strong animal who could take his protection with him anywhere he went. Another client visualized herself as a large rock in a local river. Provocation was viewed like the murky water of the spring runoff, yet she, like the rock, was solid and firmly anchored to the riverbed, not being swept away, but enduring and surviving the turgid torrents until the crystal, sparkling water of late summer returned. A final example includes a visualized analogy of anger being like a fire. The client indicated that a fire could burn the house down or warm it on a cold day. She visualized a calm, warm, glowing fire in her living room on a winter's day.

Other palliatives are in the form of calm, anger-incompatible activities. For example, one mother visualized one of two images: listening to the rain on the roof when she was a youngster, or smelling rain on the fields at her grandfather's farm. Either allowed her to endure walking a colicky child. Other activities might include things such as making a favorite cup of tea, taking a long, warm bath, or, as one client did, walking barefoot on a thickly carpeted floor because it relaxed and calmed him. The goal here is not to provide an endless list of palliatives, but to suggest that the therapist work to identify simple self-talk, images, and activities that allow clients a degree of calmness and capacity to endure frustrating events (see chap. 7, this volume, for further analysis of the use of palliatives).

Relaxation Coping Skills

If affective/physiological arousal is a significant part of the diagnostic picture (e.g., frequent, intense, and/or lengthy arousal, or anger-related psychophysiological disorders), a relaxation intervention is likely to be appropriate. Relaxation interventions directly target heightened emotional and physiological arousal, and indirectly may influence other response domains. This is so because the individual is able to think more clearly and initiate problem solving and coping when calm, perhaps developing greater self-efficacy and enhanced secondary appraisals of coping over time.

Initial research on relaxation interventions for anger reduction (Novaco, 1975) suggested that relaxation was minimally effective. However, the results for relaxation in this study may have been compromised by issues of intervention design and implementation. Subsequent research (Deffenbacher, Demm, & Brandon, 1986; Deffenbacher & Stark, 1992; Hazaleus & Deffenbacher, 1986) showed that anxiety-management training (Suinn, 1990; Suinn & Deffenbacher, 1988) could be adapted successfully to anger reduction.

This intervention typically takes about eight sessions, with added sessions as needed. The first three sessions provide: (a) a self-management treatment rationale; (b) enhanced personal awareness through self-monitoring and attention to physiological tension when practicing relaxation; (c) progressive relaxation training; (d) training in four relaxation coping skills: (i) relaxation without tension (focusing on and relaxing muscles without tensing), (ii) personal relaxation imagery (visualization of specific, relaxing memory), (iii) breathing-cued relaxation (relaxing more deeply on each of three to five slow, deep breaths), and (iv) cue-controlled relaxation (relaxing with each repetition of a word or phrase paired previously with relaxation [see Suinn & Deffenbacher, 1988, for details]; and (e) development of two moderately angering scenes (approximately 50 on a 100-point scale of anger arousal). Homework involves self-monitoring, with attention to internal cognitive-emotional-physiological characteristics of anger arousal and daily practice of progressive relaxation and relaxation coping skills. The fourth session initiates active self-management of anger arousal within sessions. The client visualizes an anger scene and experiences anger arousal for approximately 30 seconds. Then the scene is cleared, and the therapist assists the client in initiation of one or more relaxation skills. When the client signals relaxation (i.e., anger reduction), the other anger scene is presented in a similar fashion. This process is repeated several times. Homework involves development of new anger scenes and in vivo application of relaxation coping skills for anger reduction.

Initially, clients are cautioned not to expect anger reduction every time, but are told that competence will come with practice. Over subsequent sessions, anger intensity of scenes is increased (about 10–15 units of anger per session), and the degree of therapist assistance with relaxation coping skills is faded. Homework also extends relaxation coping skills to other negative emotional states, such as anxiety and depression. Scenes involving other dysfunctional emotions can be included as needed to facilitate and consolidate transfer.

If relaxation is to be used, it should be employed early in therapy. It fits readily with many clients' conceptualizations of anger, seems to increase rapport and the therapeutic alliance, and seems to reduce resistance and reactance to the early introduction of cognitive change strategies (Deffenbacher & Lynch, in press). Moreover, relaxation can be easily integrated with other interventions such as cognitive restructuring (Deffenbacher, Story, Brandon, Hogg, & Hazaleus, 1988; Deffenbacher & Stark, 1992; Deffenbacher, Story, Stark, Hogg, & Brandon, 1987; Deffenbacher, McNamara, Stark, & Sabadell, 1990a; Deffenbacher, Thwaites, Wallace, & Oetting, 1994) and social skills (Deffenbacher, McNamara, Stark, & Sabadell, 1990b).

Cognitive Restructuring

Problematic anger, for the most part, is not a function of the external or internal prompts of anger per se, but of the ways in which the individual codes these cues and makes meaning of them (Beck, 1976; Dryden, 1990; Ellis, 1977). That is, many events naturally and appropriately elicit low- to moderate-level emotions, such as irritation, frustration, annoyance, and mild to moderate anger. Goal-directed behavior is thwarted, promises are broken, jobs and opportunities are lost, relationships are terminated unwillingly, illness happens, and people die, to name just a few. However, cognitive processing of these events often makes bad situations worse and elevates anger to problematic levels. That is, the individual construes these events in anger-engendering ways and then responds to the emotional meaning of this constructed reality. The following is a list of common cognitive biases and errors in anger.

1 Overestimation and underestimation. Angry individuals tend to overestimate the probability of negative events and underestimate personal and other coping resources (i.e., primary appraisal processes are biased toward identifying threatening, trespassing, or frustrating events, whereas secondary appraisals underestimate capacities to problem solve and cope). The antidote is learning to engage in accurate estimation, in which individuals can assay negative and more positive and benign information, and more fully assess their personal and environmental resources, as well as shortcomings.

2 Misattributions and single explanations. Angry individuals tend to jump to egocentric, often highly personalized conclusions and explanations, and then respond angrily as if these interpretations are true, regardless of their veracity. Often these attributions involve ideas of injustice, intentionality, controllability, and blameworthiness (see Eckhardt & Deffenbacher, chap. 2, this volume), which further elevate anger. The antidote is multiplicative thinking, in which individuals entertain a number of possible alternative explanations and attributions, and then assess their veracity.

3 Polarized conceptualization. In making this cognitive error, angry individuals code events in dichotomous concepts (e.g., good–bad, right–wrong, strong–weak, winners–losers). Any evidence that disconfirms the positive polarity automatically triggers the extreme negative coding and the anger associated with it. The antidote is continuous thinking, in which individuals learn to employ qualifying adjectives, adverbs, and phrases that introduce the shades of gray and complexity to their world, as well as attenuation of anger.

4 Overgeneralization. Angry individuals tend to abstract broad, sweeping conclusions that go way beyond the details of specific events. These conclusions are often reduced to labels that are applied to people's self, others, events, or time (e.g., *dumb, worthless, always this way,* etc.), and the people respond to the angry meaning of the label, rather than the specifics. The antidote is for these individuals to become more discriminant thinkers and to focus on and limit conclusions, emotions, and behaviors to the specifics of a given time and place.

5 Inflammatory thinking. This cognitive distortion appears to have particular relevance to anger, and involves labeling events or people in highly negative, often obscene or nonsensical terms (e.g., *hairball, creep, asshole, bitch,* etc.). Anger escalates as individuals respond to the emotive meaning of the term. The antidote is for individuals to define their terms and recode events in realistically negative ways.

6 Catastrophizing. Individuals code events in highly negative, extreme ways (e.g., awful, terrible, devastating, can't stand it, etc.) that extend well beyond realistic negativity. The antidote is learning to code events in realistically negative ways (e.g., sad, disappointing, irritating, annoying, frustrating, etc.).

7 Demanding and commanding. These people elevate their preferences and desires to moral dictates and commandments of self and others (i.e., things should, ought to, have to, gotta be certain ways). Anger eventuates if these commandments are or might be broken. The antidote is engaging in preferential thinking, in which people hold important wants, desires, preferences, and values; work hard to pursue their preferences and values; and accept and experience the natural frustrations and disappointments that go with those not being met.

Cognitive change strategies target anger-engendering information-processing and cognitive constructs, most specifically primary and secondary appraisal processes, enduring ways of coding the world, and cognitive components of the anger response. Anger is reduced as the emotive meaning of the client's world is reconstructed from highly angering to more appropriate levels. It should be noted, however, that cognitive change, or any other strategy for that matter, does not necessarily lead to a positive world. To the contrary, it is usually aimed at helping the client not make a bad situation worse. External or internal reality may be legitimately bad, but when the individual is not inordinately angry, he or she is in a better position to cope. The individual may still have to deal with frustrating events, make and enact difficult decisions, and/or accept painful realities. These are not positive, but are natural developmental and existential tasks and realities—tasks and realities that are sidetracked by unnecessary anger.

Cognitive restructuring involves five overlapping steps or therapeutic tasks, with multiple strategies employed at each step (Beck & Emery, 1985; Deffenbacher & Lynch, in press; Dryden, 1990; Meichenbaum, 1985). The first step—enhancing awareness of the situational and experiential elements of anger—is achieved by exploring and monitoring the self-talk, imagery, and memory elements of anger in ways described previously. Cognitive therapy, however, often involves a second step not necessary with some other interventions—namely, that of having clients accept the influence of cognitive processes. That is, clients may become more aware of cognitive elements, but not necessarily understand their influence. For many angry individuals, anger is something that just wells up from within and "happens," and is quickly attributed to external events. In either case, cognition is seen as having little to do with anger. Searching for naturally occurring or generating contrasts in experience in the same situation is usually the best way to have clients begin to understand the influence of cognitive processes. For example, in going over self-monitoring homework, the therapist might note and ask clients about why dealing with a situation caused high anger on one day, but was relatively easy on another. Sometimes significant situational differences exist, but often clients will indicate that they had a different perspective on it. This leads one to explore the notion that how one thinks about situations makes a difference. The therapist might model aloud a way of thinking about events that is very different from the clients', and then ask clients how they would feel if this were the only way in which they were thinking. This, too, provides a contrast in emotional and behavioral reactions. Hyperbole may also be helpful. That is, the therapist thinks aloud in a way that is dramatically different from the clients' experiences, and that would lead the clients to experience positive feelings or relief. Although it does not fit the clients' realities, it may help make the point that perspective (cognitive processes) makes a difference, and thereby open the door to cognitive factors. In group therapy, the therapist can highlight naturally occurring differences to the same event and assist clients in outlining why individuals respond differently. Because the situation is the same, cognitive elements rise to the fore. What is needed is for the clients to understand and accept that cognitive processes influence anger, and, therefore, that changing them *will* make a difference. Without this, cognitive change often stalls out and is resisted because the clients do not know why they are doing things that do not make sense to them and that challenge basic attitudes and premises.

The third therapeutic task involves identifying and clarifying the nature of the cognitive distortions and biases. A basic strategy is the use of Socratic questions that help clients explore the limits and implications of their thinking without increasing too much reactance. For example, questions like, Where's your evidence for that? or How does that follow? may lead clients to explore dichotomous thinking, overgeneralization, or misestimation of probabilities. A series of, And then what would happen?-type questions often exposes that clients *can* handle what is labeled as *catastrophic*. A question like, And what's another way of looking at that? tends to elicit a variety of alternative perspectives and attributions, which can be juxtaposed to the clients' singular attributions. Behavioral experiments, in which clients engage in behavior that may challenge client assumptions, are often illuminating. For example, a man who reacted angrily to perceived criticism agreed, for a 4-day period, to ask others what they meant. This provided him with a variety of interpretations other than they were being hostile and critical. A few sessions later, he agreed, for a 1-week period, to admit mistakes, even when he had not made them, to see if others would automatically take advantage of and disrespect him. In fact, he found they liked and respected him better and did not take wholesale advantage of him. A college student who was angrily preoccupied with a young woman who terminated their relationship took on the assignment of interviewing 10 male and 10 female college students, who had suffered relationship losses, about how they thought and coped with these losses. This provided a range of alternative ways of thinking, rather than that she was responsible for ending his life's meaning. As noted previously, cognitive modeling can be extended. The therapist might think aloud in less demanding ways, and might ask the clients how angry they would feel if they were thinking in this manner. This provides an alternative way of thinking and a stimulus to probe the difference in thinking styles.

Role reversal may also be adapted. For example, the therapist may ask clients to help him or her as if he or she was a good friend talking about a problem. A problem is picked that taps the same general themes as the clients, but that is dissimilar in specific content. As the therapist portrays a problem, the clients begin to challenge the therapist's thinking. After several exchanges, the therapist breaks roles and contrasts the clients' thinking in role play, with their typical thinking in similar situations. Bibliotherapy and popular media may be used, wherein characters of importance to the clients are used as an alternative frame of reference. For example, one angry adolescent who was a "Star Trek freak" was repeatedly asked how Spock would think about the situation, which provided a more reasoned, rational perspective. Regardless of the method employed, the goal is clarification and understanding of the errors and anger-engendering biases.

Understanding, however, is rarely sufficient. The fourth therapeutic task is to convert the insights and understandings gained in the prior stage into concrete verbal and visual responses, which counteract and replace prior automatic anger-engendering cognitions. Over time, these are refined into specific scripts, images, principles, and metaphors with which clients can lower anger and approach difficulties in a more accepting and problem-oriented manner.

The fifth step involves rehearsal and transfer activities. Repeated practice and application is necessary if clients are to have a reliable repertoire of cognitive responses with which to counteract their usual and habitual ways of processing the world. Within sessions, cognitive responses can be rehearsed much in the manner described for relaxation procedures. That is, clients imagine anger-provoking events, become angry, and then employ alternative cognitions to counteract and lower anger. Over time, the level of anger elicited can be increased, the type of situation can be changed, and the level of therapist assistance can be lowered. Role plays and other behavioral-enactment procedures can be used. They can be stopped at different places, and new cognitions can be rehearsed to handle anger arousal. If video equipment is available, recording the role play or enacted sequence, stopping the tape at places where the clients were angered, and rehearsing alternative cognitions are also effective strategies. Homework assignments and contracted encounters should be used to consolidate new cognitive skills in the external world. Although the means of practice and transfer may vary from client to client, the importance of this practice cannot be overemphasized.

Several studies (Achmon, Granek, Golomb, & Hart, 1989; Deffenbacher et al., 1988; Hazaleus & Deffenbacher, 1986; Moon & Eisler, 1983; Novaco, 1975) have shown that cognitive restructuring can reduce anger significantly. Moreover, cognitive change procedures can be easily combined with other interventions, such as relaxation (Deffenbacher et al., 1987, 1988, 1990a, 1994; Novaco, 1975), time out, and skill building (Deffenbacher et al., 1990b). However, because there may be initial resistance and reactance to cognitive procedures when introduced in the first few sessions (Deffenbacher & Lynch, in press), other procedures, such as relaxation, should precede cognitive ones by two or three sessions. This seems to minimize reactance without any substantive loss.

Silly Humor

Silly humor probably could be considered a cognitive intervention, but it appears useful enough with anger to merit separate discussion. This intervention involves having clients reconceptualize things in a silly, humorous manner. Anger is reduced as an anger-incompatible emotion is generated, and as the client gains cognitive distance and reconceptualization. Thus, humor addresses cognitive, feeling, and physiological elements of anger. Use of humor roughly follows the steps of cognitive restructuring. First, clients are introduced to silly, humorous ways of looking at provocative situations. Humorous ideas are honed into specific self-talk and images that are then rehearsed within sessions and in vivo for anger reduction.

Several humorous interventions have proved clinically applicable. Concretization of terms and concepts is helpful, especially with inflammatory and other colorful labels. First, clients are asked to define and describe their terms concretely. This is often humorous enough, but clients are then asked to draw pictures of their terms. For example, one client kept referring to others as *incompetent shitheads*. An operationalization of this led to the description of individuals whose heads were covered and filled with fecal material, which, on reflection, accounted for their incompetence. He then drew a cartoon-type picture of this, and practiced substituting this image any time he said the words aloud or to himself. Such humorous imagery may also support other cognitive changes, such as drawing oneself as a god in dealing with absolutistic demandingness, or a vision of "all hell breaking loose" in dealing with catastrophization. Humorous reattribution of cause and motivation may be useful in reducing hostile and malevolent personalizations and interpretations. For example, others' inconsiderate driving might be attributed to them having had cases of diarrhea, another's forgetfulness might be attributed to being "a little brain damaged," or another's grumpy, depressive characteristics might be attributed to being severely constipated. In all three examples, attributions are moved away from highly personalized, intentional assaults to more benign, humorous explanations. Hyperbolous conspiracy, too, may prove of assistance, especially for personalized attributions. For example, one individual said that her co-workers did things to frustrate and anger her, and to make it so she could not get her work done. When asked if work was well organized and efficient, she responded with an incredulous and emphatic, "No." The therapist then puzzled aloud his confusion: To frustrate and anger her so efficiently would take a great deal of attention and organization (e.g., meetings, planning, monitoring to make sure plans went well, etc.). The client began to laugh, and reframed that they were just people trying to do their jobs under pressure and poor conditions. The notion of *organized conspiracies* was then used to confront other sensed intrusions, and to provide an alternative perspective.

Although humor is not always a recommended intervention in psychotherapy, it has proved useful with angry clients, not as a whole answer, but as a partial one in many cases. In recommending humor, three points should be noted. First, humor should be of the silly variety. Hostile and sarcastic humor have little place because they encourage anger and an indirect means of expressing it, thereby maintaining many of the underlying hostile attitudes and beliefs. Second, clients should not be encouraged to laugh off their problems and engage in a kind of humorous denial. To the contrary, they should be encouraged to engage in silly humor to take a brief cognitive step backward, perhaps laughing at themselves and their cognitions, to reduce their anger and then approach the situation again. The individuals may still be frustrated and face problems, but hopefully a humorous relief has left them in a better place from which to cope. Finally, humor is somewhat risky. Some clients feel laughed at or put down when humor is introduced. Therefore, it is suggested that humor be introduced a few sessions into therapy, when the therapeutic alliance is strongly established and/or when the therapist has assessed that the clients have a sense of humor, especially in regards to themselves. Nonetheless, angry clients are, as a group, durable and not fragile. Even if they are offended by an attempt at silly humor, their anger at the therapist can be used as an immediate example of anger, from which they can identify and change the anger-engendering cognitions and images they experienced when humor was introduced.

Skill Enhancement

Skill building interventions generally target forms of anger expression. However, as is suggested later, there may be other important targets as well. If individuals can handle provocative situations with greater skill, anger is reduced or prevented as escalating conflict and aggression are avoided. Over time, secondary appraisal may be affected as individuals view themselves as more able to cope with angering situations. For example, social and communication skill approaches have proved effective for general anger reduction (Deffenbacher et al., 1987, in press; Moon & Eisler, 1983). All kinds of skills may be relevant (e.g., parenting, budgeting and financial planning, marital communication, supervisory skills, or technical skills), depending on the nature of dysfunctional anger expression and the sources of anger. If skill deficits are encountered and addressed in therapy, generally some type of behavioral rehearsal program will be appropriate to develop a range of flexible behaviors and principles that are transferred to the problematic situations. The therapist may also wish to assist clients in locating appropriate classes and training programs in their environment because not all skills need to be trained in therapy.

Problem-solving skills may also be relevant for some angry clients (Moon & Eisler, 1983). Some angry individuals are behaviorally skilled, but do not appear proficient in general problem-solving skills, with which to assess situations in a calm way and generate less angry, aggressive modes of expression, which they already possess. Problem-solving training helps these clients lower their anger by developing a series of cognitive strategies for approaching and defining provocations as problems and then generating, evaluating, and implementing more effective, calm behaviors. Problem solving is discussed, modeled, rehearsed within sessions, and then transferred for in vivo application in the same general manner as cognitive restructuring.

Effective problem-solving steps might include the following: (a) coding provocation and frustrations as hassles and problems to be solved, rather than awful and horrible events to be attacked (i.e., the development of a general attitude or set with which to code events and to initiate problem solving); (b) problem identification (i.e., asking oneself questions such as, What's the problem here? or Ok, I am frustrated. Let me figure out what the problem is so I can focus on that. Ok, so where is it coming from?, to identify and begin defining the nature of the problem); (c) breaking the problem down (i.e., many provocations are either a complex of issues or a series of separate problems that have not been separated by self-instructions, such as, Break it down. I can handle the little ones much better; It's beginning to feel overwhelming, and that means that I need to break it down. Get a piece of paper and make a list of things that are going on); (d) assessing the source of the problem and identifying resources (i.e., a step in which the individual tries to identify the sources of the problem and potential resources through asking him- or herself questions such as, Ok, what are the things that I need to do in order to handle this? or What are my resources to cope with this? Can I get anyone to help?); (e) solution generation (i.e., a step in which the person generates one or more solutions to which he or she can commit action that may be reflected in self-talk, such as, Ok, now that I have thought it over, it looks like the best thing to try is . . .); and (f) solution implementation with recycling as necessary (i.e., an action-oriented step, where the individual implements a decision and takes action via self-instructions, such as, Ok, let's try that out. If it works, great. If not, I'll step back and figure something else out; or Just stay focused on trying. . ., rather than getting all pissed off. So my first step is . . .).

Two other problem-solving steps may be relevant to angry clients because they often get stuck in ineffective problem solving, thus continuing an angry attack when a strategic retreat is in order. They may benefit from: (a) ultimate control and escape self-instruction (i.e., the ability to identify escape routes and take control via a time out by self-instructions such as, Bottom line, I'm in control. If I can't handle it any other way, I will walk. I am not going to get all pissed off and do something dumb this time; or Look, athletic teams take time outs. That's what I need to do, take a time out and let a cooler head prevail), and (b) termination when no good solutions are apparent (i.e., self-instruction to abort attention and move away, rather than the angry, stubborn pursuit of a frustrating event, such as, Looks like I am stuck. No use getting all pissed about something I can't solve. So, let me turn my attention to . . . ; or Can't figure this one out. That's not the end of the world. Let it sit for awhile and come back to it later if that makes sense).

A third set of skills that may need strengthening is self-reinforcement and self-efficacy. Some angry clients, even when they are making substantive change, do not support their coping efforts and positive effects. Anger continues or drifts back to pretreatment levels of arousal and forms of expression because the clients do not support changes. Developing and employing realistic patterns of self-reinforcement and self-efficacious appraisals are often helpful. Gains and changes are discussed and integrated into self-appraisal sets that provide realistic, positive expectations in the future, support of success, support for trying to improve, and attributions of change to self. For example, clients might think things such as, "Good. I was appropriately angry and expressed my frustrations, but did not get all pissed and yell and scream," or "I am getting better at this anger management stuff. I just said, 'To hell with it' and was able to focus on work, rather than being pissed all afternoon that she was out with someone else."

A fourth set of skills is much more speculative, but both the author and Dryden (1990) observed that the hedonic tone or balance of many angry clients' lives is decidedly tipped toward the negative. That is, their lives seem to have a great many problems, hassles, and stresses, and relatively few sources of joy, pleasure, and happiness. If this is the case, the momentary emotional-physiological state is much more likely to be aversive, which in turn increases the probability of anger (Berkowitz, 1990). Some of the skills described earlier, such as cognitive restructuring, relaxation, and time out, may be appropriate for dealing with aversive conditions. However, the therapist may also want to work toward increasing the rate of positive events, and may wish to consult the cognitive–behavioral literatures on the treatment of marital dysfunction and depression for suggestions that might be adapted.

CONCLUSION

This chapter set out to address ideal treatment of adult anger problems. A review of the chapter, however, might suggest that it is nothing more than a list of issues and strategies, not a singular ideal approach to the treatment of anger. But that is exactly the point. No two angry individuals are likely to share exactly the same anger problems. What is needed is a client who owns that he or she has a personal problem with anger and who wants help for that problem. If the client does not conceptualize him- or herself as having a problem, no matter what others may think or suggest, attempting to treat anger is likely to be a waste of time. Instead, intervention should focus on enhancing client readiness. If such interventions are successful, the client may be ready to move toward anger reduction. If not, therapeutic time and energy will not have been misplaced. Once the client identifies anger as a personal issue and desires to change it, strategies for anger management become appropriate. Once again, however, angry clients do not all need the same monolithic treatment. Instead, careful initial and ongoing, collaborative assessment should provide a detailed picture of each client's anger, a picture to which varying strategies can be targeted to different elements of the client's anger issues. This is the art and science of the ideal treatment of adult anger problems.

Chapter 10

Ideal Treatment Package for Children and Adolescents with Anger Disorders

Eva L. Feindler

C.W. Post College/Long Island University

Although angry outbursts, often accompanied by aggressive behaviors, are hallmarks of early childhood, most children outgrow these displays and learn more socially acceptable expressions of dissatisfaction and frustration (Loeber, Lahey, & Thomas, 1991). Clinicians, however, anecdotally report that many referrals for child and adolescent psychotherapy are related to patterns of oppositional behavior, aversive verbal assaults, and aggression toward family members and peers. These behaviors are usually accompanied by intense emotional displays of anger, resentment, or bitterness, by both the children and the parents. The anger and aggression create extreme personal and family distress, and necessarily become the focus of clinical intervention. In fact, disruptive behavior disorders (including attention deficit hyperactivity, conduct, and oppositional defiant disorders) represent the largest group of referrals for psychotherapy intervention (Abikoff & Klein, 1992).

Following a brief case description of one such clinical referral, this chapter presents an anger-management intervention package designed to teach appropriate anger expression and to reduce aggressive temper outbursts. Of course, no package is truly ideal in terms of the knowledge that will be gained in the years ahead. However, it does represent a state-of-the-art approach to these kinds of difficulties in children and adolescents.

CASE DESCRIPTION

Erica was a 13-year-old, second child of college-educated parents. The parents' marriage was in great distress, and separation was imminent. A pleasant, sociable, and slightly overweight early adolescent, Erica performed above average academically and had no reported difficulties in school. Recently, however, interactions with peers had become increasingly volatile. In addition to the early teenage "fickleness" of friendships and the competition for male attention, Erica seemed to react excessively to teasing, name calling, gossip, and social ostracism that occurred frequently in her shifting peer group. When provoked, Erica would curse and scream at other girls in school, and on several occasions she pushed or pulled hair to "get back" at someone she perceived as being against her.

Following a history of contrariness and stubborn opposition to parental directives, Erica was becoming increasingly difficult for her mother to manage without the consistent support of Erica's father. With her self-centered adolescent perspective, Erica had begun to use her parents' deteriorating marital situation to her own advantage. She made unreasonable demands of one parent, displaying "temper tantrum-like" behavior when her demands were not met, and, finally, manipulating the other parent to get her way. This coercive behavior chain had escalated a number of times from verbal "freshness" and cursing to physical attacks on her mother. Her anger and aggression occurred when she did not receive desired material objects, when foods she desired were not prepared, and when her mother refused to complete academic or household tasks for her. Another escalating chain occurred when Erica apparently lied to her mother, about having taken money or clothing, and her mother confronted her. Erica responded with aversive verbalizations directed toward her mother's attempt to "catch her in a lie."

Erica's parents and older brother responded to her tantrums with screaming and threats of their own, until someone either was hurt or left the house. In most cases, Erica's outbursts were reinforced by having her demands met (in the short run, at least). Thus, she felt justified in fighting for what she wanted, and she saw herself as the victor. However, long-term consequences included continued anger and resentment on the part of all family members, deterioration in family communication and problem solving, and subtle emotional rejection in family affective relationships.

Erica denied that she had any difficulties, and maintained that she was simply responding to the "uncalled for" provocation of others. Nevertheless, she agreed to therapy in order to have "someone to talk to about the divorce." Although the marital situation reinforced a distorted attribution of blame for Erica's negative behavior patterns, the therapist accepted this initial premise for treatment so as to establish a working alliance (this pattern of denial, attribution of blame, and a requirement that the therapist accept the initial presentation to establish a therapeutic alliance have been discussed in detail by DiGiuseppe, chap. 8, this volume).

DIAGNOSTIC ISSUES

The case presented previously presents some interesting diagnostic issues for the clinician consulting the *DSM-IV* classification system (American Psychiatric Association, 1994). Erica's symptom picture captures the essential feature of oppositional defiant disorder (ODD): a pattern of negativistic and hostile and defiant behavior, without the more serious violations of basic rights, which are seen in conduct disorder. Other criteria for ODD include: argumentative with adults, frequent temper loss, swearing, often angry and resentful, defiance of adult rules and requests, and a tendency to blame others for own mistakes or difficulties (American Psychiatric Association, 1994). The manifestations of ODD are more prevalent in the presence of people who are familiar to the child, such as family members, and other social relationships may be affected because the hostile and oppositional attitudes are manifest in a number of environments (Samuels & Sikorsky, 1990).

It is well known that diagnostic decision making with children and adolescents is difficult. According to Kazdin (1988), there are sources of ambiguity in symptom descriptions for externalizing behavior disorders in children, as well as considerable overlap of criteria across such disorders. Further, given the developmentally related cognitive and behavior changes across the age span from childhood to adolescence, the identification of stable disorders is difficult, and normative data are not readily available. Thus, the wide range of manifestations of anger impulses and aggressive behaviors across ages, diagnostic categories, and gender makes a clear diagnosis difficult.

A review of externalizing behavior indicates that anger and aggression are associated features in all categories (Samuels & Sikorsky, 1990). For example, attention deficit/hyperactivity disorder includes: not listening when spoken to, not following through on chores, reluctance to engage in tasks that require effort, forgetfulness and easily distracted, fidgets, leaves seat in school without permission, doesn't await his or her turn, interrupts and intrudes, and so on. Similarly, features of conduct disorder include: threatening and cruel behavior, bullying, manipulation of others, intimidation and confrontational behaviors, disobeyance of parental rules, and so on.

Studies have indicated that conduct disorder and ODD are strongly and developmentally related, but also different, in that ODD shows specific and high co-morbidity with attention deficit disorder (ADD; Loeber, Lahey, & Thomas, 1991). Results from an analysis of disruptive childhood behavior disorders (see Fig. 10.1; Lahey et al., 1990) emphasize four clear behavior patterns (property violations, aggression, status violations, and oppositional behavior) across two dimensions (destructive–nondestructive and overt–covert), and may help in the development of subtypes for these diagnostic categories. The issues of co-morbidity and diagnostic dilemmas are highlighted by applying this grid to the case presented in this chapter. Although primarily falling into Category D, Erica also manifests behavior problems in each of the other areas.

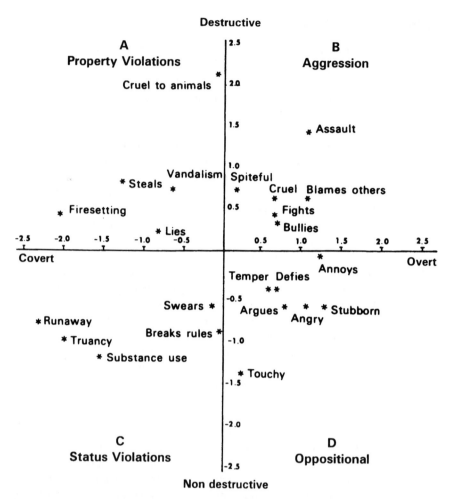

Figure 10.1 Results of the meta-analysis of factor analyses of disruptive child behavior (Lahey, Frick, Loeber, Tannenbaum, Van Horn, & Christ, 1990). Copyright is retained by Benjamin B. Lahey.

One additional consideration in regard to manifestations of anger, aggression, and diagnostic fit for children and adolescents concerns the criteria for depression and dysthymia, which also come to mind in the case presented. According to Samuels and Sikorsky (1990), depression in children and adolescents may be manifested by negativistic, aggressive behaviors, lack of cooperation, irritable mood, and an increased sensitivity to criticism or rejection. Features of dysthymia include: difficulties with social relationships, and reacting with shyness or anger toward peers and adults. Unfortunately, diagnostic criteria involving the frequency and intensity of these features are not explicit. However, when the criteria are coupled with Erica's low self-esteem, perceived extreme loss regarding the deteriorating marital situation, and pessimistic view of the world, she might also be diagnosed by some clinicians as having a mild depressive disorder. Here, then, anger and aggression are key features in the diagnosis of an internalizing disorder. Thus, as Eckhardt and Deffenbacher note in chapter 2, given the complexities of the symptom picture, it may be timely to propose a new diagnostic category having to do only with anger and aggression.

In summary, the following represents the best fit, working diagnosis according to *DSM-IV* for the case presented:

AXIS I—313.81 Oppositional defiant disorder
AXIS II—V 71.09 No diagnosis or AXIS II
AXIS III—None
AXIS IV—Problems with primary support group: impending parental separation
AXIS V—Global assessment of functioning: Current: 55, Past year: 60

ASSESSMENT ISSUES AND METHODS

We now examine assessment issues to: (a) quantify and evaluate pretreatment functioning, and (b) develop an effective intervention package. Regrettably, it is well known that diagnostic categorization neither guides treatment nor predicts response to treatment. Rather, it simply helps determine the presence or absence of a disorder (Kazdin, 1988). Of greater clinical utility is a multimethod approach to assessment, which includes different sources of information, various assessment methods, and an examination of functioning in different domains.

Attempts to objectively measure anger in children and adolescents have been complicated by difficulties in defining the anger construct, and by the complex interrelatedness of anger and aggression (Finch, Saylor, & Nelson, 1987; Kassinove & Sukhodolsky, chap. 1, this volume). Thus, a variety of methods is used.

In the assessment of ODD, parent and teacher ratings of disruptive behaviors are typically gathered. Subscales of aggression are available for the clinician from the Achenbach Child Behavior Checklist (Achenbach, 1991), the Louisville School Behavior Checklist (Miller, 1981), the Missouri Children's Behavior Checklist (Sines, Pauker, Sines, & Owens, 1969), and others. Standardized scores and norms are available, affording the clinician the opportunity to assess relative levels of the constructs and of associated behaviors. However, acts of adolescent anger and aggression are often subtle, verbal, and *covert*. Thus, parents and teachers may not be able to detect changes relevant for the treatment goal of increased self-control and/or elimination of anger and aggression.

What may be most useful to the clinician are the eight-item subscales of the Revised Behavior Problem Checklist (RBPC; Quay & Peterson, 1987), which distinguishes between and focuses on both reactive and proactive anger and aggression. Parents and/or significant others simply respond to the presence of the items presented in Table 10.1 (described in Dodge, Price, Bachorowski, & Newman, 1990).

In the case presented earlier, Erica's parents were asked to respond to this checklist. The mother and father both indicated a relatively high frequency of reactive aggression at pretreatment. In contrast, they rated only the first two proactive aggression items as occurring with any frequency. Clearly, this type of checklist is an easy way to assess the observable behaviors of a child or adolescent presenting with an anger disorder.

Anger is defined as the emotional arousal preceding impulsive, hostile, and reactive aggression (see Kassinove & Sukhodolsky, chap. 1, this volume). Thus, as noted by Salzinger (chap. 4, this volume), it is a private and subjective event that presents special assessment issues. The measurement of overt aggressive behavior, although important, may have limited utility as a means to assess the construct (Finch et al., 1987). Thus, rather than infer the experience of anger from behavior, clinicians and researchers have turned to self-report methods for assessment in children and adolescents.

For example, the Children's Inventory of Anger (CIA; Finch et al., 1987) is a 71-item self-report questionnaire designed to assess children's perceptions of their own anger in a variety of situations. Each item describes a potentially anger-provoking situation, and the respondents indicate on a Likert-type scale how angry they would feel. Psychometric studies have shown the CIA to be a reliable and valid tool; however, concurrent validity seems questionable. A lack of significant correlations between CIA responses and teachers' ratings of aggression (Wolfe, Finch, Saylor, Blount, Pallmeyer, & Carek, 1987) illustrates the complex

Table10.1 Revised Behavior Problem Checklist Aggression Scales

Subscale	Items
Reactive Aggression	
	_____Has temper tantrums
	_____Is uncooperative in group situations
	_____Is negative—tends to do the opposite of what is requested
	_____Is impertinent—talks back
	_____Is irritable, hot tempered, easily angered
	_____Argues, quarrels
	_____Sulks, pouts
	_____Blames others, denies own mistakes
Proactive Aggression	
	_____Is disruptive—annoys and bothers others
	_____Persists and nags, can't take no for an answer
	_____Tries to dominate others—bullies, threatens
	_____Picks at other children as a way of getting their attention
	_____Brags and boasts
	_____Teases others
	_____Is selfish, won't share
	_____Is deliberately cruel to others

relationship between the cognitive and emotional variable of anger and the overt behavior class of aggression. Clearly, not all anger experienced by children and adolescents results in overt aggression. Indeed, because most authors believe this to be true, correlations between self-report instruments and teachers' rating may be expected to be low.

The State–Trait Anger Expression Inventory (STAXI; Spielberger, 1988) is another self-report scale developed for use with adults; however, adolescent norms are also available. This 44-item scale forms six subscales (State Anger, Trait Anger, Anger-In, Anger-Out, Anger-Control, and Anger-Expression), and has two additional trait anger subscales (Angry Temperament and Angry Reaction). Good internal consistency and discriminant validity have been demonstrated, and there are normative data available from numerous samples in many foreign languages. A short and easy-to-use instrument, the STAXI is a good choice, especially for adolescents.

Consistent with Novaco's (1975) model of anger, which emphasizes the affective, cognitive, and behavioral components of emotional responses to frustration and/or provocation, the newly developed Children's Anger Response Checklist (CARC; Feindler, Adler, Brooks, & Bhumitra, 1993) taps each dimension as the child or adolescent responds to 10 hypothetical conflict situations. Estimations of how one would feel, think, and act are made by indicating which of the precoded reactions would likely occur. Figure 10.2 presents a sample item from the CARC. In addition to overall anger and responsivity indices, the following subscales are scored: Behavioral Aggression, Behavioral Assertion, Behavioral Submission, Cognitive Aggression, Cognitive Assertion, Cognitive Submission, Perceived Injustice, Self-Blame, Emotional Responses, and Physiological Responses. A unique feature of this measure is the assessment of each domain, such that discrete aspects of the anger response can be quantified and skill training can be directed toward these deficits. For example, in the case presented, Erica had a low emotional-physiological response index, which indicated little need for relaxation training. However, she scored extremely high on the Cognitive Aggression and Perceived Injustice subscales, hence it was apparent that cognitive restructuring and reattribution training would be important for her.

A critical variable in recent understanding of children's anger and aggression has been the predominance of hostile attributional styles and poor problem-solving abilities (Lochman & Dodge, 1994). Aggressive youth tend to make hostile interpretations of ambiguous interactions when they feel personally threatened, and they tend to attribute blame to others, which may fuel anger arousal and potentiate retaliatory responses (Fondacaro & Heller, 1990). Clinical researchers have developed several methods to assess these social cognitive processes, which are key to the development of ideal anger-control programs. Fondacaro and Heller (1990) created a structured interview, in which problem situations involving peers, parents, and other adults from the Adolescent Problems Inventory (Freedman, Rosenthal, Donahoe, Schlerndt, & McFall, 1978) were presented to aggressive adolescents. Subjects were then asked to state what they thought was

Instructions: Read the following story and check off all of the possible responses you might have in this situation. Remember you can check off as many or as few responses as you feel you might have in that situation. There is also an area marked "other" where you can put responses that you might have but are not listed on the page. Then check off how angry you would be next to the face that matches how you feel.

STORY #8

You hardly ever watch TV but while you are watching your one favorite TV program, your parent starts to nag you a lot to clean up your room. Finally, your parent comes in and shuts off the TV and sends you to your room. What would you do?

E	P	B	C	Other responses might have:
__ FEEL HAPPY?	__TIGHTEN UP MUSCLES?	__ REFUSE TO MOVE?	__THINK YOU HATE YOUR PARENT?	_____
__ FEEL NERVOUS	__CRY?	__ RUN AWAY AND HIDE?	__THINK IT'S UNFAIR?	_____
__ FEEL MAD?	__FEEL HEART POUNDING?	__ YELL AND SCREAM?	__THINK PARENT IS RIGHT?	_____
__ FEEL HURT?				_____
__ FEEL DISGUSTED?	__FEEL VERY TIRED?	__ TALK IT OVER WITH PARENT?	__THINK ABOUT HOW TO SOLVE PROBLEM?	_____
	__GET HOT AND SWEATY?	__ GO TO ROOM QUIETLY AND TRY TO FORGET ABOUT IT?	__ THINK THAT YOU DON'T CARE?	_____

1 ____   2 ____   3 ____   4 ____   5 ____

Figure 10.2 Sample item from Children's Anger Response Checklist (CARC; Feindler, Adler, Brooks, & Bhumitra, 1993).

the major cause of the problem, and to rate their causal attributions on dimensions of self-blame versus other blame, and behavioral other blame versus characterological other blame. This is assessed by two items, such as:

Does the cause have to do with:
Something about you   Something about the other person
1   2   3   4   5   6   7   8   9

Does the cause have to do with:
The kind of person   The way he acted in this
he is (personality)   specific situation
1   2   3   4   5   6   7   8   9

The assessment of these attributional styles can provide the clinician with important information about the development of effective cognitive interventions because this dimension is viewed as a key in triggering anger arousal. From a clinical standpoint, relevant problem situations can be identified for each individual client, who then can rate these aspects of causality. Additional ratings of level of hostile intent can be added.

In a similar vein, Guerra, Huesmann, and Zelli (1990) developed the Assessment for Social Failure (ASF) scale, in which stories involving social situations of interpersonal frustration (e.g., peer group reentry, blocked attainment of a goal, etc.) were presented to adolescents. They were asked, Why would this happen to you?, and then were asked further questions that probed three dimensions: controllability, external–internal, and stability. These cognitive dimensions may require assessment because evidence suggests that anger arousal and subsequent aggressive responding may increase when others' actions are seen as intentional, hostile, and directed toward controlling one's own behavior (Dodge et al., 1990).

Of course, clinicians would be wise to consider an individualized approach to the assessment of attributional biases when planning an anger-management intervention. Understanding adolescents' specific cognitive distortions will help determine the most effective cognitive restructuring strategies. In the case presented, it was quite clear that Erica misperceived many social cues from peers (e.g., "Where did you get those shoes?") as intentional and hostile provocations/criticisms that required an angry, defensive response. Further, she viewed the deteriorating family situation as intentional (her parents were purposefully trying to "screw her up") and as beyond her control ("Nothing I say or want matters to them"). These cognitive responses would be emphasized in her subsequent treatment.

Another area requiring assessment, prior to intervention for anger control, is that of problem-solving skills and deficiencies. Because aggressive children and adolescents generate fewer verbal-assertion solutions and show an excess of nonverbal, direct, action-oriented solutions in response to social problems (Lochman & Dodge, 1994), problem-solving skills are often limited and require training. Kennedy (1982) described the development and use of the Adolescent Social Problem Solving (ASPS) scale, which presents seven social problems in a story-completion format. The variables scored include: alternative solutions generated, mention of effects of time on solution strategies, consideration of obstacles to problem resolution, and expectations of success and personal experience with such a problem (see Kennedy, Felner, Cauce, & Primavera, 1988, for further description). Probing these areas of a youth's interpersonal problem-solving skills provides a general assessment of cognitive assets and deficiencies assumed to be related to anger arousal and aggression in interpersonal conflict situations.

A similar, but more relevant, problem-solving measure is the Problem-Solving Measure for Conflict (PSM–C), as described by Lochman and Dodge (1994). The PSM–C presents six stories of conflict between peers, between student and teacher, and between child and parent. Responses that are offered as potential solutions to the problem are then categorized into the following domains: verbal assertion, direct action, help seeking, nonconfrontational, physical aggression, verbal aggression, and compromise or bargaining. The clinical application of this measure might be to assist in the determination of the clients' predominant response set to the hypothetical conflict situations involving antagonism and frustration, and to determine the need for problem-solving training.

A final problem-solving measure easily adapted for clinical use with children and adolescents is the Kidcope (Spirito, Stark, & Williams, 1988). Youths are asked to select a problem encountered in the previous month (for anger-assessment purposes, the youths could select an anger provocation, altercation, or interpersonal conflict) and rate each of 10 coping items according to frequency of use and effectiveness of the strategy. The 10 coping strategies are: distraction, social withdrawal, wishful thinking, self-criticism, blaming others, problem solving, emotional regulation, cognitive restructuring, social support, and resignation. Use of this checklist may help the clinician probe current coping strategies and target others for intervention. In the clinical case presented, Erica selected a peer conflict involving her perception of a rumor being spread about her liking an undesirable boy in her grade. After wishing she had never worked on a science project with this boy, her overt response was to confront the girls, call them names, and mildly threaten them with retribution (i.e., getting her other friends to reject them). Thus, the strategies she endorsed on Kidcope were: wishful thinking, blaming others, and social support. When probed for alternative solutions using the PSM–C format, Erica's responses were coded primarily on the physical aggression (hitting them, throwing books at them), verbal aggression (threatening, insulting, or yelling at them; spreading retaliatory rumors), and bargaining (trying to snare loyalties of some of the "in" group by inviting them to her house or to the movies) domains. Clearly, Erica was grounded in emotional reasoning when angered by this type of social rejection. She was unable to generate any assertive or compromise solutions, and she was unable to cope via control of her own emotional arousal or cognitive restructuring (i.e., her interpretation of the provocation).

The final method suggested for the multimodal assessment of childhood and adolescent anger is a self-monitoring data-collection system. This allows for an ongoing recording of provocation incidents, anger experienced, cognitive and behavioral responses to the provocation, and the outcome of the provocation situation. Such self-recording has been used in studies wherein college students were asked to record certain emotions (including anger) and related thoughts over a 24-hour period (Wickless & Kirsch, 1988) to substantiate a cognitive theory of emotion. Deffenbacher and colleagues (Deffenbacher, Story, Brandon, Hogg, & Hazaleus, 1988) added an "anger log" to the assessment package to evaluate the effects of an 8-week anger-management program for self-referred college students. Students recorded: (a) an anger situation, which described their personal, ongoing situation provoking the greatest anger, and asked for a rating of the amount of anger experienced; (b) the anger symptom, which asked for a quantification of self-reported physiological reactivity when angered; and (c) the anger log, in which subjects listed the most provocative situation of the day, across all weeks of the study, and rated amount of anger experienced. Such an individualized assessment approach would not only enable the clinician to determine direct application of newly acquired anger-management skills to daily situations, but would also provide a rich source of data for the development of in-session role plays.

This has been the case in my own anger-management programs for adolescents (Ecton & Feindler, 1990; Feindler, 1990; Feindler & Ecton, 1986). In the original work with institutionalized delinquent youths, a "hassle log" was constructed in a checklist format to reduce response cost of compliance to self-monitoring instructions. Whenever a *hassle*, defined as an interpersonal provocation, occurred, youths were instructed to check off items reflecting situational antecedents or setting events, the actual trigger (e.g., somebody teased me, somebody took something of mine), the responses (both appropriate and inappropriate), and a self-rating of both anger and outcome. Because such data recording by antisocial youths is probably inaccurate and unreliable, with opportunity for both positive and negative impression management, these self-monitoring logs were neither quantified nor used as a database on which to evaluate the program. However, the self-assessment has become a crucial element in anger-management training. It provides a subtle way to introduce terminology and sequences of events, to direct the youths' attention to alternative responses to interpersonal problems, and to provide real-life examples for in-session role plays.

With more compliant youths, a less structured self-monitoring method may be employed. In the present clinical case, an "anger diary" was constructed, and Erica was directed to make entries whenever she found herself in an anger situation. The diary's questions directly corresponded to the components of an anger reaction hypothesized to precede aggressive behavior. Further, it was necessary to understand Erica's cognitive distortions, specifically to provocations, so that specific cognitive treatments could be planned.

Two of the early therapy sessions were devoted specifically to instructions regarding completion of the anger diary and to a review of her responses. Subsequently, 10 minutes were set aside at the beginning of each treatment session to review her diary from the preceding week, and to note any incorporation of previously learned anger-management skills. The diary situations that Erica chose to share with the therapist supported previous assessments and highlighted her frequent flare-ups with her parents and girlfriends. They showed Erica's tendency to presume the other person was intentionally trying to provoke her, a justification of her aggression by externalizing blame for the situation, and few assertive solutions to problem situations. Erica was asked to continue the anger diary assessment throughout the course of her 15-session therapy contract.

SUMMARY OF THE COMPREHENSIVE ANGER ASSESSMENT

In reference to the clinical case presented, Table 10.2 summarizes the multi-method approach to anger assessment conducted during the initial four sessions of treatment. Although such a comprehensive assessment is rarely done in clinical practice, it is likely that treatments directly linked in conceptual ways to these assessment methods may be readily identified as most salient by the client, and therefore clinical efficiency may be enhanced. Results from Erica's assessment revealed: (a) frequent aggressive outbursts toward parents, (b) clear cognitive biases in regard to intentionality and legitimacy of her retaliation, (c) little physiological reactivity, (d) impulsive responding, and (e) few appropriate interpersonal problem-solving responses. These results enabled an individualized, and therefore "ideal," treatment to be developed.

EFFECTIVE ANGER-MANAGEMENT STRATEGIES FOR CHILDREN AND ADOLESCENTS

Recent clinical work with youths diagnosed with either oppositional defiant disorder or conduct disorder has focused on multimodal treatment packages (Kazdin, 1987). Ideally, a comprehensive intervention package would include: (a) training to remediate deficits in prosocial and problem-solving skills, and (b) training for the parents to reduce coercive family interaction patterns and teach effective child-management strategies. In addition, what seems imperative is an

Table 10.2 Clinical Assessment of Erica's Anger Difficulties

Session	Procedure
Session 1	Intake interview with 13-year-old client and her parents
Session 2	Structured assessment session. Client administered the following:
	• RBPC Aggression Scales (parents)
	• STAX1 (Erica)
	• CARC (Erica)
	• Kidcope (Erica)
Sessions 3 and 4	Anger diary presentation and review of completed data sheets

emphasis on the preceding and/or accompanying anger components. According to Novaco (1975) and Feindler (1990), aggressive behavior is influenced by heightened states of emotional and physiological arousal *and* by cognitive distortions, including misperceptions of social stimuli and hostile attributions. Accordingly, effective interventions have been designed to address these individual response components of anger disorders. This section describes these anger-management techniques, and shows how they were implemented in the case of Erica.

Arousal-Management Training

Anger arousal is marked by increased physiological activity in the endocrine, cardiovascular, and skeletal muscular systems (Feindler, 1990). Increases in heart and breathing rate, muscle tension, and skin temperature have been documented by Novaco (1979), and are hypothesized to interfere with appropriate cognitive and behavioral responses to interpersonal provocation. Lochman, White, and Wayland (1991) suggested that the ways in which aggressive children perceive or label the arousal experienced during conflict constrains their behavioral responses. Aggressive children have a distorted affect-labeling process, and are inclined to label any situation that elicits physiological arousal as an *anger situation*, rather than consider it as a sadness, fear, guilt, or anxiety situation. For these reasons, an ideal anger-management intervention begins with a focus on teaching skills to identify the onset of physiological arousal, and then to label and manage the arousal so as to remain relatively calm and controlled when faced with provocation or conflict.

Although there are numerous reports of effective relaxation therapy for college students and adults with anger disorders (e.g., Hazaleus & Deffenbacher, 1986; Novaco, 1979), there have been few investigations of the effectiveness of this component for adolescents or children. However, building on evidence linking stress to depression, Reynolds and Coats (1986) implemented relaxation training as an active treatment for moderately depressed high school students. Following 10 sessions of group intervention, adolescents reported decreases in anxious and depressive symptoms, and increases in self-esteem and academic self-concept. These authors suggested that relaxation provides a coping skill that may increase a sense of personal mastery over arousal. The link between stress and anger experiences, and/or the blurred relationship between depression and anger in children and adolescents, provide a basis for the extension of relaxation training to aggressive youths.

As part of the self-management training component of their anger-coping program for aggressive boys, Lochman and his colleagues (Lochman et al., 1984, 1991; Lochman & Curry, 1986) described methods to teach identification of physiological and affective anger arousal. Children are asked to identify environmental (anger-arousing stimuli) and physiological cues of anger, and are encouraged to differentiate their experiences on a dimension of intensity. This helps them conceptualize anger as occurring on a continuum, and children can then be taught to identify symptoms at lower and more manageable levels (Lochman et al., 1991).

Our own anger-control interventions with aggressive and delinquent adolescents (Feindler, Marriot, & Ivata, 1984; Feindler, Ecton, Dubey, & Kingsley, 1986; Feindler & Guttman, 1994) have built on these identification and discrimination skills by incorporating techniques designed to reduce physiological arousal. Deep breathing, pleasant imagery, and various relaxation training methods are used to gain control over impulsive response tendencies to provocation, and to help "let go" of anger. Adolescents are encouraged to practice diaphragmatic breathing by imagining they have a balloon in their stomach and that they have to blow it up slowly without moving any other part of their body. Brief relaxation exercises that focus on tensing and relaxing only a few muscle groups (typically facial, arm, and stomach muscles) are modeled and rehearsed.

Case Application

Two therapy sessions were devoted to arousal-management skills training with Erica. Following a review of her anger diary sheets, it was noted that Erica responded minimally to the "physical reaction" section. Nevertheless, she was able to identify a few typically occurring physiological cues to anger-provocated arousal. Erica identified feeling hot, and noticed that her heart would "begin to pound" during several interactions with her mother surrounding household responsibilities and chores. On reflection, she was also able to describe a sinking feeling in her stomach while she was verbally arguing with her mother, and she described an accompanying impulse to become physically aggressive.

Session 5 was therefore devoted to a detailed review of several anger-provoking incidents, to the identification of physiological cues that occur during anger arousal, to discrimination of these physiological cues from others accompanying pleasant events, and to increasing Erica's awareness of her overall physiological reactivity. Erica seemed able to understand the importance of recognizing these physiological responses as cues for impending temper outbursts, and as signals to use self-control skills. Clearly, this model emphasizes a sequence of stimulus–response units, and implies critical points for anger-management intervention.

Session 6 was devoted to physiological arousal-reduction training to build self-control over previously impulsive and aggressive responses to provocation. Conceptually, two objectives are emphasized: (a) learning how to stem the physiological arousal to stay calm and have time to consider alternate responses to the perceived provocation, and (b) learning to identify internal cues and reduce accumulated anger arousal. Specifically, Erica was taught the deep, diaphragmatic breathing strategy to use whenever she recognized the onset of the hot, heart pounding sensation. This included: (a) a long, slow inhalation with eyes closed or at least diverted from the provocation, (b) an immediate, but slow exhalation with visualization of the balloon inside her stomach deflating, and (c) thinking the word *relax* or *calm down* during exhalation. Further, Erica was encouraged to instruct her body to slow down. She imagined reducing her body temperature and slowing down her heart beat. These autogenic suggestions seemed to increase her sense of control over her own reactions, and she learned that she could keep control during a seemingly uncontrollable anger-provoking incident. Each session concluded with instructions to practice the various strategies, and to note the improved control in her anger diary.

Cognitive Restructuring

The development of anger-management programs for children and adolescents is largely based on Novaco's (1979) conceptualization of anger arousal in adults and Dodge's (1986) model of social information processing with children. A critical variable in a reaction to a potentially anger-arousing event is children's perception and appraisal of the event. Children who display angry temper outbursts tend to have difficulties encoding appropriate social cues, to make hostile-biased attributions about intentionality, to display an egocentric perspective, and to invoke a set of beliefs that maintain aggressive behavior and external blame (Lochman & Lenhart, 1993). In her review of these distortions in social information processing, Feindler (1991) indicated that aggressive youths misperceive neutral events as intentional, foreseeable, and direct attacks, and that this "assume-the-worst" interpretation justifies their aggressive responding.

Numerous intervention studies designed to reduce aggressive responding in aggressive youths have focused on restructuring this cognitive component of anger arousal. Building on verbal-mediation deficits, self-instructional training has been used effectively to generate internal verbal commands that control impulsive behavior and guide appropriate social behavior. These self-instructions are designed to teach a more adaptive appraisal of provoking events, thoughtful consideration of alternative responses to provocation, and control of physiological and verbal–nonverbal responses. In support of this part of the ideal intervention model, the clinical research literature reports the successful training of self-instructions (Snyder & White, 1979), thinking ahead (Perry, Perry, & Rasmussen, 1986), attribution retraining (Lochman, 1987; Slaby & Guerra, 1988), and problem solving (Bash & Camp, 1985; Guerra & Slaby, 1990).

From a clinical standpoint, it is hypothesized that aggressive youths have developed an idiosyncratic set of hostile beliefs and biased thoughts that include the incomplete utilization of environmental cues, selective attention to aggressive cues, and overattribution of hostile intent (Lochman & Lenhart, 1993). Thus, the content of self-instructional training focuses on: (a) prompting information seeking and attention to other cues, (b) discounting aggressive and emphasizing nonaggressive cues, and (c) considering neutral or accidental intentions. Attitude change techniques, which might include self-statements refuting the use of aggression and the legitimacy of retaliation (Guerra & Slaby, 1990) or which emphasize nonpersonal characteristics of the provoker, are used to develop less hostile interpretations. In fact, Feindler (1991) suggested that cognitive interventions designed to lessen the recall of anger-inducing events, to relabel affect experienced as less intense, to shift attributions toward external and/or accidental causes, and to provide explanations stressing mitigating circumstances are beneficial in the reduction of anger and aggression.

Case Application

Pretherapy assessment results and completed anger diary entries showed that much of Erica's anger arousal was fueled by misperceptions of social cues, hostile attributions concerning intentionality to harm her, and ruminations of aggression and getting back at others. Specifically, Erica seemed to filter out many positive aspects of social situations, and focused on seemingly hostile cues that she used to assume that others did not like her, and wanted to hurt and reject her.

One peer interaction example involved Erica's approach toward a group of girls standing near her locker at school. In her anger diary, she recorded the following faulty assumptions: (a) "They were probably planning to get together without me," (b) "They might even be talking about me," and (c) "I hate them and don't trust them." As she approached, two girls turned toward her. However, Erica also observed (i.e., interpreted) that a third girl "made a face and rolled her eyes." This led Erica to feel "justifiably angry," and to make a sarcastic comment about the girl's outfit.

Session 7 was organized around these types of misperceptions of social cues, faulty assumptions based on lack of information, and on Erica's egocentric interpretations of others' behavior. Using a series of self-talk prompts, Erica was instructed to: (a) focus on something positive in the situation (Erica decided to attend to the person she liked most in a group), (b) assume that the girls wanted to interact with her, unless they specifically said otherwise (Erica chose to prompt herself to smile back at whoever smiled first), and (c) figure out nonpersonal reasons why one peer might not be responsive to her (Erica seemed to enjoy the assumption that the more "snotty" peers probably were suffering from premenstrual syndrome [PMS]).

These alternative, more positive cognitive responses were modeled for Erica out loud by the therapist, and were then written on individual index cards. Several additional hypothetical peer situations were discussed, and Erica was asked to generate appropriate, alternative attributions. Further, whenever Erica made a hostile interpretation or conclusion concerning another's intentions (e.g., "She's always trying to upset me"), she was asked to provide evidence for the conclusion.

The next session extended these alternative attributions to negative interactions with family members. A critical cognitive shift occurred when Erica prompted herself to consider (believe) that her mother's deteriorating marital situation was not intentional, not desired, and certainly not invoked to make Erica's life more miserable. This nonhostile view enabled Erica to reinterpret her mother's angry and irritable behavior to her own unhappiness, and even prompted Erica to express empathy toward her mother. Additional cognitive distortions, consonant with Beck's (1976) description of depressive thought patterns, were also noted upon further discussion of the notations in Erica's anger diary. These were all-or-none thinking, selective abstraction, arbitrary inference, personalization, and catastrophizing.

Throughout this session, the numerous cognitive strategies summarized by Reeder (1991) were invoked. These included: (a) questioning the evidence, (b) examining options and alternatives, (c) decatastrophizing (e.g., "What if" or "What's the worst that could happen?"), (d) advantages and disadvantages (e.g., listing pros and cons of a belief or behavior to gain perspective and move away from all-or-none thinking), (e) turning adversity to advantage or challenge, (f) paradox or exaggeration (i.e., taking an idea to the extreme), and (g) cognitive rehearsal (i.e., visualizing an event and an appropriate behavioral and cognitive response). Erica was given a list of various cognitive distortions from *Feeling Good* (Burns, 1990), and she began to discriminate the various responses she had by adding these terms to her anger diary.

Session 9 was the final session for this cognitive restructuring component, and included calming/coping self-talk, thinking ahead before responding to assess probable consequences, and positive self-evaluative statements.

Behavioral Skills Training

The next phase of an ideal and comprehensive anger-management program for children and adolescents presenting with oppositional behavior and temper outbursts involves multicomponent treatment in prosocial skills. Theoretically, aversive and aggressive behaviors stem from deficits in specific areas such as assertiveness, communication, problem solving, and other social skills. Children and adolescents who become angry in response to a perceived provocation resort to temper outbursts and aggressive behavior if unable to verbally express frustration and concern, generate alternative nonaggressive solutions, and/or use appropriate social skills to achieve well-functioning relationships. Thus, most social skills training programs target five clusters of behaviors: (a) cooperation, (b) assertion, (c) responsibility, (d) empathy, and (e) self-control, which are all key responses required to not experience (or at least control) anger and respond in a nonaggressive fashion (see Morrison & Sandowicz, 1994, for a comprehensive review of social skills training).

The comprehensive anger-management programs described by Feindler (1990); Goldstein, Glick, Zimmerman, and Reiner (1987); and Larson (1994) all include a skills training section. Generally, more appropriate interpersonal responses are taught through use of instructions, modeling, role playing, and performance feedback. Depending on the clinical assessment, both nonverbal skills, such as appropriate response latency, eye contact, facial expression, and gestures, and verbal skills, such as appropriate vocal loudness and response content, are taught (Feindler, 1990). The treatment manual of Feindler and Guttman (1994) details the following specific assertion techniques that can be taught as alternative social responses to interpersonal provocation: broken record, empathetic assertion, escalating assertion, and fogging. Further, Feindler and Ecton (1986) described training in the use of "I-message" assertion, wherein aggressive youths are taught to express their feelings and needs directly, and to accept responsibility for these feelings.

Aggression replacement training, as described by Goldstein et al. (1987), stresses a series of social skills that emphasize effective communication (listening, responding, expressing feelings), conflict resolution (negotiation and contracting), cooperation with others, decision making, and problem solving. Evaluations of this program have indicated that disruptive and delinquent adolescents in residential treatment centers can acquire a set of prosocial skills that transfer to situations outside of the training session and that seem to help decrease both the frequency and intensity of aversive, angry, and aggressive behaviors (Goldstein et al., 1987).

Finally, because cognitive deficiencies in the various aspects of problem solving, such as generating sufficient nonaggressive solutions to interpersonal conflicts (Lochman, Meyer, Rabiner, & White, 1991), generating assertive responses rather than aggressive ones (Slaby & Guerra, 1988), or evaluating solutions and deciding on the ones producing the best outcomes (Lochman & Lenhart, 1993), have all been clearly identified with angry and aggressive youths, teaching appropriate and effective problem solving becomes another crucial component of anger-management programs. In Lochman and Curry's (1986) comprehensive anger coping program, youths are asked to describe problem situations, identify all possible solutions (appropriate and inappropriate), identify and evaluate the consequences of various solutions, and choose the best solution. Evaluation data from various outcome studies (Lochman & Lenhart, 1993) indicate vastly improved problem-solving abilities subsequent to training. This problem-solving component is also an important part of other comprehensive anger-management programs (Feindler, 1990; Feindler & Guttman, 1994; Feindler & Ecton, 1986).

Case Application

Sessions 10 and 11 were based on the skill deficiencies exhibited by Erica during the assessment phase, and on evidence presented in her anger diary during treatment. Areas of greatest concern were Erica's interpersonal problem-solving skills, assertive responses to provocation, and competence to effectively communicate her emotions and desires to peers and family members.

Following a review of situations from her anger diary, which illustrated the need for assertiveness training, the concept of *assertion* and several specific strategies were presented, discussed, and modeled. First, Erica was presented with definitions of assertive behavior; although her right to express herself was supported, the rights of others and the need for mutual respect were emphasized.

A variety of communication skills were discussed in terms of attaining cooperative solutions to interpersonal conflicts. Specifically, Erica was taught to: (a) see conflict as a situation in which two people participate, (b) consider the desires of all persons involved in the conflict, (c) understand the attitudes and motivations of the other person, (d) express her feelings and attitudes about the particular situation using "I messages," and (e) practice negotiating a compromise decision, which reflects a cooperative solution. Erica was also taught specific assertive skills, as described in Feindler and Guttman (1994). Of particular importance to Erica was her new level of confidence and her skill to express her anger directly. After considering a wide number of possible affective terms reflecting anger intensity (e.g., *irritation, frustration, annoyance*, etc.), Erica practiced "I-message" communication of her feelings. She quickly realized that this had a much greater impact on the interpersonal interaction, and it led more quickly to a positive response from others. Another readily accepted strategy was the use of "fogging," which enabled Erica to quickly respond to a peer's sarcastic or teasing comment. She enjoyed shocking her peers as she "interpreted" their criticism as an apparent compliment. For example, she preferred quick retorts, such as, "I know you think so . . . Thanks for the compliment."

Session 11 was devoted to problem-solving training because these skills have been clearly identified as crucial to prosocial competence and better adjustment (Kennedy, Felner, Cauce, & Primavera, 1988), and to the reduction of angry outbursts and aggressive behavior (Lochman & Lenhart, 1993). Morrison and Sandowicz (1994) described key skills that were presented to and rehearsed with Erica. These included:

- alternate thinking—generating a number of different solutions to problems
- consequential thinking—projecting short- and long-term consequences of both angry and prosocial responses
- means–ends thinking—planning methods of attaining interpersonal goals
- social causal thinking—recognizing that one's actions and feelings are reciprocally related to the actions and feelings of others

Using specific situations described in her anger diary, Erica was helped to clearly define the problem, generate alternate solutions, select a solution, and, finally, implement that solution. One example involved her frustration and resentment at having to complete some household responsibilities. Discussion revealed that Erica was resentful because her brother had fewer responsibilities (apparently because he was involved in a school sport). She also believed that as her mother's attention focused more on the imminent marital separation, some of the necessary household chores fell to Erica. In an assertive and direct fashion, Erica was able to express her fears about the increased work load and her unhappiness with the inequitable family distribution of chores. Erica then engaged her mother in a problem-solving analysis. She and her brother were each required to choose two chores per day from a larger list. This prosocial process helped Erica behave more appropriately at home, and she significantly reduced her previous responses of defiance, abusive verbalizations toward her mother, and intense negative affect.

Family Involvement

Although individual skills training, as described previously, is the main focus of anger-management training, it is not sufficient to achieve transfer and maintenance of treatment gains (Kazdin, 1987). Significant others, usually parents and siblings, must also be targeted for intervention. In their review of the influences of parent behavior and parent social cognition on the development of angry and aggressive behavior patterns, Lochman and Lenhart (1993) indicated that aversive parenting practices and marital aggression are critical areas for treatment. Poor problem-solving and communication skills among family members, in addition to a belief that anger and aggression are effective and appropriate methods of control, are important and specific targets for intervention. In fact, in a recent study examining the efficacy of problem-solving skills and parent-management training, Kazdin, Siegel, and Bass (1992) found that the combination was more effective than either treatment alone in the reduction of aggression in antisocial boys. Specifically, Patterson and Bank (1989) hypothesized that aggressive, conduct-disordered behavior patterns develop via a series of social exchanges that are initiated in the home environment. Three key variables combine to result in ineffective parental discipline and monitoring, and to provide models for the development of aggressive responses. These are: (a) a lack of parental social skills, (b) aggressive parental behavior and beliefs and child traits such as having a difficult temperament, and (c) disruptive stressors such as marital conflict. Clearly, a parent-training component must be included in comprehensive anger management.

Case Application

Following a discussion with Erica and a telephone contact in which the rationale for parental involvement was presented (see Braswell, 1991, for helpful guidelines), two family sessions were planned, in which the development of appropriate conflict-resolution strategies between Erica and her parents was the focus. Clear limitations on the content of the session were set, and it was not considered appropriate for the marital situation to be reviewed.

Session 12 focused on the basics of contingency management and contracts. Erica's parents were asked to list the top five rules and responsibilities to which they expected Erica to conform. These included: (a) adhering to specific phone times, (b) eating dinner with the family, (c) not cursing when communicating with the parents, (d) respecting time curfews during the week and on weekends, and (e) completing homework. Household responsibilities included: (a) making her bed, (b) cleaning her room, (c) putting her clothes away, (d) emptying the dishwasher, and (e) feeding the cat. Erica agreed that these were reasonable, and that they generally corresponded to the expectations her parents had of her brother. Additionally, a reward list was constructed and included privileges, an allowance, and material objects.

Contingencies and contract principles were described to the parents, including the Premack principle (Premack, 1965), positive reinforcement, and response cost strategies. Homework focused on the determination of specific contingencies surrounding the timely completion of her responsibilities and adherence to the rules. Daily and weekly contingencies, as well as agreement of equity by all parties, were required. An example of a mutually agreed on contingency contract was as follows: Completion of all five household responsibilities per day will earn Erica the privilege of being driven to school by either her mother or father the next morning.

The second family session focused on improving communication between Erica and her parents (communication between the parents was extremely hostile, and it was suggested that they seek help for themselves). The following skills from a violence-prevention program (Hammond & Yung, 1991) were presented and rehearsed in role plays taken from those described in previous anger diaries:

Givin' It: calmly and respectfully expressing criticism, disappointment, anger, or displeasure.

Takin' It: listening, understanding, reflecting, empathizing, and appropriately reacting to criticism and the anger of others.

Workin' It Out: listening, identifying problems and possible solutions, suggesting alternatives when disagreements persist, and learning to compromise.

Although Erica and her parents understood each of these skills, and were able to rehearse them in session, this was only accomplished with firm limit setting by the therapist. There was obviously too much family distress for a single session of skill training to be adequate. In recognition of this, the family contracted for five additional sessions following the termination of Erica's individual treatment.

Summary and Postassessment

Session 14 was designed as a comprehensive review of all of the skills and strategies taught to Erica in her anger-management program. She was asked to reflect and describe the content of Sessions 5 through 13, and a summary table (Table 10.3) was generated.

With the therapist, Erica described the skills learned in each session on nine separate index cards. She was encouraged to refer to them whenever she was frustrated with her parents or peers. Further, Erica was encouraged to continue her anger diary because it was a genuine reflection of her growth and maturity. Indeed, Erica took pride in reviewing these diary sheets; she was able to note the differences in how she had learned to handle provocations and manage her own anger reactions.

Table 10.3   Anger-Management Intervention Procedures

Session	Procedure
Session 5	Arousal management—deep diaphragmatic breathing, identification of physiological cues, pausing
Session 6	Brief relaxation training
Session 7	Cognitive restructuring: identifying misperceptions and hostile attributions, alternate attributions, and disputing irrational beliefs
Session 8	Coping self-talk: reminders to ignore, stay calm, and think of other reasons why things are happening
Session 9	Thinking-ahead procedures, coping self-talk, and redirecting attention to nonhostile cues
Session 10	Assertiveness training, direct expression of anger, I messages, listening to others and reflecting their feelings, fogging
Session 11	Social problem-solving training: alternative, consequential, means–ends, and social causal thinking
Session 12	Family session: contingency contracting and positive discipline strategies
Session 13	Family session: communication skills and conflict-negotiation training

Session 15 was structured as a postassessment session in which self-report and parent rating checklists were completed, as had been done prior to intervention. Data from the pre- to postcomparison were shared with Erica because they reflected positive changes in her anger-management skills. In particular, on the State–Trait Anger Expression Inventory (STAXI), Erica showed increased scores on anger-control and anger-expression, and decreases on both trait and state anger. On the Children's Anger Response Checklist (CARC), subscales indicated more appropriate cognitive and behavioral responses in the assertiveness domain. A readministration of the Causal Dimension Scale, related to both a family and peer conflict situation, indicated a shift in Erica's ability to view conflict as related to nonegocentric causes, and to be situation-specific rather than global. Finally, ratings by Erica's parents on the Revised Behavior Problem Checklist (RBPC) showed mild decreases in individual items, particularly on the Reactive Aggression subscale.

CONCLUSION

In summary, this case was successful because it followed an ideal, state-of-the-art format. A formal preintervention assessment was used for diagnostic purposes and, more important, to identify those areas of behavioral, physiological/emotional, and cognitive functioning that were likely leading to anger and aggression. This assessment included interview, structured assessment, and anger diary data. The treatment included a set of specific and planned relaxation, cognitive, and behavioral procedures. Finally, the parents were invited to join in later sessions to help them understand some of the problems and techniques used, and to introduce contingency contracting and to improve communication among the family members. Utilizing this type of treatment package, or similar adaptations, highlights how children and adolescents can learn to understand and control their anger. This control and education will help them adjust to their present life situations, and hopefully will provide a solid basis for a healthy emotional life in the future.

Chapter 11

An Anger Model and a Look to the Future

Howard Kassinove

Hofstra University, Hempstead, New York

Christopher I. Eckhardt

University of North Carolina at Wilmington

Human phenomena such as anger can be studied from a variety of differing perspectives, and many of these have been previously discussed. In this chapter, we relate the contributions made by these perspectives to an overall model for the formation and regulation of anger experiences and expressions. However, we initiate our discussion by expressing agreement with the conclusion recently reached by Berkowitz (1994). He wrote, "Any really close and thorough examination of the psychological research into the origins of anger and emotional aggression must leave the thoughtful reader somewhat dissatisfied" (p. 35). For the scientist, there are many research findings that are either inconsistent or unexplainable. For the practitioner, there are all too many cases where anger was predicted to appear but did not, or where strong anger was expected to dissipate but, instead, led to violent aggression. Therefore, we present our model not as a final product, but as one that we hope stimulates further investigations into understanding anger—the "forgotten emotion."

We begin by restating what is, by now, obvious. Anger is a frequent, negative, often disruptive psychobiological experience that varies in intensity, frequency, and duration. It is phenomenologically felt and subjectively labeled, and is associated with specific cognitive distortions and deficiencies, physiological changes, and socially constructed and reinforced behaviors, which become manifest as organized scripts. Anger has not been widely studied, compared with other affective states such as anxiety and depression, or to more easily measured behaviors such as aggression. However, the move by social scientists from rigid adherence to logical positivism to the acceptance of alternate philosophies, such as that of social constructivism (Averill, 1982; González, Biever, & Gardner, 1994), has opened the door to a more comprehensive investigation of anger and anger-related variables. This is beneficial because it will help bridge the gap between knowledge developed by scientists and the activities of practitioners who work with angry clients on a daily basis.

A MODEL FOR ANGER FORMATION

Figure 11.1 presents a comprehensive model for the formation of states of anger and aggression. It takes into account the many positions stated in earlier chapters. It begins with an activating aversive event, and ends with either a positive or negative outcome for the individual. Before looking at the factors in this model, however, we want to identify those permanent, semipermanent, and situational forces that help to mold anger experiences.

Permanent biological factors include genetics and temperament, and the particular kinds of sensory mechanisms people's bodies are equipped with, because they help people organize stimuli into perceptions. Some forces are labeled *semipermanent* because they appear and may disappear at different ages. For example, older people simply may not become angry because they can no longer hear or see the stimuli that led to anger when they were younger. Of course, stronger bifocals and hearing aids may bring these stimuli back into focus. Another example would be the development of diabetes and sugar imbalances at some point in life, which will likely affect anger levels, depending on how the body processes the injected insulin or other chemicals used to regulate the imbalance. Finally, forces such as alcohol and drug ingestion are classified as *situational*. The perception of aversive stimuli (such as discovering that a spouse has been having an extramarital affair) and people's reactions to such events are clearly affected by the level of alcohol or the particular drug taken. Alcohol may exacerbate the anger experience and disinhibit aggressive behavior patterns. In contrast, heroin users may not react much at all because they are focused on achieving their next "high." In addition to these biological factors, individual patterns of learning and sociocultural forces also shape every portion of the anger experience. As noted by Kassinove and Sukhodolsky in chapter 1, acquisition of display rules for anger can be observed from the first year of life. Parents generally encourage and reinforce positive emotions and discourage negative feelings such as anger. However, anger experiences and aggression displays in children and adolescents are not only a function of socialization. Evidence has shown that aggressive children have distorted and deficient social information-processing mechanisms, including hostile attributional biases and cue-detection deficits. This leads them to experience anger in situations wherein nonaggressive children simply "see" the situation differently. The socialization of anger involves children's incorporation of rules about what to feel angry about, under what circumstances to feel angry,

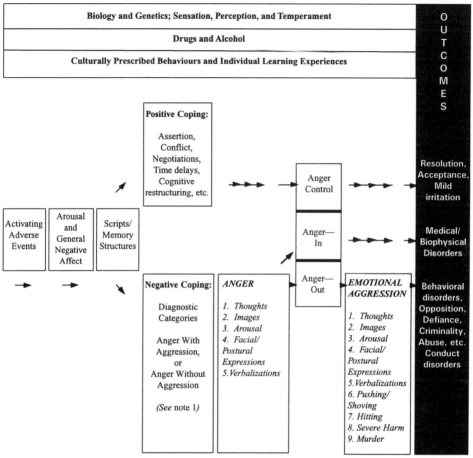

Note 1. We recognize that use of diagnostic categorization in clinical practice
would occur at the end of this chain. The proposed diagnoses are placed
here for illustrative purposes, to demonstrate what is likely to follow in
cases where there are repeated patterns of anger, with or without anger–
out/aggression.

(H. Kassinove, Ph.D. © 1994)

Figure 11.1   Model for the formation of states of anger and aggression.

and to whom to show the anger. These rules, as Tanaka-Matsumi (chap. 5, this
volume) and Nisbett (1993) have shown, vary both by culture and geographic
region.

   Let us now review our model for the sequential formation of states of anger
and aggression. We begin with some kind of *activating event that* is *perceived to
be negative*. As noted throughout this book, events such as not being invited to a
party, the use of profanity, playing the stereo very loudly, or receiving a grade of
"B" on a school paper must first be perceived as aversive to set off the possibility
of anger. Just as one person's rags may be another person's riches, a grade of "B"
may lead to happiness in one student and anger in another. Thus, the anger chain

begins when a client with an anger problem takes an event and perceives it to be negative. This, then, can be the first point of intervention. Clinicians can teach their clients either the wisdom that Shakespeare promoted in *Hamlet* ("There is nothing good or bad, but thinking makes it so"), or what the Stoic philosopher Epictetus (1956) said: "Men are disturbed not by the things which happen, but by the opinions about the things" (p. 172). This kind of insight is an important part of the cognitive therapies, and has been particularly promoted by Ellis (1962, 1973, 1994) in his rational-emotive behavior therapy.

If an event is perceived as aversive, or if there are other aversive stimuli in the environment such as foul odors, a general level of negative affect develops (Berkowitz, 1993). This arousal has been shown in numerous studies to increase the likelihood of experiencing anger and expressing it outwardly (i.e., aggressing; for a review, see Zillman, 1988). This negative affect or arousal is determined not only by environmental or situational forces. It has also been shown to be a reliable individual difference factor (Costa & McCrae, 1986) that may predispose certain individuals to enter otherwise neutral situations with a negatively valenced affect state. Researchers investigating contributions of the five-factor model (FFM) of personality for understanding emotional disorders (cf. Costa & Widiger, 1994) equate negative affectivity with the Neuroticism factor. To date, however, few systematic investigations have been undertaken to apply the FFM to angry individuals. When such studies do emerge, the results may help clarify the role of stable individual difference factors that affect the probability of angry and aggressive outcomes.

The stage is now set in our model for a positive or negative response to the perceived aversive event. Consider the case of a parent whose adolescent child has not followed through on a promise to apply immediately for a much needed part-time job. When the parent discovers this, memories of similar situations and the behavioral programs previously used in such situations are brought into play. Thus, as noted by Eron and colleagues (Eron, 1994; Huesmann & Eron, 1984), behavior is controlled by programs learned during early development. These scripts are stored in memory and are used to guide people's behavior in conflict or problem-solving situations. As noted by behaviorists such as Salzinger (chap. 4, this volume), they are learned by observation, modeling, reinforcement, and so on in the personal and unique experiences people have in the early years of life. They are encoded in memory, ready to be retrieved in situations that are similar to those in which they were learned. However, referring to children, Eron (1994) noted, ". . . not all scripts which are retrieved are translated into behavior. Once a script is retrieved, the child evaluates its appropriateness in light of existing internalized norms and also evaluates the likely consequences" (p. 7). Of course, the same kind of evaluation is performed by adults, and thus there is the possibility for psychotherapists to intervene at this point in the chain of events.

In our example, a positive, nonangry, nonaggressive outcome might emerge if the parent has positive coping skills and has used them in the past. For example, the parent might use assertion ("I feel disappointed that you didn't apply for that job. I can't afford to keep giving you an allowance because of other expenses. I would really be appreciative if you would apply for a job tomorrow"), or some kind of negotiation ("If you get a part-time job, as you promised to do, I will also save some money and we can then buy a car for you"). If these kinds of activities have worked in the past, the parent will likely access these strategies to manage the situation, and anger will not emerge. However, if they have not worked, or if the parent is unskilled in using assertion, negotiation, or other skill-based techniques, it is likely that other scripts, such as those for anger and aggression, will emerge.

Anger scripts can be organized into identifiable patterns or syndromes, as suggested by Eckhardt and Deffenbacher (chap. 2, this volume). For some individuals, the chronic and intense experience of anger is limited to specific situations (i.e., situational anger disorder). The presence of a particular stimulus (e.g., being stuck in traffic) cues relevant affectively laden memories, and scripts that call for intense anger experiences, belligerence, and in some cases expressive anger-out behaviors (e.g., reckless driving, verbal threats, physical altercations) are accessed. For others, the chronic and intense experience of anger appears across situations (i.e., general anger disorder). Perhaps, because of hostile attributional biases or temperamental predispositions, a wide variety of situations cue aversive affective states. These states allow for easy accessibility of anger-relevant scripts that, when applied, tend to be highly functional in the short term, thus reinforcing the utility of the script.

When anger does emerge, it seems to involve thoughts, images, autonomic nervous system arousal, and a series of facial and postural expressions, as well as verbalizations. As stated in the model developed by Spielberger (1988; also see chap. 3, this volume), the anger can be expressed outwardly (anger-out), kept hidden from others (anger-in), or deliberately reduced and managed (anger-control). He further differentiates "anger-control in" (e.g., simmering down) and "anger-control out" (e.g., controlling behavioral expression). If it is controlled, acceptance of the event and the experience and expression of appropriate levels of annoyance or irritation will likely occur. For example, if the person adopts the position advocated by Ellis (1994), a series of cognitive reconstructions will occur following the activating event. The person would conclude that it is only unfortunate (and not awful or horrible) that the adolescent did not apply for the job, and that it continues to be preferable (not absolutely necessary) that the child get a job. Further, the parent would believe that it is standable and tolerable that the adolescent did not apply for the job (and would not say, "I can't stand knowing that he or she didn't apply for the job"), and would see the adolescent as a fallible, mistake-making person (rather than "a jerk" or "a dumb kid," etc.). Because there is clear evidence that highly angry and abusive men (Eckhardt & Kassinove, 1995), and probably women, emit a variety of such irrational verbalizations and cognitive distortions, psychotherapists would be wise to teach clients to reconstruct their evaluations of situations to reduce or eliminate intense anger. It is likely that similar irrational thinking styles are present in highly angry women as well, and future investigations are warranted to clarify gender similarities and differences.

If the anger is held in, and if this kind of reaction persists over the years, a pattern of angry ruminations is likely. Evidence suggests that such ruminations may lead to a variety of medical problems (Greer & Morris, 1975; Harburg, Blakelock, & Roeper, 1979; Harburg, Gleiberman, Russell, & Cooper, 1991; Kalis, Harris, Bennett, & Sokolow, 1961; Spielberger, Crane, Kearns, Pellegrin, & Rickman, 1991). Thus, anger-in reaction patterns also require intervention by therapists. Assertion training with role playing and reinforcement is helpful because the main goal of assertion is, ". . . the socially appropriate verbal and motor expression of any emotion other than anxiety" (Wolpe, 1990, p. 135).

The final option is that the anger is expressed outwardly. If the expressive consequence to the perceived aversive event involves an anger-out strategy, it may become emotional aggression. Aggression in our view significantly overlaps the anger-out concept. However, although recognizing its merits, we do not endorse the position of radical behaviorists such as Salzinger, who suggest that anger and aggression are one unified concept with the same controlling operant or respondent forces. Anger-in and anger-control options make the issue more complex. Figure 11.1 defines *emotional aggression* as consisting of the same five anger elements (i.e., thoughts, images, autonomic system arousal, and facial and postural expressions and verbalizations) plus motor behaviors such as shoving or pushing. In our example, the parent might (a) become physically aroused, (b) yell ("Damn it, I told you to get a job!"), (c) imagine hitting the child, and (d) actually hit, severely harm, or even murder the child.

In children and adolescents, the outcome of the chain of events depicted in Fig. 11.1 is oppositional defiant disorder, or conduct disorder. Children who have these diagnoses, as noted by Feindler (chap. 10, this volume), are often involved in angry and aggressive interactions with peers and adults. In adults, anger-out and emotional aggression may also consist of opposition and defiance, but may involve criminal acts such as marital assault (Eckhardt & Kassinove, 1995) and other violent crimes (Ford, 1991; Welsh & Gordon, 1991).

TREATMENT

Averill (1982, 1983) reported that the ratio of reported beneficial to harmful consequences of anger was 3:1 for angry persons and 2.5:1 for the target of anger. Anger incidents, of course, were perceived as unpleasant, but the consequences were often considered as positive. However, Averill used a normal group of college students and community residents. For those who present clinically, anger is frequently highly disruptive, is persistent over time, often appears as a personality characteristic (i.e., trait anger), and is associated with emotional aggression. Given that aggression present as early as age 8 predicts criminal behavior at age 30 (e.g., arrests, convictions, traffic offenses, DWIs, spouse abuse, etc.), it is obviously important to develop programs to prevent and reduce anger and aggression (Huesmann, Eron, Lefkowitz, & Walder, 1984). Indeed, this is a pressing issue. Eron (1994) noted that his own attempts, and those of others (e.g., Kazdin, 1987), to develop effective aggression treatment programs based on behavioral and cognitive methods have met with only mixed success. He attributed this to two factors. First, the programs are brief. Second, the contexts in which maladaptive feelings and behaviors are learned and exhibited are highly variable.

With regard to anger, the authors in this book have reached some rather specific conclusions. First, in his meta-analysis, Tafrate (chap. 7, this volume) concluded that strategies that target self-statements, physiological arousal, and development of behavioral skills seem to be rather effective. Thus, programs such as those discussed and developed by Deffenbacher (chap. 9, this volume) and Feindler (chap. 10, this volume), which begin with relaxation training and move on to analysis and remediation of cognitive errors and social skill improvements, are likely to be helpful for children, adults, and families. However, Deffenbacher has mainly worked with distressed college student samples in a program that typically lasts for less than 10 sessions, and he has done most of the acceptable published work in this area. It seems important to now extend his treatment model to more severely disturbed groups, which will likely require more sessions of intervention. When confounding factors such as alcoholism, medical problems, low socioeconomic status, and so on enter the picture, it will be of interest to discover whether 10 sessions of treatment suffice. In chapter 8, DiGiuseppe noted that persons with anger problems are not likely to seek therapy on their own, and that it is particularly difficult to establish a therapeutic alliance with them if they do enter treatment. Research on this element of treatment will likely lead to improved techniques for the development of the alliance. We also reinforce Tafrate's call to test the efficacy of other forms of intervention, such as Beck's (1976) cognitive therapy, Ellis' (1974) rational-emotive behavior therapy, and exposure- and catharsis-based interventions. The small number of outcome studies in the literature that address anger with specified interventions is clearly a call to action.

THE FUTURE

The past has not been too kind to anger research. More than 60 years ago, Meltzer (1933) called anger, "the chief enemy of public happiness and private peace" (p. 285). Yet Kassinove and Sukhodolsky (chap. 1, this volume) showed that relatively little research has been carried out in this area. Research on emotion has tended to drift in and out of popularity, and most studies have been devoted to anxiety and depression. As noted earlier, DiGiuseppe, Tafrate, and Eckhardt (1994) called anger the *forgotten emotion*.

In contrast to the past, the present gives many signs of hope. The shift from acceptance of only logical positivism to other approaches, such as social constructivism, has opened the door for work such as that initiated by Averill (1982,

1983) and extended by others (Baryk, Kassinove, & Quick, 1995; Kassinove & Sukhodolsky, 1995; Kassinove, Eckhardt, Tsytsarev, Sukhodolsky, & Solovyova, 1995). Developments in psychometric approaches, as represented by Spielberger's (1988) State–Trait Anger Expression Inventory (STAXI), will allow for reliable analysis of anger experiences and modes of expression, which can be used in psychotherapy outcome studies with angry clients. Finally, the current and popular focus on cultural analyses in science, as represented by the writings of Tanaka-Matsumi (chap. 5, this volume), as well as that on multicultural perspectives in psychotherapy, which blend well with social constructivism (González, Biever, & Gardner, 1994), have also boosted the acceptance of research that accepts self-report data as meaningful and important.

The future, of course, is unknown. However, we are optimistic. The work of the authors in this book, as well as that of many others, have yielded important findings for the understanding and treatment of anger and aggression. In this final chapter, we have offered not only a summary of their findings, but also a tentative framework to help understand the overall picture. Ultimately, we believe it is crucial to ask the following question: How can we better understand the causes and consequences of anger to alleviate the suffering associated with the felt experience and the expression of anger, including anger-out or aggression? There is a pressing need to address the epidemic levels of aggression and violence observed in communities around the world, and to understand the observable acts of aggression as well as the antecedents existing both in the person (i.e., anger) and the situation (cues that facilitate retrieval of anger scripts). We believe that the future holds promise for increases in clinical research leading to practical advancements for practitioners who work with clients who present with anger disorders.

References

Abelson, R. (1981). The psychological status of script concepts. *American Psychologist, 36,* 715–729.

Abikoff, H., & Klein, R.G. (1992). Attention-deficit hyperactivity and conduct disorder: Comorbidity and implications for treatment. *Journal of Consulting and Clinical Psychology, 60,* 881–892.

Achenbach, T. (1991.) *Manual for the Child Behavior Checklist/4–18 and 1991 profile.* Burlington, VT: University of Vermont Press.

Achmon, J., Granek, M., Golomb, M., & Hart, J. (1989). Behavioral treatment of essential hypertension: A comparison between cognitive therapy and biofeedback of heart rate. *Psychosomatic Medicine, 51,* 152–164.

Adler, A. (1931). *What life should mean to you.* New York: Blue Ribbon Books.

Alexander, F.G. (1939). Emotional factors in essential hypertension: Presentation of a tentative hypothesis. *Psychosomatic Medicine, 1,* 175–179.

Alexander, F.G. (1948). Emotional factors in hypertension. In F. Alexander & T.M. French (Eds.), *Studies in psychosomatic medicine: An approach to the cause and treatment of vegetative disturbances* (pp. 289–297). New York: Ronald.

Alexander, F.G., & French, T.M. (Eds.). (1948). *Studies in psychosomatic medicine: An approach to the cause and treatment of vegetative disturbances.* New York: Ronald.

American Psychiatric Association. (1994). *Diagnostic and Statistical Manual of Mental Disorders* (4th ed.). Washington, DC: Author.

Anastasi, A., Cohen, N., & Spatz, D. (1948). A study of fear and anger in college students through the controlled diary method. *Journal of Genetic Psychology, 73,* 243–249.

Asch, S.E. (1955). Opinions and social pressure. *Scientific American, 193,* 31–35.

Averill, J.R. (1977, November). *Anger.* Paper presented at the Nebraska Symposium on Motivation.

Averill, J.R. (1979). Anger. In H. Howe & R. Dienstbier (Eds.), *Nebraska Symposium on Motivation* (Vol. 26). Lincoln, NE: University of Nebraska Press.

Averill, J.R. (1982). *Anger and aggression: An essay on emotion.* New York: Springer-Verlag.

Averill, J.R. (1983). Studies on anger and aggression: Implications for theories of emotion. *American Psychologist, 38,* 1145–1160.

Averill, J.R. (1993). Illusions of anger. In R.B. Felson & J.T. Tedeschi (Eds.), *Aggression and violence: Social interactionist perspectives* (pp. 171–192). Washington, DC: American Psychological Association.

Ax, A.F. (1953). The physiological differentiation between fear and anger in humans. *Psychosomatic Medicine, 15,* 433–442.

Bach, G., & Goldberg, H. (1974). *Creative aggression.* Garden City, NY: Anchor Books.

Bandura, A. (1973). *Aggression: A social learning analysis.* Englewood Cliffs, NJ: Prentice-Hall.

Barlow, D.H., Craske, M.G., Cerny, J.A., & Klosko, J.S. (1989). Behavioral treatment of panic disorder. *Behavior Therapy, 20,* 261–282.

Baron, R.A. (1977). *Human aggression.* New York: Plenum.

Baryk, D., Kassinove, H., & Quick, K. (1995). *Self-reported anger experiences in high school and college students.* Manuscript submitted for publication.

Bash, M.A., & Camp, B.W. (1985). *Think aloud: Increasing social and cognitive skills—A problem solving program for children.* Champaign, IL: Research Press.

Beck, A.T. (1963). Thinking and depression. *Archives of General Psychiatry, 9,* 324–333.

Beck, A.T. (1971). Cognition, affect, and psychopathology. *Archives of General Psychiatry, 24,* 495–500.

Beck, A.T. (1976). *Cognitive therapy and the emotional disorders.* New York: International Universities Press.

Beck, A.T. (1988). *Love is never enough.* New York: Harper & Row.

Beck, A.T., & Emery, G. (1985). *Anxiety disorders and phobias.* New York: Basic Books.

Bedford, E. (1957). Emotions. *Aristotelian Society Proceedings, 57,* 281–304.

Bem, S.L. (1981). *Bem Sex-Role Inventory: Professional manual.* Palo Alto, CA: Consulting Psychologists Press.

Bendig, A.W. (1962). Factor analytic scales of covert and overt hostility. *Journal of Counseling Psychology, 26,* 200.

Benedict, R. (1946). *The chrysanthemum and the sword.* Boston: Houghton Mifflin.

Benson, H. (1975). *The relaxation response.* New York: William Morrow.

Berkowitz, L. (1962). *Aggression: A social psychological analysis.* New York: McGraw-Hill.

Berkowitz, L. (1964). Aggressive cues in aggressive behavior and hostility catharsis. *Psychological Review, 71,* 104–122.

Berkowitz, L. (1970). Experimental investigations of hostility catharsis. *Journal of Consulting and Clinical Psychology, 35,* 1–7.

Berkowitz, L. (1989). Frustration-aggression hypothesis: Examination and reformulation. *Psychological Bulletin, 106,* 59–73.

Berkowitz, L. (1990). On the formation and regulation of anger and aggression: A cognitive-neoassociationistic analysis. *American Psychologist, 45,* 494–503.

Berkowitz, L. (1993). *Aggression: Its causes, consequences, and control.* New York: McGraw-Hill.

Berkowitz, L. (1994). Is something missing? Some observations prompted by the cognitive-neoassociationist view of anger and emotional aggression. In L.R. Huesmann (Ed.), *Aggressive behavior: Current perspectives* (pp. 35–60). New York: Plenum.

Berry, J.W., Poortinga, Y., Segall, M., & Dasen, P. (1992). *Cross-cultural psychology.* New York: Cambridge University Press.

Biaggio, M.K. (1980). Assessment of anger arousal. *Journal of Personality Assessment, 44,* 289–298.

Biaggio, M.K., & Maiuro, R.D. (1985). Recent advances in anger assessment. In C.D. Spielberger & J.N. Butcher (Eds.), *Advances in personality assessment* (Vol. 5, pp. 71–111). Hillsdale, NJ: Erlbaum.

Biaggio, M.K., Supplee, K., & Curtis, N. (1981). Reliability and validity of four anger scales. *Journal of Personality Assessment, 45,* 639–648.

Blashfield, R., Sprock, J., & Fuller, K. (1990). Suggested guidelines for including or excluding categories in the DSM-IV. *Comprehensive Psychiatry, 31,* 15–19.

Boky, I., & Tsytsarev, S. (1987). Pathological craving for alcohol in alcoholic patients during remissions. In I. Boky, O. Eryshev, & T. Rybakova (Eds.), *Remissions in alcoholism: Collected scientific papers* (pp. 7–19). Leningrad, Russia: The Bekhterev Institute Press.

Booth-Kewley, S., & Friedman, H.S. (1987). Psychological predictors of heart disease: A quantitative review. *Psychological Bulletin, 101,* 343–362.

Bordin, E.S. (1979). The generalizability of the psychoanalytic concept of the working alliance. *Psychotherapy: Theory, Research, and Practice, 16,* 252–260.

Boucher, J.D., & Brandt, M.E. (1981). Judgment of emotions: American and Malay antecedents. *Journal of Cross-Cultural Psychology, 12,* 272–283.

Bower, G.H. (1981). Mood and memory. *American Psychologist, 36*, 129–148.

Braswell, L. (1991). Involving parents in cognitive-behavioral therapy with children and adolescents. In P.C. Kendall (Ed.), *Child and adolescent therapy: Cognitive-behavioral procedures* (pp. 316–352). New York: Guilford.

Briggs, J.L. (1970). *Never in anger: Portrait of an Eskimo family*. Cambridge, MA: Harvard University Press.

Brooks, M.L., Walfish, S., Stenmark, D.E., & Canger, J.M. (1981). Personality variables in alcohol abuse in college students. *Journal of Drug Education, 11*, 185–189.

Burke, R.J. (1982). Interpersonal behavior and coping styles of Type A individuals. *Psychological Reports, 51*, 971–977.

Burns, D.D. (1980). *Feeling good: The new mood therapy*. New York: Morrow.

Burns, D.D. (1989). *The feeling good handbook*. New York: Plume.

Buss, A.H. (1961). *The psychology of aggression*. New York: Wiley.

Buss, A.H., & Durkee, A. (1957). An inventory for assessing different kinds of hostility. *Journal of Counseling Psychology, 21*, 343–349.

Buss, A.H., & Perry, M. (1992). The aggression questionnaire. *Journal of Personality and Social Psychology, 63*, 452–459.

Caine, T.M., Foulds, G.A., & Hope, K. (1967). *Manual of the hostility and direction of hostility questionnaire (HDHQ)*. London: University of London Press.

Caldwell-Colbert, A.T., & Jenkins, J.O. (1982). Modification of interpersonal behavior. In S.M. Turner & R.T. Russell (Eds.), *Behavior modification in black populations* (pp. 171–207). New York: Plenum Press.

Cannon, W.B. (1914). The interrelations of emotions as suggested by recent physiological research. *American Journal of Psychology, 25*, 252–282.

Cannon, W.B. (1929). *Bodily changes in pain, hunger, fear, and rage*. New York: Branford.

Casriel, D. (1974). *A scream away from happiness*. New York: Grosset & Dunlap.

Cavanaugh, D.J., Kanonchoff, A.D., & Bartels, R.L. (1987). *Menstrual irregularities in athletic women may be predictable based on pretraining menses*. Unpublished manuscript, Ohio State University, Columbus, OH.

Chesney, M.A. (1985). Anger and hostility: Future implications for behavioral medicine. In M.A. Chesney & R.H. Rosenman (Eds.), *Anger and hostility in cardiovascular and behavioral disorders* (pp. 277–290). Washington, DC: Hemisphere.

Clore, G.L., Ortony, A., & Foss, M. (1987). The psychological foundations of the affective lexicon. *Journal of Personality and Social Psychology, 53*, 751–766.

Cohen, J. (1977). *Statistical power analysis for the behavioral sciences* (rev. ed.). New York: Academic Press.

Conoley, C.W., Conoley, J.C., McConnell, J.A., & Kimzey, C.E. (1983). The effect of the ABC's of rational emotive therapy and the empty chair technique of gestalt therapy on anger reduction. *Psychotherapy: Theory, Research and Practice, 20*(1), 112–117.

Costa, P.T., & McCrae, R.R. (1986). Personality stability and its implications for clinical psychology. *Clinical Psychology Review, 6*, 407–423.

Costa, P.T., & McCrae, R.R. (1992). *Revised NEO Personality Inventory (NEO-PI-R) and NEO Five-Factor Inventory (NEO-FFI) professional manual*. Odessa, FL: Psychological Assessment Resources.

Costa, P.T., & Widiger, T.A. (Eds.). (1994). *Personality disorders and the five-factor model of personality*. Washington, DC: American Psychological Association.

Cox, W.M., & Klinger, E. (1990). Incentive motivation, affective change, and alcohol use: A model. In W. Cox (Ed.), *Why people drink: Parameters of alcohol as a reinforcer* (pp. 291–314). New York: Garden Press.

Cramer, D. (1985). Irrational beliefs and strength versus inappropriateness of feelings. *British Journal of Cognitive Psychotherapy, 3*, 81–83.

Cramer, D., & Fong, J. (1991). Effect of rational and irrational beliefs on intensity and "inappropriateness" of feelings: A test of rational-emotive theory. *Cognitive Therapy and Research, 15,* 319–329.

Crick, N.R., & Dodge, K.A. (1994). A review and reformulations of social information-processing mechanisms in children's social adjustment. *Psychological Bulletin, 115,* 74–101.

Cook, W.W., & Medley, D.M. (1954). Proposed hostility and pharisaic-virtue scales for the MMPI. *Journal of Applied Psychology, 18,* 414–418.

Crane, R.S. (1981). The role of anger, hostility, and aggression in essential hypertension (Doctoral dissertation, University of South Florida, 1981). *Dissertation Abstracts International, 42,* 2982B.

Croyle, R.T., Jemmott, J.B., III, & Carpenter, B.D. (1988). Relations among four individual difference measures associated with cardiovascular dysfunction and anger coping style. *Psychological Reports, 63,* 779–786.

Curtis, G., Kinder, B., Kalichman, S., & Spana, R. (1988). Affective differences among subgroups of chronic pain patients. *Anxiety Research: An International Journal, 1,* 65–73.

D'Andrade, R.G.D. (1984). Cultural meaning systems. In A. Shweder & R.A. LeVine (Eds.), *Culture theory. Essays on mind, self, and emotion* (pp. 88–122). New York: Cambridge University Press.

Darwin, C. (1965). *The expression of emotions in man and animals.* Chicago: University of Chicago Press. (Original work published 1872)

Davison, G.C., Robins, C., & Johnson, M.K. (1983). Articulated thoughts during simulated situations: A paradigm for studying cognition in emotion and behavior. *Cognitive Therapy and Research, 7,* 17–40.

Deffenbacher, J.L. (1991). La inoculacion de estres (Stress innoculation). In V.E. Caballo (Ed.), *Manual de tecnicas de terapia y modificacion de conducta (Manual of psychology and behavior modification techniques)* (pp. 627–654). Madrid: Siglo XXI.

Deffenbacher, J.L. (1992). Trait anger: Theory, findings and implications. In C.D. Spielberger & J.N. Butcher (Eds.), *Advances in personality assessment* (Vol. 9, pp. 177–201). Hillsdale, NJ: Erlbaum.

Deffenbacher, J.L. (1993). General anger: Characteristics and clinical implications. *Psicologia Conductual, 1,* 49–67.

Deffenbacher, J.L. (1994). Anger reduction: Issues, assessment, and intervention strategies. In A.W. Siegman & T.W. Smith (Eds.), *Anger, hostility, and the heart* (pp. 239–269). Hillsdale, NJ: Erlbaum.

Deffenbacher, J.L. (in press). Cognitive-behavioral treatment of anger. In K. S. Dobson & K. Craig (Eds.), *Progress in cognitive-behavioral therapy.* Newbury Park, CA: Sage.

Deffenbacher, J.L., Demm, P.M., & Brandon, A.D. (1986). High general anger: Correlates and treatment. *Behaviour Research and Therapy, 24,* 481–489.

Deffenbacher, J.L., & Lynch, R.S. (in press). Cognitive/behavioral intervention for anger reduction. In V.E. Caballo & R.M. Turner (Eds.), *International handbook of cognitive/behavioral treatment of psychiatric disorders.* Madrid, Spain: Siglo XXI.

Deffenbacher, J.L., McNamara, K., Stark, R.S., & Sabadell, P.M. (1990a). A combination of cognitive, relaxation, and behavioral coping skills in the reduction of general anger. *Journal of College Student Development, 31,* 351–358.

Deffenbacher, J.L., McNamara, K., Stark, R.S., & Sabadell, P.M. (1990b). A comparison of cognitive-behavioral and process oriented group counseling for general anger reduction. *Journal of Counseling and Development, 69,* 167–172.

Deffenbacher, J.L., & Sabadell, P.M. (1992). Comparing high trait anger individuals to low trait anger individuals. In M. Muller (Ed.), *Anger and aggression in cardiovascular disease.* Germany: Han Huber Verlag.

Deffenbacher, J.L., & Stark, R.S. (1992). Relaxation and cognitive-relaxation treatments of general anger. *Journal of Counseling Psychology, 39,* 158–167.

Deffenbacher, J.L., Story, D., Brandon, A., Hogg, J., & Hazaleus, S. (1988). Cognitive and cognitive-relaxation treatments of anger. *Cognitive Therapy and Research, 12,* 167–184.

Deffenbacher, J.L., Story, D.A., Stark, R. S., Hogg, J.A., & Brandon, A.D. (1987). Cognitive-relaxation and social skills interventions in the treatment of general anger. *Journal of Counseling Psychology, 34,* 171–176.

Deffenbacher, J.L., & Thwaits, G.A. (1991, April). *Consequences of trait anger.* Paper presented at the Rocky Mountain Psychological Association, Denver, CO.

Deffenbacher, J.L., Thwaites, G.A., Wallace, T.L., & Oetting, E.R. (1994). Social skills and cognitive-relaxation approaches to general anger reduction. *Journal of Counseling Psychology, 41,* 386–396.

Dembroski, T.M., MacDougall, J.M., Williams, R.B., & Haney, T.L. (1984). Components of Type A, hostility, and anger-in: Relationship to angiographic findings. *Psychosomatic Medicine, 47,* 219–233.

Deshields, T.L. (1986). Anger and assertiveness in essential hypertension. *Dissertation Abstracts International, 42,* 3212B.

de Sousa, R. (1980). The rationality of emotions. In A.O. Rorty (Ed.), *Explaining emotions* (pp. 127–152). Berkeley, CA: University of California Press.

Diamond, E.L., Schneiderman, N., Schwartz, D., Smith, J.C., Vorp, R., & Pasin, R.D. (1984). Harassment, hostility, and type A as determinants of cardiovascular reactivity during competition. *Journal of Behavioral Medicine, 7,* 171–189.

Diamond, E. (1982). The role of anger and hostility in essential hypertension and coronary heart disease. *Psychological Bulletin, 92,* 410–433.

DiGiuseppe, R. (Speaker). (1991). *What do I do with my anger?* New York: Institute for Rational-Emotive Therapy.

DiGiuseppe, R., Eckhardt, C.I., & Tafrate, R.C. (1993). *Toward an anger/hostility disorder for DSM Axis I classification.* Unpublished manuscript.

DiGiuseppe, R., Tafrate, R.C., & Eckhardt, C.I. (1994). Critical issues in the treatment of anger. *Cognitive and Behavioral Practice, 1,* 111–132.

Dix, T. (1991). The affective organization of parenting. *Psychological Bulletin, 110,* 3–25.

Docherty, J.P., Feister, S.J., & Shea, T. (1986). Syndrome diagnosis and personality disorder. In A. Frances & R. Hales (Eds.), *Psychiatry update: The American Psychiatric Association annual review* (Vol. 5, pp. 215–355). Washington, DC: American Psychiatric Press.

Dodge, K., Price, J., Bachorowski, J., & Newman, J. (1990). Hostile attributional biases in severely aggressive adolescents. *Journal of Abnormal Psychology, 99,* 385–392.

Dodge, K.A., & Coie, J.D. (1987). Social-information-processing factors in reactive and proactive aggression in children's peer groups. *Journal of Personality and Social Psychology, 53,* 1146–1158.

Dollard, J., Doob, L., Miller, N., Mowrer, O., & Sears, R. (1939). *Frustration and aggression.* New Haven, CT: Yale University Press.

Dryden, W. (1990). *Dealing with anger problems: Rational-emotive therapeutic interventions.* Sarasota, FL: Practitioner's Resource Exchange.

D'Zurilla, T.J. (1988). Problem-solving therapies. In K. Dobson (Ed.), *Handbook of cognitive behavioral therapies* (pp. 85–135). New York: Guilford.

D'Zurilla, T.J., & Goldfried, M.R. (1971). Problem solving and behavior modification. *Journal of Abnormal Psychology, 78,* 107–126.

Eckhardt, C.I. (1993, August). *A diagnostic category for dysfunctional anger and hostility.* Paper presented at the annual meeting of the American Psychological Association, Toronto, Canada.

Eckhardt, C.I. (1994, August). *Assessment of anger/hostility disorders by structured interview.* Paper presented at the annual meeting of the American Psychological Association, Los Angeles, CA.

Eckhardt, C.I., DiGiuseppe, R., & Tafrate, R.C. (1994). *Diagnostic criteria for anger disorders: Self-report and structured interview data.* Manuscript submitted for publication.

Eckhardt, C.I., & Kassinove, H. (1995). *Articulated irrational thoughts in maritally violent men.* Manuscript submitted for publication.

Ecton, R.B., & Feindler, E.L. (1990). Anger control training for temper control disorders. In E.L. Feindler & G.R. Kalfus (Eds.), *Adolescent behavior therapy handbook* (pp. 351–371). New York: Springer.

Ekman, P. (1972). Universal and cultural differences in facial expressions of emotions. In J.K. Cole (Ed.), *Nebraska symposium on motivation, 1971* (pp. 207–283). Lincoln: University of Nebraska Press.

Ekman, P. (1973). *Darwin and facial expression: A century of research in review.* San Diego, CA: Academic Press.

Ekman, P. (1974). Universal facial expression of emotions. In R. LeVine (Ed.), *Culture and personality: Contemporary readings* (pp. 8–15). Chicago: Aldine.

Ekman, P., & Friesen, W. (1976). *Pictures of facial affect.* Palo Alto, CA: Consulting Psychologists Press.

Ekman, P., & O'Sullivan, M. (1988). The role of context in interpreting facial expression: Comment on Russell & Fehr (1987). *Journal of Experimental Psychology: General, 117,* 86–88.

Ellis, A.E. (1962). *Reason and emotion in psychotherapy.* New York: Lyle Stuart.

Ellis, A.E. (1973). *Humanistic psychotherapy.* New York: McGraw-Hill.

Ellis, A.E. (1977). *Anger. How to live with it and without it.* New York: Citadel Press.

Ellis, A.E. (1989). Comments on my critics. In M. Bernard & R. DiGiuseppe (Eds.), *Inside rational emotive therapy: A critical appraisal of the theory and therapy of Albert Ellis* (pp. 199–233). Orlando, FL: Academic Press.

Ellis, A.E. (1994). *Reason and emotion in psychotherapy: Revised and updated.* New York: Carol Publishing.

Ellis, A.E., & DiGiuseppe, R. (1994). Are inappropriate or dysfunctional feelings in rational-emotive therapy qualitative or quantitative? *Cognitive Therapy and Research, 17,* 471–477.

Ellis, A.E., & Dryden, W. (1987). *The practice of rational-emotive therapy.* New York: Springer.

Ellis, A.E., & Harper, R. (1975). *A new guide to rational living.* North Hollywood, CA: Wilshire Books.

Epictetus (1956). The enchiridion. In M. Aurelins & Epictetus. *Meditations and enchiridion.* Chicago, IL: Gateway.

Epictetus (1890). *The collected works of Epictetus.* Boston: Little, Brown.

Erikson, K. (1966). *Wayward Puritans: A study in the sociology of deviance.* New York: Wiley.

Eron, L.D. (1994). Theories of aggression: From drives to cognitions. In L.R. Huesmann (Ed.), *Aggressive behavior: Current perspectives* (pp. 3–12). New York: Plenum.

Evans, D.R., & Stangeland, M. (1971). Development of the reaction inventory to measure anger. *Psychological Reports, 29,* 412–414.

Farley, F. (1986, May). The big T in personality. *Psychology Today,* pp. 44–52.

Fava, M., Anderson, K., & Rosenbaum, J. (1990). "Anger attacks": Possible variants of panic and major depressive disorder. *American Journal of Psychiatry, 147,* 867–870.

Fava, M., Rosenbaum, J.F., McCarthy, M., Pava, J., Steingard, R., & Bless, E. (1991). Anger attacks in depressed outpatients. *Psychopharmacology Bulletin, 27,* 275–279.

Fava, M., Rosenbaum, J.F., Pava, J., McCarthy, M.K., Steingard, R.J., & Bouffides, E. (1993). Anger attacks in unipolar depression: Part 1. Clinical correlates and response to fluoxetine treatment. *American Journal of Psychiatry, 150,* 1158–1163.

Fehr, B., & Russell, J.A. (1984). Concept of emotion viewed from a prototype perspective. *Journal of Experimental Psychology: General, 113,* 464–486.

Feindler, E.L. (1990). Adolescent anger control: Review and critique. In M. Hersen, R. Eisler, & P. Miller (Eds.), *Progress in behavior modification* (Vol. XXV, pp. 11–59). Newbury Park, CA: Sage.

Feindler, E.L. (1991). Cognitive strategies in anger control interventions. In P. Kendall (Ed.), *Child and adolescent behavior therapy: Cognitive-behavioral procedures* (pp. 56–97). New York: Guilford.

Feindler, E.L., Adler, N., Brooks D., & Bhumitra, E. (1993). The development and validation of the Children's Anger Response Checklist: CARC. In L. VandeCreek (Ed.), *Innovations in clinical practice* (Vol. 12, pp. 337–362). Sarasota, FL: Professional Resources Press.

Feindler, E.L., & Ecton, R. (1986). *Adolescent anger control: Cognitive-behavioral techniques.* New York: Pergamon.

Feindler, E.L., Ecton, R.B., Dubey, D., & Kingsley, D. (1986). Group anger control training for institutionalized psychiatric male adolescents. *Behavior Therapy, 17,* 109–123.

Feindler, E.L., & Guttman, J. (1994). Cognitive-behavioral anger control training for groups of adolescents: A treatment manual. In C. W. LeCroy (Ed.), *Handbook of child and adolescent treatment manuals* (pp. 170–199). New York: Lexington Books.

Feindler, E.L., Marriot, S.A., & Ivata, B. (1984). Group anger control for junior high school delinquents. *Cognitive Therapy and Research, 8*(3), 299–311.

Feshbach, S. (1964). The function of aggression and the regulation of aggressive drive. *Psychological Review, 71,* 257–272.

Feshbach, S. (1970). Aggression. In P.H. Mussen (Ed.), *Carmichael's manual of child psychology* (Vol. 2, pp. 159–261). New York: Wiley.

Finch, A.J., Saylor, C., & Nelson, W.M. (1987). Assessment of anger in children. In R.J. Prinz (Ed.), *Advances in behavioral assessment of children and families* (Vol. 3, pp. 235–265). New York: JAI Press.

Fondacaro, M.R., & Heller, K. (1990). Attributional style in aggressive adolescent girls. *Journal of Abnormal Child Psychology, 18,* 75–89.

Fontaine, J.R.J., & Poortinga, Y.H. (1994, July). *The cognitive structure of emotions in Indonesia and the Netherlands: A preliminary report.* Paper presented at the XIIth Congress of Cross-Cultural Psychology, Pamplona, Spain.

Ford, B.D. (1991). Anger and irrational beliefs in violent inmates. *Personality and Individual Differences, 12,* 211–215.

Frankl, V.E. (1955). *The doctor of the soul: An introduction to logotherapy.* New York: Knopf.

Freedman, B.J., Rosenthal, L., Donahoe, C., Schlerndt, D., & McFall, R. (1978). A social-behavioral analysis of skill deficits in delinquent and non-delinquent adolescent boys. *Journal of Consulting and Clinical Psychology, 46,* 1448–1462.

Freud, S. (1920). *A general introduction to psychoanalysis* (G. S. Hall, Trans.). New York: Boni & Liveright.

Freud, S. (1924). *Collected papers* (Vol. 1). London: Hogarth.

Freud, S. (1927). *Beyond the pleasure principle.* New York: Boni & Liverright.

Freud, S. (1936). *The problem of anxiety.* New York: W.W. Norton.

Freud, S. (1959). Why war? In J. Strachey (Ed.), *Collected papers* (Vol. 5). London: Hogarth. (Original work published 1933)

Frijda, N.H., & Mesquita, B. (1994). The social roles and functions of emotions. In S. Kitayama & H.R. Markus (Eds.), *Emotion and culture* (pp. 51–87). Washington, DC: American Psychological Association.

Funkenstein, D.H., King, S.H., & Drolette, M.E. (1954). The direction of anger during a laboratory stress-inducing situation. *Psychosomatic Medicine, 16,* 404–413.

Gates, G.S. (1926). An observational study of anger. *Journal of Experimental Psychology, 9,* 325–331.

Geen, T. (1990). *Human aggression.* Pacific Grove, CA: Brooks/Cole.

Gentry, W.D. (1972). Biracial aggression: 1. Effect of verbal attack and sex of victim. *Journal of Social Psychology, 88,* 75–82.

Gentry, W.D., Chesney, A.P., Gary, H.G., Hall, R.P., & Harburg, E. (1982). Habitual anger-coping styles: 1. Effect on mean blood pressure and risk for essential hypertension. *Psychosomatic Medicine, 44,* 195–202.

Gentry, W.D., Chesney, A.P., Hall, R.P., & Harburg, E. (1981). Effect of habitual anger-coping pattern on blood pressure in black/white, high/low stress area respondents. *Psychosomatic Medicine, 43,* 88.

Glass, D.C. (1977). *Behavior patterns, stress, and coronary disease*. Hillsdale, NJ: Lawrence Erlbaum Associates.

Goffaux, J., Wallston, B.S., Heim, C.R., & Shields, S.L. (1987, March). *Type A behaviors, hostility, anger and exercise adherence*. Paper presented at the eighth annual session of the Society of Behavioral Medicine, Washington, DC.

Goldstein, A. (1992, June). *Criminal responsibility assessments: When can we look backwards?* Paper presented at the conference on International Perspectives: Crime, Justice and Public Order, St. Petersburg, Russia.

Goldstein, A. (1994). Aggression towards persons and property in America's schools. *The School Psychologist, 48*, 6–16.

Goldstein, A.P., Glick, B., Zimmerman, D., & Reiner, S. (1987). *Aggression replacement training: A comprehensive intervention for the acting out delinquent*. Champaign, IL: Research Press.

González, R.C., Biever, J.L., & Gardner, G.T. (1994). The multicultural perspective in therapy: A social constructivist approach. *Psychotherapy, 31*, 515–524.

Goodenough, F. (1931). *Anger in young children*. Minneapolis: University of Minnesota Press.

Gorkin, L., Appel, M., Holroyd, K.A., Saab, P.G., & Stauder, L. (1986). *Anger management style and family history status as risk factors for essential hypertension*. Unpublished manuscript, Ohio University, Athens, OH.

Graham, S., Hudley, C., & Williams, E. (1992). Attributional and emotional determinants of aggression among African-American and Latino young adolescents. *Developmental Psychology, 28*, 731–740.

Greer, S., & Morris, T. (1975). Psychological attributes of women who develop breast cancer. A controlled study. *Journal of Psychosomatic Research, 19*, 147–153.

Guerra, N., Huesmann, L.R., & Zelli, A. (1990). Attributions for social failure and aggression in incarcerated delinquent youth. *Journal of Abnormal Child Psychology, 18*, 347–355.

Guerra, N.G., & Slaby, R.G. (1990). Cognitive mediators of aggression in adolescent offenders: 2. Intervention. *Developmental Psychology, 26*, 269–277.

Guldan, V. (1989). Motivation of criminal behavior in psychopathic individuals. In V. Kudriavtsev (Ed.), *Criminal motivation*. Moscow: Nauka. (In Russian)

Hammond, R., & Yung, B. (1991). *Dealing with anger: A violence prevention program for African American youth*. Champaign, IL: Research Press.

Harburg, E., Blakelock, E.H., & Roeper, P.J. (1979). Resentful and reflective coping with arbitrary/ authority and blood pressure: Detroit. *Psychosomatic Medicine, 3*, 189–202.

Harburg, E., Erfurt, J.C., Hauenstein, L.S., Chape, C., Schull, W.J., & Schork, M.A. (1973). Socioecological stress, suppressed hostility, skin color, and black- white male blood pressure: Detroit. *Psychosomatic Medicine, 35*, 276–296.

Harburg, E.H., Gleiberman, L., Russell, M., & Cooper, L. (1991). Anger coping styles and blood pressure in black and white males. *Psychosomatic Medicine, 53*, 153–164.

Harburg, E., & Hauenstein, L. (1980). Parity and blood pressure among four race-stress groups of females in Detroit. *American Journal of Epidemiology, 111*, 356–366.

Harburg, E., Schull, W.J., Erfurt, J.C., & Schork, M.A. (1970). A family set method for estimating heredity and stress-1. *Journal of Chronic Disease, 23*, 69–81.

Harré, R.M. (Ed.). (1986). *The social construction of emotions*. Oxford, England: Basil Blackwell.

Hartfield, M.T. (1985). Appraisals of anger situations and subsequent coping response in hypertensive and normotensive adults: A comparison (Doctoral dissertation, University of California, 1985). *Dissertation Abstracts International, 46*, 4452B.

Hartmann, H., Kris, E., & Loewenstein, R. (1949). Notes on the theory of aggression. *Psychoanalytic Study of the Child, 3*, 9–36.

Haynes, S.G., Levine, S., Scotch, N., Feinleib, M., & Kannel, W.B. (1978). The relationship of psychosocial factors to coronary heart disease in the Framingham Study: I. Methods and risk factors. *American Journal of Epidemiology, 107*, 362–383.

Hazaleus, S.L., & Deffenbacher, J.L. (1986). Relaxation and cognitive treatments of anger. *Journal of Consulting and Clinical Psychology, 54*, 222–226.

Hedges, L.V., & Olkin, I. (1985). *Statistical methods for meta-analysis.* San Diego, CA: Academic Press.

Hedges, L.V., & Olkin, I. (1986, October). Meta analysis: A review and a new view. *Educational Researcher,* pp. 14–22.

Heider, K.G. (1991). *Landscape of emotion: Mapping three cultures in Indonesia.* Cambridge, England: Cambridge University Press.

Herschberger, P. (1985). *Type A behavior in non-intensive and intensive care nurses.* Unpublished master's thesis, University of South Florida, Tampa, FL.

Herskovits, M.J. (1948). *Man and his works: The science of cultural anthropology.* New York: Knopf.

Hillbrand, M., Foster, H., Jr., & Hirt, M. (1988). Variables associated with violence in a forensic population. *Journal of Interpersonal Violence, 3,* 371–380.

Hochschild, A.R. (1979). Emotion work, feeling rules, and social structure. *American Journal of Sociology, 85,* 551–575.

Hochschild, A.R. (1983). *The managed heart: Commercialization of human feelings.* Berkeley: University of California Press.

Hofstede, G. (1980). *Culture's consequences: International differences in work-related values.* London, England: Sage.

Horney, K. (1950). *Neurosis and human growth.* New York: Norton.

Horvath, A.O., & Symonds, B.D. (1991). Relation between working alliance and outcome in psychotherapy: A meta-analysis. *Journal of Consulting and Clinical Psychology, 38,* 139–149.

Horvath, A., & Luborsky, L. (1993). The role of the therapeutic alliance in psychotherapy. *Journal of Consulting and Clinical Psychology, 61*(4), 561–573.

Hoshmand, L.T., & Austin, G.W. (1985). Criteria in lay self-judgment of anger control. *Journal of Research in Personality, 19,* 89–94.

Hoshmand, L.T., & Austin, G.W. (1987). Validation studies of a cognitive-behavioral anger control inventory. *Journal of Personality Assessment, 51,* 417–432.

Huesmann, L.R., & Eron, L.D. (1984). Cognitive processes and the persistence of aggressive behavior. *Aggressive Behavior, 10,* 243–251.

Huesmann, L.R, Eron, L.D., Lefkowitz, M.M., & Walder, L.O. (1984). The stability of aggression over time and generations. *Developmental Psychology, 20,* 1120–1134.

Imber, S.D., Pilkonis, P.A., Sotsky, S.M., Elkin, I., Watkins, J.T., Collins, J.F., Shea, M.T., Leber, W.R., & Glass, D.R. (1989). Mode-specific effects among three treatments for depression. *Journal of Consulting and Clinical Psychology, 58,* 352–359.

Isen, A., Shalker, T., Clark, M., & Karp, L. (1978). Affect, accessibility of material in memory, and behavior: A cognitive loop? *Journal of Personality and Social Psychology, 36,* 1–12.

Izard, C.E. (1971). *The face of emotion.* New York: Appleton-Century-Crofts.

Izard, C.E. (1977). *Human emotions.* New York: Plenum.

Izard, C.E. (1980). Cross-cultural perspectives on emotion and emotion communication. In H. Triandis & W. Lonner (Eds.), *Handbook of cross-cultural psychology: Basic processes* (Vol. 3, pp. 185–222). Boston: Allyn & Bacon.

Izard, C.E. (1989). The structure and function of emotions: Implications for cognition, motivation, and personality. In I.S.Cohen (Ed.), *The G. Stanley Hall lecture series* (Vol. 9, pp. 35–74). Washington, DC: American Psychological Association.

Izard, C.E. (1994). Innate and universal facial expressions: Evidence from developmental and cross-cultural research. *Psychological Bulletin, 115,* 288–299.

Jacobson, E. (1938). *Progressive muscle relaxation.* Chicago: University of Chicago Press.

James, W. (1952). *The principles of psychology.* Chicago: Encyclopedia Britannica, Inc. (Original work published 1891)

James. W. (1890). *The principles of psychology.* New York: Holt.

Janisse, M.P., Edguer, N., & Dyck, D.G. (1986). Type A behavior, anger expression, and reactions to anger imagery. *Motivation and Emotion, 10,* 371–385.

Janov, A. (1970). *The primal scream.* New York: Perigee Books.

Johnson, B.T. (1989). *DSTAT: Software for the meta-analytic review of research literatures.* Hillsdale, NJ: Erlbaum.

Johnson, E.H. (1984). *Anger and anxiety as determinants of elevated blood pressure in adolescents.* Unpublished doctoral dissertation, University of South Florida, Tampa, FL.

Johnson, E.H., & Broman, C.L. (1987). The relationship of anger expression to health problems among Black Americans in a national survey. *Journal of Behavioral Medicine, 10,* 103–169.

Johnson, E.H., Spielberger, C., Worden, T., & Jacobs, G. (1987). Emotional and familial determinants of elevated blood pressure in black and white adolescent males. *Journal of Psychosomatic Research, 31,* 287–300.

Johnson, E.J., & Tversky, A. (1983). Affect, generalization and the perception of risk. *Journal of Personality and Social Psychology, 45,* 20–31.

Johnson, F.A. (1993). *Dependency and Japanese socialization.* New York: New York University Press.

Johnson-Saylor, M.T. (1984). *Relationships among anger expression, hostility, hardiness, social support, and health risk.* Unpublished doctoral dissertation, University of Michigan, Ann Arbor, MI.

Kalis, B., Harris, R., Bennett, C., & Sokolow, M. (1961). Personality and life history factors in persons who are potentially hypertensive. *Journal of Nervous and Mental Disorders, 132,* 457–468.

Kassinove, H., Eckhardt, C.I., & Endes, R. (1993). Assessing the intensity of "appropriate" and "inappropriate" emotions in rational-emotive therapy. *Journal of Cognitive Psychotherapy: An International Quarterly, 7,* 227–240.

Kassinove, H., Eckhardt, C.I., Tsytsarev, S., Sukhodolsky, D., & Solovyova, S. (1995). *Self reported anger experiences in Russian medical students.* Manuscript submitted for publication.

Kassinove, H., & Sukhodolsky, D. (1995, August). *Anger experiences in Russian high school students.* Paper accepted for presentation at the annual meeting of the American Psychological Association, New York.

Kaufmann, H. (1970). *Aggression and altruism.* New York: Holt, Rinehart, & Winston.

Kazdin, A. (1987). Treatment of antisocial behavior in children: Current status and future directions. *Psychological Bulletin, 102,* 187–203.

Kazdin, A. (1988). The diagnosis of childhood disorders: Assessment issues and strategies. *Behavioral Assessment, 10,* 67–94.

Kazdin, A., Siegel, T., & Bass, D. (1992). Cognitive problem solving skills training and parent management training in the treatment of antisocial behavior in children. *Journal of Consulting and Clinical Psychology, 60,* 733–747.

Kearns, W.D. (1985). *A laboratory study of the relationship of mode of anger expression to blood pressure.* Unpublished master's thesis, University of South Florida, Tampa, FL.

Kelly, G. (1955). *The psychology of personal constructs.* New York: Norton.

Kemper, T.D. (1978). *A social interaction theory of emotions.* New York: Wiley.

Kemper, T.D. (1991). An introduction to the sociology of emotions. In K. T. Strongman (Ed.), *International review of studies of emotion* (pp. 301–349). New York: Wiley.

Kemper, T.D., & Collins, R. (1990). Dimensions of microinteractions. *American Journal of Sociology, 96,* 32–98.

Kennedy, M., Felner, R., Cauce, A., & Primavera, J. (1988). Social problem solving and adjustment in adolescence: The influence of moral reasoning level, scoring alternatives and family climate. *Journal of Clinical Child Psychology, 17,* 73–83.

Kennedy, R.E. (1982). Cognitive-behavioral approaches to the modification of aggressive behavior in children. *School Psychology Review, 11*(1), 47–55.

Kinder, B., Curtis, G., & Kalichman, S. (1986). Anxiety and anger as predictors of MMPI elevations in chronic pain patients. *Journal of Personality Assessment, 50,* 651–661.

Kitayama, S., & Markus, H.R. (Eds.). (1994). *Emotion and culture.* Washington, DC: American Psychological Association.

Knight, R.G., Chisholm, B.J., Paulin, J.M., & Waal-Manning, H.J. (1988). The Spielberger Anger Expression Scale: Some psychometric data. *Journal of Clinical Psychology, 27*, 279–281.

Kon, I. (1988). *Introduction to sexology.* Moscow: Medicina. (In Russian)

Koop, C.E., & Lundberg, G.D. (1992). Violence in America: A public health emergency. *Journal of the American Medical Association, 267*, 3075–3076.

Kopper, B.A., & Epperson, D.L. (1991). Women and anger: Sex and sex-role comparisons in the expression of anger. *Psychology of Women Quarterly, 15*, 7–14.

Kostogiannis, C., & Tanaka-Matsumi, J. (1994, July). *Subjective meanings and experiences of melancholia and depression among Greeks and Americans.* Paper presented at the XII International Congress of Cross-Cultural Psychology, Pamplona, Spain.

Krasner, S.S. (1986). *Anger, anger control, and the coronary prone behavior pattern.* Unpublished master's thesis, University of South Florida, Tampa, FL.

Lahey, B.B., Frick, P.J., Loeber, R., Tannenbaum, B.A., Van Horn, Y., & Christ, M.A.G. (1990). *Oppositional conduct disorder: I. A meta-analytic review.* Unpublished manuscript, University of Georgia, Athens, GA.

Laird, J.D. (1974). Self attribution of emotion: The effects of expressive behavior on the quality of emotional experience. *Journal of Personality and Social Psychology, 29*, 475–486.

Laird, J.D. (1984). The role of facial expression in the experience of emotion. A reply to Tourangeau and Ellsworth, and others. *Journal of Personality and Social Psychology, 47*, 475–486.

Laird, J.D., Cuniff, M., Sheehan, K., Shulman, D., & Strum, G. (1989). Emotion specific effects of facial expressions on memory for life events. *Journal of Personality and Social Psychology, 4*, 87–98.

Lakoff, G. (1987). *Women, fire, and dangerous things: What categories reveal about the mind.* Chicago: The University of Chicago Press.

Lange, C.G., & James, W. (1922). *The emotions.* Baltimore, MD: Williams & Wilkins.

Larsen, R.J., & Diener, E. (1987). Affect intensity as an individual difference characteristic: A review. *Journal of Research in Personality, 21*, 1–39.

Larsen, R.J., Diener, E., & Cropanzano, R.S. (1987). Cognitive operations associated with individual differences in affect intensity. *Journal of Personality and Social Psychology, 53*, 767–774.

Larson, J. (1994). Cognitive-behavioral treatment of anger-induced aggression in the school setting. In M. Furlong & D. Smith (Eds.), *Anger, hostility and aggression: Assessment, prevention and intervention strategies for youth* (pp. 393–440). Brandon, VT: Clinical Psychology Publishing.

Lazarus, R. (1984). On the primacy of cognition. *American Psychologist, 39*, 124–129.

Lazarus, R. (1991). *Emotion and adaptation.* New York: Oxford.

Lebra, T. (1984). Nonconfrontational strategies for management of interpersonal conflicts. In E. Kraus, T. Rohlen, & P. Steinhoff (Eds.), *Conflict in Japan.* Honolulu: University of Hawaii Press.

LeDoux, J.E. (1986). Sensory systems and emotions: A model of affective processing. *Integrative Psychiatry, 4*, 237–243.

Lemerise, E.A., & Dodge, K.A. (1993). The development of anger and hostile interactions. In M. Lewis & J.M. Haviland (Eds.), *Handbook of emotions* (pp. 537–546). New York: Guilford.

Levy, R.I. (1973). *Tahitians. Mind and experience in the society islands.* Chicago: University of Chicago Press.

Levy, R.I. (1984). The emotions in comparative perspective. In K.R. Scherer & P. Ekman (Eds.), *Approaches to emotions* (pp. 397–412). Hillsdale, NJ: Erlbaum.

Lewis, M. (1993). The emergence of human emotions. In M. Lewis & J.M. Haviland (Eds.), *Handbook of emotions* (pp. 233–236). New York: Guilford.

Lewis, M., Alessandrini, S.M., & Sullivan, M.W. (1990). Violation of expectancy, loss of control, and anger expressions in young children. *Developmental Psychology, 26*, 745–751.

Lewis, M., & Haviland, J.M. (Eds.). (1993). *Handbook of emotions.* New York: Guilford.

Lewis, W.A., & Bucher, A.M. (1992). Anger, catharsis, the reformulated frustration-aggression hypothesis, and health consequences. *Psychotherapy, 29*(3), 385–392.

Livesley, W.J., Schroeder, M.L., Jackson, D.N., & Jang, K.L. (1994). Categorical distinctions in the study of personality disorder: Implications for classification. *Journal of Abnormal Psychology, 103*, 6–17.

Lochman, J.E. (1987). Self and peer perceptions and attributional biases of aggressive and non-aggressive boys in dyadic interactions. *Journal of Consulting and Clinical Psychology, 55*(3), 404–410.

Lochman, J.E., Burch, P.R., Curry, J.F., & Lampron, L.B. (1984). Treatment and generalization effects of cognitive-behavioral and goal setting interventions with aggressive boys. *Journal of Consulting and Clinical Psychology, 52*(5), 915–916.

Lochman, J.E., & Curry, J.F. (1986). Effects of social problem solving training and self instructional training with aggressive boys. *Journal of Child Clinical Psychology, 15*, 159–164.

Lochman, J.E., & Dodge, K.A. (1994). Social-cognitive processes of severely violent, moderately aggressive, and non-aggressive boys. *Journal of Consulting and Clinical Psychology, 62*, 366–374.

Lochman, J.E., & Lenhart, L.A. (1993). Anger coping intervention for aggressive children: Conceptual models and outcome effects. *Clinical Psychology Review, 13*, 785–805.

Lochman, J.E., Meyer, B., Rabiner, D., & White, K. (1991). Parameters influencing social problem solving of aggressive children. In R. Prinz (Ed.), *Advances in behavioral assessment of children and families* (Vol. 5, pp. 31–63). Greenwich. CT: JAI Press.

Lochman, J.E., White, K.J., & Wayland, K.K. (1991). Cognitive-behavioral assessment and treatment with aggressive children. In P.C. Kendall (Ed.), *Child and adolescent therapy: Cognitive-behavioral procedures* (pp. 25–65). New York: Guilford.

Loeber, R., Lahey, B., & Thomas, C. (1991). Diagnostic conundrum of oppositional defiant disorder and conduct disorder. *Journal of Abnormal Psychology, 100*, 379–390.

Lorenz, K. (1966). *On aggression.* New York: Harcourt, Brace.

Lubinski, D., & Thompson, T. (1993). Species and individual differences in communication based on private states. *Behavioral and Brain Sciences, 16*, 627–680.

Lutz, C. (1982). The domain of emotion words on Ifaluk. *American Ethnologist, 9*, 113–128.

Lutz, C. (1988). *Unnatural emotions: Everyday sentiments on a Micronesian atoll and their challenge to Western theory.* Chicago: University of Chicago Press.

Lutz, C., & White, G.M. (1986). The anthropology of emotions. *Annual Review of Anthropology, 15*, 405–436.

Malatesta, C., & Haviland, J. (1982). Learning display rules: The socialization of emotion expression in infancy. *Child Development, 53*, 991–1003.

Margolin, G., John, R.S., & Gleberman, L. (1988). Affective responses to conflictual discussion in violent and nonviolent couples. *Journal of Consulting and Clinical Psychology, 56*, 24–33.

Markus, H.R., & Kitayama, S. (1991). Culture and the self: Implications for cognition, emotion, and motivation. *Psychological Review, 98*, 224–253.

Markus, H.R., & Kitayama, S. (1994). The cultural construction of self and emotion: Implications for social behavior. In S. Kitayama & H.R. Markus (Eds.), *Emotion and culture* (pp. 89–132). Washington, DC: American Psychological Association.

Masters, J.C., Burish, T.G., Hollon, S.D., & Rimm, D.C. (1987). *Behavior therapy.* San Diego: Harcourt, Brace & Jovanovich.

Matsumoto, D. (1990). Cultural similarities and differences in display rules. *Motivation and Emotion, 14*, 195–214.

Matsumoto, D. (1993). Ethnic differences in affect intensity, emotion judgments, display rule attitudes, and self-reported emotional expression in an American sample. *Motivation and Emotion, 17*, 107–123.

Mausner, B. (1954). The effect of prior reinforcement on the interaction of observer pairs. *Journal of Abnormal and Social Psychology, 49*, 65–68.

Mayer-Gross, W., Slater, E., & Roth, M. (1974). *Clinical psychiatry.* Baltimore, MD: Williams & Wilkins.

McDougall, W. (1908). *An introduction to social psychology.* London: Methuen.

McElroy, S.L., Hudson, J.I., Pope, H.G., Keck, P.E., & Aisley, H.G. (1992). The DSM III-R impulse control disorders not elsewhere classified: Clinical characteristics and relationships to other psychiatric disorders. *American Journal of Psychiatry, 149*, 318–327.

Meichenbaum, D.H. (1985). *Stress inoculation training.* New York: Pergamon.

Meichenbaum, D.H., & Cameron, R. (1973). Training schizophrenics to talk to themselves. *Behavior Therapy, 4*, 515–535.

Meichenbaum, D.H., & Goodman, J. (1971). Training impulsive children to talk to themselves. *Journal of Abnormal Psychology, 77*, 127–132.

Melton, G., Petrila, J., Poythress, & Slobogin, N. (1987). *Psychological evaluations for the courts: A handbook for mental health professionals and lawyers.* New York: Guilford.

Meltzer, H. (1933). Students' adjustment in anger. *Journal of Social Psychology, 4*, 285–309.

Mesquita, B., & Frijda, N.H. (1992). Cultural variations in emotions: A review. *Psychological Bulletin, 112*, 179–204.

Miller, L.C. (1981). *School Behavior Checklist.* Los Angeles, CA: Western Psychological Services.

Miller, P., & Sperry, L.L. (1987). The socialization of anger and aggression. *Merrill-Palmer Quarterly, 33*, 1–31.

Moon, J.R., & Eisler, R.M. (1983). Anger control: An experimental comparison of three behavioral treatments. *Behavior Therapy, 14*, 493–505.

Morrison, G.M., & Sandowicz, M. (1994). Importance of social skills in the prevention and intervention of anger and aggression. In M.J. Furlong & D.C. Smith (Eds.), *Anger, hostility and aggression: Assessment, prevention and intervention strategies for youth* (pp. 345–392). Brandon, VT: Clinical Psychology Publishing.

Morsbach, H. (1973). Aspects of nonverbal communication in Japan. *Journal of Nervous and Mental Disease, 157*, 262–278.

Mossman, D. (1994). Assessing predictions of violence: Being accurate about accuracy. *Journal of Consulting and Clinical Psychology, 62*, 783–792.

Moyer, K.E. (1976). *The psychobiology of aggression.* New York: Harper & Row.

Nakane, C. (1970). *Japanese society.* Berkeley, CA: University of California Press.

Neimeyer, G.J., & Lyddon, W.J. (1993). Constructivist psychotherapy: Principles into practice. *Journal of Cognitive Psychotherapy, 7*(3), 183–194.

Nemchin, T.A., & Tsytsarev, S.V. (1989). *Personality and alcoholism.* Leningrad: Leningrad University Press. (In Russian)

Nisbett, R.E. (1993). Violence and U.S. regional culture. *American Psychologist, 48*, 441–449.

Nisbett, R.E., & Wilson, T.D. (1977). Telling more than we can know: Verbal reports on mental processes. *Psychological Review, 84*, 231–259.

Novaco, R.W. (1975). *Anger control: The development and evaluation of an experimental treatment.* Lexington, MA: D.C. Heath.

Novaco, R.W. (1977). A stress inoculation approach to anger management in training of law enforcement officers. *American Journal of Community Psychology, 5*, 327–346.

Novaco, R.W. (1979). The cognitive regulation of anger and stress. In P.C. Kendall & S.D. Hollon (Eds.), *Cognitive-behavioral interventions: Theory, research, and procedures* (pp. 241–285). New York: Academic Press.

Novaco, R.W. (1985). Anger and its therapeutic regulation. In M.A. Chesney & R.H. Rosenman (Eds.), *Anger and hostility in cardiovascular and behavioral disorders* (pp. 203–226). Washington, DC: Hemisphere.

Novello, A., Shosky, S., & Froehlke, R. (1992). From the Surgeon General, U. S. Public Health Service: A medical response to violence. *Journal of the American Medical Association, 267*, 3007.

Oatley, J. (1993). Social construction in emotions. In M. Lewis & J.M. Haviland (Eds.), *Handbook of emotions* (pp. 341–352). New York: Guilford.

O'Leary, K.D., & Murphy, C. (1992). Clinical issues in the assessment of spouse abuse. In R.T. Ammerman & M. Hersen (Eds.), *Assessment of family violence* (pp. 22–46). New York: Wiley.

Olweus, D. (1979). Stability of aggressive reaction patterns in males: A review. *Psychological Bulletin, 86*, 852–875.

Ortony, A., Clore, G.L., & Collins, A. (1988). *The cognitive structure of emotions.* New York: Cambridge University Press.

Ortony, A., Turner, T.J., & Antos, S.J. (1983). A puzzle about affect for recognition memory. *Journal of Experimental Psychology: Learning, Memory, and Cognition, 9,* 725–729.

Pallone, N., & Hennessy, J. (1992). *Criminal behavior: A process psychology analysis.* New Brunswick, NJ: Transaction Publishers.

Patterson, G. (1986). Performance models for antisocial boys. *American Psychologist, 41,* 432–444.

Patterson, G.R. (1979). A performance theory for coercive family interactions. In R. Cairns (Ed.), *Social interaction: Methods, analysis and illustration.* Hillsdale, NJ: Erlbaum.

Patterson, G.R., & Bank, L. (1989). Some amplifying mechanisms for pathologic processes in families. In M. Gunnar (Ed.), *Minnesota symposium in child development* (pp. 167–209). Hillsdale, NJ: Erlbaum.

Peele, S. (1989). *Diseasing of America: Addiction treatment out of control.* Lexington, MA: D.C. Heath.

Perry, D.G., Perry, L.C., & Rasmussen, P. (1986). Cognitive social learning mediators of aggression. *Child Development, 57*(3), 700–711.

Plutchik, R. (1962). *The emotions.* New York: Random House.

Plutchik, R. (1980). A general psychoevolutionary theory of emotion. In R. Plutchik & H. Kellerman (Eds.), *Emotion: Theory, research, and experience, Volume 1: Theories of emotion* (pp. 3–31). New York: Academic Press.

Plutchik, R. (1994). *The psychology and biology of emotion.* New York: Harper Collins.

Pollans, C.H. (1983). *The psychometric properties and factor structure of the Anger Expression (AX) Scale.* Unpublished master's thesis, University of South Florida, Tampa, FL.

Premack, D. (1965). *Reinforcement theory. Nebraska symposium on motivation.* Lincoln, NE: University of Nebraska Press.

Prochaska, J., & DiClemente, C. (1988). *The transtheoretical approach to therapy.* Chicago: The Dorsey Press.

Prochaska, J., DiClemente, C., & Norcross, J. (1992). In search of how people change: Application to addictive behaviors. *American Psychologist, 47*(9), 1102–1115.

Quay, H.C., & Peterson, D.R. (1987). *Manual for the Revised Behavior Problem Checklist.* Coral Gables, FL: University of Miami Press.

Radke-Yarrow, M., & Kochanska, G. (1990). Anger in young children. In N.L. Stein, B. Leventhal, & T. Trabasso (Eds.), *Psychological and biological approaches to emotion* (pp. 297–310). Hillsdale, NJ: Erlbaum.

Rajita, S., Lovallo, W.R., & Parsons, D.A. (1992). Cardiovascular differentiation of emotions. *Psychosomatic Medicine, 54,* 422–435.

Reeder, D.M. (1991). Cognitive therapy of anger management: Theoretical and practical considerations. *Archives of Psychiatric Nursing, 3,* 147–150.

Rehm, L.P., & Rokke, P. (1988). Self-management therapies. In K. Dobson (Ed.), *Handbook of cognitive behavioral therapies* (pp. 136–166). New York: Guilford.

Reynolds, W.M., & Coates, K.I. (1986). A comparison of cognitive-behavioral therapy and relaxation training for the treatment of depression in adolescents. *Journal of Clinical and Consulting Psychology, 54,* 653–660.

Richardson, F. (1918). *The psychology and pedagogy of anger.* Baltimore, MD: Warwick & York.

Richardson, F.C., & Suinn, R.M. (1973). A comparison of traditional systematic desensitization, accelerated massed desensitization, and anxiety management training in the treatment of mathematics anxiety. *Behavior Therapy, 4,* 212–218.

Robin, M., & Eckhardt, C.I. (1993, August). *Clinical assessment of anger/hostility disorder.* Paper presented at the annual meeting of the American Psychological Association, Toronto, Canada.

Rogachevsky, L.A. (1984). *Emotions and crime.* St. Petersburg: Znanie Society. (In Russian)

Rogers, C. (1951). *Client centered therapy.* Boston: Houghton Mifflin.

Rosenbaum, A., & O'Leary, K.D. (1986). The treatment of marital violence. In N.S. Jacobson & A.S. Gurman (Eds.), *Clinical handbook of marital therapy* (pp. 385–406). New York: Guilford.

Rosenbaum, J.F., Fava, M., Pava, J., McCarthy, M.K., Steingard, R.J., & Bouffides, E. (1993). Anger attacks in unipolar depression: Part 2. Neuroendocrine correlates and changes following fluoxetine treatment. *American Journal of Psychiatry, 150,* 1164–1168.

Rosenberg, M., O'Carroll, P., & Powell, K. (1992). Let's be clear, violence is a public health problem. *Journal of the American Medical Association, 267,* 3071–3072.

Rosenthal, R. (1979). The file drawer problem and tolerance for null results. *Psychological Bulletin, 86,* 638–641.

Rosenthal, R. (1984). *Meta-analytic procedures for social sciences.* Beverly Hills, CA: Sage.

Rosenzweig, S. (1976). Aggressive behavior and the Rosenzweig picture frustation study. *Journal of Clinical Psychology, 32,* 885–891.

Rosenzweig, S. (1978). *The Rosenzweig Picture Frustration (P-F) Study basic manual and adult form supplement.* St. Louis, MO: Rana.

Rubin, J. (1986). The emotion of anger: Some conceptual and theoretical issues. *Professional Psychology: Research and Practice, 17,* 115–124.

Russell, J.A. (1991). Culture and categorization of emotions. *Psychological Bulletin, 110,* 426–450.

Russell, J.A. (1994). Is there universal recognition of emotion from facial expression? A review of the cross-cultural studies. *Psychological Bulletin, 115,* 102–141.

Russell, J.A., & Fehr, B. (1987). Relativity in the perception of emotion in facial expressions. *Journal of Experimental Psychology: General, 116,* 223–237.

Russell, J.A., Suzuki, N., & Ishida, N. (1993). Canadian, Greek, and Japanese freely produced emotion labels for facial expressions. *Motivation and Emotion, 17,* 337–351.

Russell, S.F. (1981). *The factor structure of the Buss-Durkey hostile inventory.* Unpublished master's thesis, University of South Florida, Tampa, FL.

Sabini, J., & Silver, M. (1982). *Mortalities of everyday life.* Oxford, England: Oxford University Press.

Salzinger, K. (1993, August). *Reinforcement history and other concepts neglected by behavior analysts.* Invited address delivered at the annual meeting of the American Psychological Association, Toronto, Canada.

Salzinger, K., Fairhurst, S.P., Freimark, S.P., & Wolkoff, F.D. (1973). Behavior of the goldfish as an early warning system for the presence of pollutants in water. *Journal of Environmental Systems, 3,* 27–40.

Salzinger, K., & Pisoni, S. (1958). Reinforcement of affect responses of schizophrenics during the clinical interview. *Journal of Abnormal and Social Psychology, 57,* 84–90.

Salzinger, K., & Pisoni, S. (1960). Reinforcement of verbal affect responses of normal subjects during the interview. *Journal of Abnormal and Social Psychology, 60,* 127–130.

Salzinger, K., & Pisoni, S. (1961). Some parameters of the conditioning of verbal affect responses in schizophrenic subjects. *Journal of Abnormal and Social Psychology, 63,* 511–516.

Salzinger, K., & Portnoy, S. (1964). Verbal conditioning in interviews: Application to chronic schizophrenics and relationship to prognosis for acute schizophrenics. *Journal of Psychiatric Research, 2,* 1–9.

Salzinger, K., Portnoy, S., & Feldman, R.S. (1964). Verbal behavior of schizophrenic and normal subjects. *Annals of the New York Academy of Sciences, 105,* 845–860.

Samuels, S.K., & Sikorsky, S. (1990). *Clinical evaluations of school age children.* Sarasota, FL: Professional Resource Exchange.

Schachter, S., & Singer, J.E. (1962). Cognitive, social and physiological determinants of emotional state. *Psychological Review, 69,* 379–399.

Schaef, A. (1987). *When society becomes an addict.* San Francisco: Harper & Row.

Schaef, A., & Fassel, D. (1988). *The addictive organization.* San Francisco: Harper & Row.

Schachter, S. (1971). *Emotions, obesity, and crime.* New York: Academic Press.

Scherer, K.R. (Ed.). (1988). *Facets of emotion.* Hillsdale, NJ: Erlbaum.

Scherer, K.R., Summerfield, A.B., & Wallbott, H.G. (1983). Cross-national research on antecedents and components of emotion: A progress report. *Social Science Information, 3,* 355–385.

Scherer, K.R., Wallbott, H.G., Matsumoto, D., & Kudoh, T. (1988). Emotional experience in cultural context: A comparison between Europe, Japan, and the United States. In K.R. Scherer (Ed.), *Facets of emotion: Recent research* (pp. 5–30). Hillsdale, NJ: Erlbaum.

Scherer, K.R., Wallbott, H.G., & Summerfield, A.B. (Eds.). (1986). *Experiencing emotion: A cross-cultural study.* Cambridge, England: Cambridge University Press.

Schlosser, M.B. (1986, August). *Anger, crying, and health among females.* Paper presented at the 94th annual convention of the American Psychological Association, Washington, DC.

Schlosser, M.B., & Sheeley, L.A. (1985a, August). *The hardy personality: Females coping with stress.* Paper presented at the 93rd annual convention of the American Psychological Association, Los Angeles, CA.

Schlosser, M.B., & Sheeley, L.A. (1985b, August). *Subjective well-being and the stress process.* Paper presented at the 93rd annual convention of the American Psychological Association, Los Angeles, CA.

Schneider, R.H., Egan, B., & Johnson, E.H. (1986). Anger and anxiety in borderline hypertension. *Psychosomatic Medicine, 48,* 242–248.

Schultz, S.D. (1954). A differentiation of several forms of hostility by scales empirically constructed from significant items on the MMPI. *Dissertation Abstracts, 17,* 717–720.

Schwarz, N., & Clore, G.L. (1983). Mood, misattribution, and judgments of well-being: Information and directive functions of affective states. *Journal of Personality and Social Psychology, 45,* 513–523.

Seligman, M. (1975). *Helplessness: On depression, development and death.* San Francisco: W. H. Freeman.

Shaver, P., Schwartz, J., Kirson, D., & O'Connor, C. (1987). Emotion knowledge: Further exploration of a prototype approach. *Journal of Personality and Social Psychology, 52,* 1061–1086.

Shaver, P.R., Wu, S., & Schwartz, J.C. (1992). Cross-cultural similarities and differences in emotion and its representation. A prototype approach. In M.S. Clark (Ed.), *Emotion. Review of personality and social psychology 13* (pp. 175–212). Newbury Park, CA: Sage.

Sherif, M. (1935). A study of some social factors in perception. *Archives of Psychology, 27*(187).

Shipley, R.H. (1979). Implosive therapy: Theory and technique. *Psychotherapy: Theory, Research, and Practice, 16*(2), 140–147.

Siegel, S. (1956). The relationship of authoritarianism. *Journal of Abnormal and Social Psychology, 52,* 368–373.

Sigler, R.T. (1989). *Domestic violence in context: An assessment of community attitudes.* Lexington, MA: Lexington Books.

Sines, J.O. (1986). Normative data: Revised Missouri Children's Behavior Checklist-Parent Form (MCBC-P). *Journal of Abnormal Child Psychology, 14,* 89–94.

Skinner, B.F. (1945). The operational analysis of psychological terms. *Psychological Review, 52,* 270–277.

Slaby, R.G., & Guerra, N.G. (1988). Cognitive mediators of aggression in adolescent offenders: 1. Assessment. *Developmental Psychology, 24*(4), 580–588.

Smith, T.W. (1992). Hostility and health: Current status of a psychosomatic hypothesis. *Health Psychology, 11,* 139–150.

Snyder, J., & White, M. (1979). The use of cognitive self-instruction in the treatment of behaviorally disturbed adolescents. *Behavior Therapy, 10,* 227–235.

Soloman, R.C. (1976). *The passions.* Garden City, NY: Doubleday/Anchor.

Soloman, R.C. (1984). Getting angry: The Jamesian theory of emotions in anthropology. In R. Shweder & R. LeVine (Eds.), *Culture theory: Essays on mind, self, and emotion* (pp. 238–255). Cambridge, England: Cambridge University Press.

Sommers, S. (1988). Understanding emotions: Some interdisciplinary considerations. In C. Z. Stearns & P.N. Stearns (Eds.), *Emotion and social change* (pp. 23–39). New York: Holmes & Meier.

Spiegler, M.D., & Guevremont, D.C. (1993). *Contemporary behavior therapy* (2nd ed.). Belmont, CA: Brooks/Cole.

Spielberger, C.D. (1980). *Preliminary manual for the State-Trait Anger Scale (STAS)*. Tampa, FL: University of South Florida, Human Resources Institute.

Spielberger, C.D. (1983). *Manual for the State-Trait Anxiety Inventory: STAI (Form Y)*. Palo Alto, CA: Consulting Psychologists Press.

Spielberger, C.D. (1988). *Manual for the State-Trait Anger Expression Inventory (STAXI)*. Odessa, FL: Psychological Assessment Resources.

Spielberger, C.D. (1992, August). *Anger/hostility, heart disease and cancer.* Paper presented at the American Psychological Association, Washington, DC.

Spielberger, C.D., Crane, R.S., Kearns, W.D., Pellegrin, K.L., & Rickman, R.L. (1991). Anger and anxiety in essential hypertension. In C.D. Spielberger, I.G. Sarason, Z. Kulcsar, & G.L. Van Heck (Eds.), *Stress and emotion: Anxiety, anger, and curiosity* (pp. 265–279). New York: Taylor & Francis.

Spielberger, C.D., Gorsuch, R.L., & Lushene, R.D. (1970). *Manual for the State-Trait Anxiety Inventory (STAI)*. Palo Alto: Consulting Psychologists Press.

Spielberger, C.D., Jacobs, G., Russell, S., & Crane, R.S. (1983). Assessment of anger: The state-trait anger scale. In J.N. Butcher & C.D. Spielberger (Eds.), *Advances in personality assessment* (Vol. 2, pp. 161–190). Hillsdale, NJ: Erlbaum.

Spielberger, C.D., Johnson, E.H., Russell, S.F., Crane, R.J., Jacobs, G.A., & Worden, T.J. (1985). The experience and expression of anger: Construction and validation of an anger expression scale. In M.A. Chesney & R.H. Rosenman (Eds.), *Anger and hostility in cardiovascular and behavioral disorders* (pp. 5–30). New York: Hemisphere.

Spielberger, C.D., Krasner, S.S., & Solomon, E.P. (1988). The experience, expression and control of anger. In M.P. Janisse (Ed.), *Health psychology: Individual differences and stress* (pp. 89–108). New York: Springer-Verlag.

Spielberger, C.D., & Maes, S. (1985–1986). *A Dutch adaptation of the State-Trait Anger Expression Inventory.* Unpublished manuscript, Tilburg University, The Netherlands.

Spielberger, C.D., & Sydeman, S.J. (1994). State-Trait Anxiety Inventory and State-Trait Anger Expression Inventory. In M.E. Maruish (Ed.), *The use of psychological tests for treatment planning and outcome assessment* (pp. 292–321). Hillsdale, NJ: Erlbaum.

Spirito, A., Stark, L.J., & Williams, C. (1988). Development of a brief checklist to assess coping in pediatric populations. *Journal of Pediatric Psychology, 13*, 555–574.

Spivack, G., Platt, J., & Shure, M. (1976). *The problem solving approach to adjustment.* San Francisco: Jossey-Bass.

Stampfl, T.G., & Levis, D.J. (1967). Essentials of implosive therapy: A learning theory-based psychodynamic behavioral therapy. *Journal of Abnormal Psychology, 72*, 496–503.

Stearns, C.Z., & Stearns, P.N. (1986). *Anger: The struggle for emotional control in America's history.* Chicago: University of Chicago Press.

Storr, A. (1968). Human aggression. New York: Atheneum.

Story, D., & Deffenbacher, J.L. (1986, April). *A test of state-trait anger theory.* Paper presented at the meeting of the Rocky Mountain Psychological Association, Denver, CO.

Straus, M.A., & Gelles, R.J. (1986). Societal change and change in family violence from 1975 to 1985 as revealed by two national surveys. *Journal of Marriage and the Family, 48*, 465–479.

Suarez, E.C., & Williams, R.B. (1989). Situational determinants of cardiovascular and emotional reactivity in high and low hostile men. *Psychosomatic Medicine, 51*, 404–418.

Suinn, R.M. (1990). *Anxiety management training.* New York: Plenum.

Suinn, R.M., & Deffenbacher, J.L. (1988). Anxiety management training. *Counseling Psychologist, 16*, 31–49.

Sydeman, S.J. (1995). *The control of suppressed anger.* Unpublished master's thesis, University of South Florida, Tampa, FL.

Tafrate, R.C. (1995). *Anger control among adult males: Exposure to the barb with rational, typical, and irrelevant self-statements.* Unpublished doctoral dissertation, Hofstra University, Hempstead, NY.

Tanaka-Matsumi, J., Attivissimo, D., Nelson, S., & D'Urso, T. (1994). *Context effects on the judgment of basic emotions in the face.* Manuscript submitted for publication.

Tanaka-Matsumi, J., & Boucher, J.D. (1978). Jyodo, Ganmen Hyojyo, Oyobi Bunkateki Sai (Emotion, facial expression, and cross-cultural differences). *Japanese Journal of Psychology, 49,* 167–172.

Tanaka-Matsumi, J., Boucher, J.D., & Hasegawa, K. (1989). Emic and etic antecedents to emotional experience: Japanese and American situations. In D.M. Keats, D. Munro, & L. Munn (Eds.), *Heterogeneity in cross-cultural psychology* (pp. 443–451). Lisse: Swets & Zeitlinger.

Tanaka-Matsumi, J., & Higginbotham, N.H. (in press). Behavioral approaches to counseling across cultures. In P.B. Pedersen, J.G. Draguns, W.J. Lonner, & J.E. Trimble (Eds.), *Counseling across cultures* (4th ed.). Thousand Oaks, CA: Sage.

Tanaka-Matsumi, J., & Marsella, A.J. (1976). Cross-cultural variations in the phenomenological experiences of depression: I. Word association studies. *Journal of Cross-Cultural Psychology, 7,* 379–396.

Tanaka-Matsumi, J., Seiden, D., Xydas, M., & Lam, K. (1994, July). *Method factors in facial emotion recognition.* Paper presented at the Congress of the International Association for Cross-Cultural Psychology, Pamplona, Spain.

Tavris, C. (1982). *Anger: The misunderstood emotion.* New York: Simon & Schuster.

Tavris, C. (1989). *Anger: The misunderstood emotion* (2nd ed.). New York: Touchstone.

Tavris, C. (1992). *The mismeasure of woman.* New York: Simon & Schuster.

Tedeschi, J.T. (1983). Social influence theory and aggression. In R.G. Green & E.I Donnerstein (Eds.), *Aggression: Theoretical and empirical reviews* (Vol. 1, pp. 135–162). New York: Academic Press.

Thayer, S. (1980). The effect of expression sequence upon judgments of emotion. *Journal of Social Psychology, 111,* 305–306.

Thoits, P.A. (1985). Self-labeling process in mental illness: The role of emotional dissonance. *Journal of Sociology, 91*(2), 221–249.

Thoits, P.A. (1989). The sociology of emotions. *Annual Review of Sociology, 15,* 317–342.

Thomas, S.P. (1989). Gender differences in anger expression: Health implications. *Research in Nursing and Health, 12,* 389–398.

Thomas, S.P. (Ed.). (1993). *Women and anger.* New York: Springer.

Tomkins, S. (1979). Script theory: Differential magnification of affect. In H.E. Howe & R.A. Dienstbier (Eds.), *Nebraska symposium of motivation 1978* (pp. 201–236). Lincoln, NE: University of Nebraska Press.

Toufexis, A. (1994, April 25). Workers who fight firing with fire. *Time Magazine,* pp. 34–37.

Triandis, H.C. (1972). *The analysis of subjective culture.* New York: Wiley.

Triandis, H.C. (1994). Major cultural syndromes and emotion. In S. Kitayama & H.R. Markus (Eds.), *Emotion and culture* (pp. 285–306). Washington, DC: American Psychological Association.

Trull, T.J., & McCrae, R.R. (1994). A five-factor perspective on personality disorder research. In P.T. Costa & T.A. Widiger (Eds.), *Personality disorders and the five-factor model of personality* (pp. 59–72). Washington, DC: American Psychological Association.

Tsytsarev, S.V. (1987). Objects and methods of psychological evaluations for the courts. In V.V. Melnik, S.V. Tsytsarev, & Y.M. Yakovlev (Eds.), *Foundations of forensic psychological evaluations in criminal cases: A textbook* (pp. 9–19). St. Petersburg, Russia: The University Press.

Tsytsarev, S.V. (1989). Psychological analysis of pathological craving for alcohol. *Proceedings of the 7th All-Union Congress of Soviet Psychologist, 3.*

Tsytsarev, S.V., & Callahan, C. (1995). Motivational approach to violent behavior: A cross-cultural perspective. In L. Adler & F. Denmark (Eds.), *Violence and the prevention of violence* (pp. 3–10). New York: Praeger.

Underwood, M.K., Coie, J.D., & Herbsman, C.R. (1992). Display rules for anger and aggression in school aged children. *Child Development, 63,* 366–380.

United States Department of Justice. (1991). *Uniform Crime Reports, 1990*. Washington, DC: U.S. Government Printing Office.

van der Ploeg, H.M. (1988). The factor structure of the State-Trait Anger Scale. *Psychological Reports, 63*, 978.

van der Ploeg, H.M., van Buuren, E.T., & van Brummelen, P. (1988). The role of anger in hypertension. *Psychotherapy and Psychosomatics, 43*, 186–193.

Vitaliano, P.P. (1984). *Identification and intervention with students at high risk for distress in medical school*. Unpublished doctoral dissertation, University of Washington, Seattle, WA.

Vitaliano, P.P., Maiuro, R.D., Russo, J., Mitchell, E.S., Carr, J.E., & van Citters, R.L. (1986). A biopsychosocial model to explain personal sources of medical student distress. *Proceedings of the 26th Annual Conference on Research in Medical Education, 26*, 228–234.

Walen, S.R., DiGiuseppe, R., & Dryden, W. (1992). *A practitioner's guide to rational emotive therapy* (2nd ed.). New York: Oxford University Press.

Walen, S.R., DiGiuseppe, R., & Wessler, R. L. (1980). *A practitioners guide to rational-emotive therapy*. New York: Oxford University Press.

Wallbott, H.G. (1988). Faces in context: The relative importance of facial expression and context information in determining emotion attributions. In K.R. Scherer (Ed.), *Facets of emotion. Recent research* (pp. 139–160). Hillsdale, NJ: Erlbaum.

Wallbott, H.G., & Scherer, K.R. (1986). The antecedents of emotional experiences. In K.R. Scherer, H.G. Wallbott, & A.B. Summerfield (Eds.), *Experiencing emotion: A cross-cultural study* (pp. 69–85). Cambridge, England: Cambridge University Press.

Warren, R., & Kurlychek, R.T. (1981). Treatment of maladaptive anger and aggression: Catharsis vs. behavior therapy. *Corrective and Social Psychiatry and Journal of Behavior Technology, 27*(3), 135–139.

Welsh, W.N., & Gordon, A. (1991). Cognitive mediators of aggression. Test of a causal model. *Criminal Justice and Behavior, 18*, 125–145.

Wessler, R. (1992). Constructivism and rational-emotive therapy: A critique. *Psychotherapy, 29*, 620–625.

Westberry, L.G. (1980). *Concurrent validation of the Trait-Anger Scale and its correlation with other personality measures*. Unpublished master's thesis, University of South Florida, Tampa, FL.

White, G.M. (1993). Emotions inside out: The anthropology of affect. In M. Lewis & J.M. Haviland (Eds.), *Handbook of emotions* (pp. 29–39). New York: Guilford.

Whiteman, M., Fanshel, D., & Grundy, J. (1987). Cognitive-behavioral intervention aimed at anger of parents at risk of child abuse. *Social Work, 32*(6), 469–474.

Wickliss, C., & Kirsch, I. (1988). Cognitive correlates of anger, anxiety and sadness. *Cognitive Therapy and Research, 12*, 367–377.

Widiger, T.A., & Trull, T.J. (1993). Borderline and narcissistic personality disorders. In H. Adams & P. Sutker (Eds.), *Comprehensive handbook of psychopathology* (2nd ed., pp. 371–394). New York: Plenum.

Wierzbicka, A. (1986). Human emotions: Universal or culture-specific? *American Anthropologist, 88*, 584–593.

Wierzbicka, A. (1992). *Semantics, culture, and cognition: Universal human concepts in culture specific configurations*. New York: Oxford University Press.

Wierzbicka, A. (1994). Emotion, language, and cultural scripts. In S. Kitayama & H. R. Markus (Eds.), *Culture and emotion* (pp. 133–196). Washington, DC: American Psychological Association.

Williams, R.B., Jr., Barefoot, J.C., & Shekelle, R.B. (1985). The health consequences of hostility. In M.A. Chesney & R.H. Rosenman (Eds.), *Anger and hostility in cardiovascular and behavioral disorders* (pp. 173–185). New York: Hemisphere/McGraw-Hill.

Wolfe, V.V., Finch, A.J., Saylor, C., Blount, R., Pallmeyer, T., & Carek, D. (1987). Negative affectivity in children: A multitrait-multimethod investigation. *Journal of Consulting and Clinical Psychology, 55*, 245–250.

Wolpe, J. (1958). *Psychotherapy by reciprocal inhibition*. Stanford, CA: Stanford University Press.

Wolpe, J. (1982). *The practice of behavior therapy* (3rd ed.). Oxford: Pergamon.

Wolpe, J. (1990). *The practice of behavior therapy* (4th ed.). New York: Pergamon.

Woods, P.J. (1987). Reductions in type A behavior, anxiety, anger, and physical illness as related to changes in irrational beliefs: Results of a demonstration project in industry. *Journal of Rational Emotive Psychotherapy, 5,* 213–237.

Wundt, W. (1896). *Outlines of psychology.* New York: Dustav E. Stechert.

Yerkes, R.M., & Dodson, J.D. (1908). The relation of strength of stimulus to rapidity of habit formation. *Journal of Comparative and Neurological Psychology, 18,* 459–482.

Young, P.T. (1943). *Emotion in man and animal.* New York: Wiley.

Zajonc, R.B. (1984). On the primacy of affect. *American Psychologist, 39,* 117–123.

Zajonc, R.B. (1985). Emotion and facial efference: A theory reclaimed. *Science, 228,* 15–21.

Zajonc, R.B. (1989). Feeling and facial efference: Implications of the vascular theory of emotion. *Psychological Review, 96,* 395–416.

Zajonc, R.B., Murphy, S.T., & Inglehart, M. (1989). Feeling and facial efference: Implications of the vascular theory of emotion. *Psychological Review, 96,* 395–416.

Zelin, M.L., Adler, G., & Myerson, P.G. (1972). Anger self-report: An objective questionnaire for the measurement of aggression. *Journal of Consulting and Clinical Psychology, 39,* 340.

Zillman, D. (1971). Excitation transfer in communication-mediated aggressive behavior. *Journal of Experimental Social Psychology, 7,* 419–434.

Zillman, D. (1988). Cognition-excitation interdependence in aggressive behavior. *Aggressive Behavior, 14,* 46–51.

Zillman, D., & Bryant, J. (1974). Effect of residual excitation on the emotional response and delayed aggressive behavior. *Journal of Personality and Social Psychology, 30,* 782–791.

Index